The Concept of Justice

Continuum Studies in Political Philosophy

Continuum Studies in Political Philosophy presents cutting-edge scholarship in the field of political philosophy. Making available the latest high-quality research from an international range of scholars working on key topics and controversies in political philosophy and political science, this series is an important and stimulating resource for students and academics working in the area.

Also available from Continuum:

Rawls, Dewey, and Constructivism – Eric Thomas Weber

Forthcoming:

Limits of Reason in Hobbes's Commonwealth – Michael P. Krom
Morality, Leadership and Public Policy – Eric Thomas Weber
Nozick's Libertarian Project – Mark D. Friedman
Perfecting Justice in Rawls, Habermas and Honneth – Miriam Bankovsky
Ricoeur, Rawls and Capability Justice – Eric Thomas Weber

The Concept of Justice

Is Social Justice Just?

Thomas Patrick Burke

continuum

Continuum International Publishing Group

The Tower Building   80 Maiden Lane
11 York Road   Suite 704
London SE1 7NX   New York, NY 10038

www.continuumbooks.com

British Library Cataloguing-in-Publication Data
A catalogue record for this book is available from the British Library.

ISBN: HB: 978-1-4411-6991-4

Library of Congress Cataloging-in-Publication Data
A catalog record for this book is available from the Library of Congress.

Typeset by Newgen Imaging Systems Pvt Ltd, Chennai, India
Printed and bound in Great Britain

Dedicated to Roger Scruton
maestro di color che sanno.

Contents

Preface

The position I wish to advance in this book is that states of affairs can be just or unjust only to the extent that rational agents can be held to account for them. And rational beings can be held to account only for those states of affairs which issue directly or indirectly from their own will. In particular, the injustice of a state of affairs is either the direct result of an unjust action, or involves the willful or negligent mistreatment of persons. Mistreatment comes in many forms. The father who spends on drink the money that his children need for their education; the drug addict who makes no effort to cure himself of his habit, even though his wife is being destroyed by it; the man who drugs a woman in order to make sexual use of her; the woman who neglects her sick child with the result that it dies: all these are forms of mistreatment, and all of them involve injustice. In some cases the injustice is deliberately intended; in other cases it arises by negligence or weakness of will; in other cases still it arises from a culpable ignorance (the drug addict who turns a blind eye to the consequences of his habit). But in all these cases a state of affairs is being imputed to the will of an agent. This idea of "imputation" is one that I will discuss in detail later. For the present it is sufficient to recognize that the will is manifest in many ways: as intention, as omission, as neglect, as "acting in ignorance." All these are ways in which someone makes himself responsible for the causal consequences of his own behavior. And in the end it is this idea of responsibility that is pivotal for understanding the concept of justice. Where there is injustice, there is somebody responsible for it. And where there is no one responsible, there cannot be injustice. The idea that there can be "social injustice," even though there is no agent to whom this can be imputed, is incoherent.

Part One

The Question

Chapter 1

The Problem of Justice

Few things are of more importance to a society than its conception of justice, and few are capable of arousing more intense emotion, because it is justice which provides the chief criterion for the legitimate use of force. In the name of justice people are arrested, handcuffed, put on trial, fined, sent to prison, and sometimes put to death. The concept of justice provides every society with its most fundamental rule of social order.

During the twentieth century, however, a revolution took place in the Western world's conception of justice. Our ordinary idea of it, which we employ in dealing with other individuals in the ordinary transactions of daily life, making an agreement, paying a bill, resolving a dispute, putting criminals in jail, a conception of justice at least as old as recorded history and familiar to all people everywhere, was superseded by a new conception which focuses instead on society as a whole. The question the new theory seeks to answer is not: what is the right and the wrong thing for a particular person in particular circumstances to do? but: how should power be distributed in society? This question has now been widely elevated to the status of the main concern of ethics. "The primary subject of justice," according to John Rawls, celebrated proponent of the new theory, is no longer the individual person in his actions toward others but "the basic structure of society." According to the new theory, which goes by such names as "social justice," or "economic justice," "justice as fairness," or (chiefly in the United States) "the liberal theory of justice," justice demands equality of power in society. It is no longer merely unfortunate that some people should be poor and powerless while others are rich and powerful; it is unjust.

"Social justice" is a demand addressed to society as a whole and not to the individual; and as such it is a demand that can be met only by the state. To make "social justice" into the basic principle of social order is to endorse the wholesale transfer of responsibility from individuals to the state, and inevitably to endorse the expansion of the state and the increase of its coercive powers.

The more one considers the matter, the clearer it becomes that redistribution is in effect far less a redistribution of free income from the richer to the poorer, as we imagined, than redistribution of power from the individual to the state.[1]

By contrast, to emphasize the ordinary conception of justice, as the regulative principle of individual transactions, is to advocate individual freedom and accountability, in the face of the coercive powers that are opposed to them.

Many people have welcomed the new theory, seeing the changes it has wrought as desirable and necessary. For some Christians, "social justice" is the implementation of the message of the Christian Gospel to love and help the poor. Governmental programs of "social justice" have provided substantial economic and other benefits to many individuals and groups. On the other hand, these benefits come at the expense of other citizens and at a substantial cost to society as a whole, including hidden costs to those it is intended to benefit. If "social justice" is merely an extension of ordinary justice, this may be right and proper. However, "social justice" is not merely an extension of ordinary justice, but essentially conflicts with it. Some recent examples will show the contrast between the two.

In order to show this, we must assume some preliminary understanding of "social justice." In later chapters we will trace the very different meanings this term has had in the course of its history, from which the difficulty will become apparent of providing any exact definition of it that covers all usage. At the end of Chapter 5, however, we offer a definition of the conception we are most directly concerned with. To anticipate, it is the view that there is a particular state of affairs in society, namely inequality of power or economic inequality, which is *ipso facto* unjust, irrespective of how it came about. In the course of Chapter 5 we will demonstrate that the principle of non-discrimination as currently construed belongs squarely within this concept, since it is not understood by its proponents to rule out all discrimination, but only that which offends against equality, discrimination for the purpose of creating equality ("affirmative action" or "reverse discrimination") being considered not only permissible but necessary. In the same chapter we will also show that the concept of "human rights" as reflected in the United Nations Universal Declaration of Human Rights embodies this concept of "social justice." This is why in what follows I consider several cases which might not seem at first sight to come under the rubric of "social justice."

The Conflict

In Philadelphia (where I live) a new social-justice policy of the city threatens to evict a noble organization, the Boy Scouts, from their historic home. In 1929 the organization constructed, at the city's request on city land but at their own expense, a large building for their own use which they donated to the city in return for the right to rent it back for an annual payment of $1. The building has been in use continuously till the present time as the headquarters of the local organization. According to the ordinary and traditional conception of justice, the Scouts have a strict right to occupy the building, since one of the basic principles of ordinary justice is that "*pacta sunt servanda*," "agreements must be kept." However, it has been one of the rules of the organization since its inception, a rule that is undoubtedly within its moral and legal rights and has always been considered reasonable, given the nature and purpose of the Boy Scouts, that no one who is openly homosexual can be a member. In 1993, however, the city passed a "social justice" ordinance prohibiting the use of public funds to support any organization that engages in "discriminatory practices." In 2003 a local scout challenged the organization's policy by announcing on television that he was homosexual, and was expelled from membership. The city thereupon demanded that the Boy Scouts either change their policy or pay the market rent for the building, which would be about $200,000 per year, far beyond their means. Consequently the Scouts are in danger of being forced to leave their historic home (they have filed a lawsuit to prevent this; at the time of writing the outcome is in doubt). The requirements of "social justice" (as interpreted by a particular conception of "discriminatory practices") here clearly contradict the demands of ordinary justice.[2]

Likewise in Philadelphia under the same law a sandwich shop owner was charged with discrimination for asking his customers to order their sandwiches in the English language. Joe Vento, a locally famous vendor of cheesesteak sandwiches in an area containing large numbers of immigrants, put a small sign up which said, "This is America. When ordering, please speak English." From the perspective of ordinary justice such a sign is fully within the proprietor's rights. It commits no crime or injustice and inflicts no harm on anyone. It does not even refuse service to those who order in a foreign language, but simply makes a request. Both the purchase and the sale of sandwiches are entirely voluntary. The request is not unreasonable, because this particular sandwich is noted locally for having its own traditional ordering vocabulary.[3] The sign might even be considered patriotic. It has not exactly been concealed from immigrants that they live in a country where English is the common language, and they must expect to have to speak English to carry out many of the ordinary tasks of life, such as shopping or traveling. However, the sign has been held to offend against "social justice" because it suggests a certain kind of inequality between those who speak English and those who do not. The chairman of the city's Commission on Human Relations complained to the Commission that the sign was "discriminatory," and the Commission summoned the vendor to appear before it to answer the charge. In the wake of heavy publicity supporting him, the Commission has recently found in favor of Mr. Vento by a vote of 2 to 1, but the charge itself, together with the fact that the outcome was long uncertain and that one of three members of the Commission agreed with the charge, points to the potential conflict that exists between the demands of ordinary justice and those of "social justice." Both cannot be satisfied at the same time.[4]

Moreover, wherever it is applied, "social justice" trumps ordinary justice. During 2006 (the latest year for which these statistics are available at the time of writing) the Equal Employment Opportunity Commission, a U.S. federal agency, filed over 200 lawsuits against employers over rules requiring employees to speak English. One of these employers was the Salvation Army, whose language policy requiring English had been specifically upheld by a federal judge in Boston in 2002.

In May 2010, a New York court declared the Swiss pharmaceutical corporation Novartis fully liable in a sexual discrimination lawsuit brought by female sales representatives, the second largest such case in history. In a class action, 5,600 women accused Novartis of discriminating against women on the basis of pregnancy, as well as paying women less than similarly experienced men. The suit was brought both as a case of disparate treatment and also disparate impact. An important part of the evidence was a statistical study showing the company paid the women on average $75 a month less than the men. According to the plaintiffs' brief the purpose of the lawsuit was "to eliminate the adverse effects" of the discrimination in their lives, careers, and working conditions. After a month-long trial and four days of deliberation, the jury found against the company on all charges, awarding $3.3 million in compensatory damages and $250 million in punitive damages. The jury consisted of five women and four men, and the judge was female.[5]

Ordinary justice depends on *desert*: the person found guilty of a punishable offence must deserve the punishment. But it seems very doubtful that Novartis deserved this extraordinary verdict. "Social justice," however, as we shall see in more detail, is not concerned with desert, but aims at producing equality in society. For ordinary justice there must be an evil intention, *mens rea*; but an argument from statistical averages is not such an argument. Here again, the conflict is manifest between the requirements of ordinary justice and those of social justice. From the viewpoint of desert, the question would have to be raised, in what sense the effects of such discrimination are "adverse." The women suffered no injury; were not robbed or swindled; they did not lose anything. Others were simply paid more than they were. The company had no obligation to employ any of them, and did them the favor of giving them each a job, which they knowingly and willingly applied for. At the time of their application for their job they could have asked whether women were paid less than men, and if the firm had assured them they were paid equally with the men, and this led them to accept the offer of work, but it turned out not to be true, they would have had grounds in ordinary justice for some kind of counter claim. But the women did not ask this. A verdict of this nature clearly contradicts ordinary justice.[6]

In Great Britain, consider the case of a widow who has no assets from her former marriage save a house, and who rents the house out to a tenant in order to live from the rent. The traditional and ordinary idea of justice tells us that it would be an injustice for the tenant to withhold the rent agreed, or to stay in the house beyond the expiration of the tenancy, or in any way to exclude the widow from her property. A first principle of ordinary justice, as we have noted, is that contracts are to be upheld. In 1977, however, the British government introduced a Rent Act which imposed rent control and gave tenants security of tenure. The arguments given for this legislation at the time concerned "social justice": the unequal position of tenants vis-à-vis landlords must be rectified, exploitation of the propertyless by the propertied must be prevented, and so on. The widow is forced to accept a rent below that agreed to and less than her living costs; she loses the possession of her house, which the tenant, younger than her, now has for life, and she is effectively ruined. "Social justice" has demanded a result here that would be widely condemned as an injustice to the widow.[7]

Likewise in Great Britain, the question of the right of self-defense has led to two contrasting approaches. On the traditional view of justice, as explained for example by Locke, the right of self-defense entitles one to kill an intruder who uses force.

This makes it lawful for a man to kill a thief, who has not in the least hurt him, nor declared any design upon his life, any farther than, by the use of force, so to get him in his power, as to take away his money, or what he pleases, from him; because using force, where he has no right, to get me into his power, let his pretence be what it will, I have no reason to suppose, that he who would take away my liberty, would not, when he had me in his power, take away everything else. And therefore it is lawful for me to treat him as one who has put himself into a state of war with me, i.e. kill him if I can; for to that hazard does he justly expose himself, whoever introduces a state of war, and is aggressor in it.[8]

And again:

> . . . force, or a declared design of force, upon the person of another, where there is no common superior on earth to appeal to for relief, is the state of war: and it is the want of such an appeal gives a man the right of war even against an aggressor, tho' he be in society and a fellow subject. Thus a thief, whom I cannot harm, but by appeal to the law, for having stolen all that I am worth, I may kill, when he sets on me to rob me but of my horse or coat; because the law, which was made for my preservation, where it cannot interpose to secure my life from present force, which, if lost, is capable of no reparation, permits me my own defence, and the right of war, a liberty to kill the aggressor, because the aggressor allows not time to appeal to our common judge, nor the decision of the law, for remedy in a case where the mischief may be irreparable.[9]

But from the perspective of "social justice," the criminal should also be considered a victim, namely of disadvantaged societal or perhaps biological circumstances. This entails a very different and much weaker view of the right of self-defense, which tends to defend the rights of the criminal as ardently as those of his victim, and construe strictly the penalties that can be levied against him. The Court of Appeal (England and Wales) has formulated the rule of self-defense as follows:

> It is not, as we understand it, the law that a person threatened must take to his heels and run, but what is necessary is that he should demonstrate by his actions that he does not want to fight. He must demonstrate that he is prepared to temporise and disengage and perhaps to make some physical withdrawal. This is a necessary feature for the justification of self-defence, whether the charge is a homicide charge or something less serious.[10]

One example out of many can illustrate the new and very diminished right of self-defense in the United Kingdom. In 1999, in a celebrated case,

Tony Martin, a 55-year-old Norfolk farmer living alone in a shabby farmhouse, awakened to the sound of breaking glass as two burglars, both with long criminal records, burst into his home. He had been robbed six times before, and his village, like the majority of rural English communities, had no police presence. He sneaked downstairs with a shotgun and shot at the intruders. Martin received life in prison for killing one burglar, 10 years for wounding the second, and a year for having an unregistered shotgun. The wounded burglar, having served 18 months of a three-year sentence, is now free and has been granted £5,000 of legal assistance to sue Martin.[11]

These examples from real life should be sufficient to make it clear that whether "social justice" is right or wrong, it is not merely different from ordinary justice, but is in conflict with it. Wherever it is applied, and wherever they are in conflict, "social justice" trumps ordinary justice. Let us now look a little further into the reasons for this.

Chapter 2

Elements of the Problem

Our aim in this chapter is not to make a complete case for our ultimate view but to explain a little more fully some further aspects or dimensions of the problem, providing a prefatory outline of assertions that will be justified in the subsequent chapters.

Ordinary Justice

The traditional conception of justice is well summarized in Justinian's *Digests* taken from the Roman jurist Ulpian: "These are the commandments of the law: to live uprightly, not to harm others, and to give to each person what belongs to him."[12] The outstanding or paradigmatical instances of injustice in this view are traditional crimes, acts such as murder, robbery, and rape. These are considered unjust because they inflict undeserved harm on individuals. The individuals who commit them are viewed as responsible for their actions, and therefore it is believed that they deserve to be punished.

These instances of injustice share certain features. A first feature to notice is that they are *actions* performed by individuals. There is a difference between an action and a *state of affairs*. An action is something someone *does*. A state of affairs is *not* something someone does. For ethics the difference between these two is crucial, because ethics has to do with actions. An action can *produce* a state of affairs, as its effect, but the distinction always remains between the action, which is the cause, and the state of affairs which is its effect. A state of affairs is the way things are at some particular time and place. It is a static condition: a state of affairs just *is*; it is the kind of thing we would describe as a fact or a situation. An action, by contrast, is an event, a transient happening, carried out by a person, usually for some purpose. A robbery is not a state of affairs, but an action. Poverty is not an action, but a state of affairs. The same is true of inequality. Some states of affairs are the result of actions, but many, especially in the realm of nature, are not the result of any action, but just happen. Poverty can be one of these. In traditional ethics, human actions are at the center of the stage.

To say that justice and injustice are qualities of actions is to say they are qualities of the *will.* I am using "action" here as an umbrella term to include all those ways in which the will can produce an effect in the world, including through such things as willful omission, neglect, culpable ignorance, and weakness of will – in short, all those ways in which people make themselves *responsible* for states of affairs, as suggested in the Preface.[13]

An action has certain features that are especially important in the traditional view of ethics. One of these is its interior dimension, the state of mind in which it is done. From the viewpoint of traditional ethics the *intention* and the interior mentality with which the person does the action is a vital consideration. When we judge an action to be ethical or unethical, we pay attention not only to the external or visible action, but to the state of mind in which it is done. When I put the $100 lying on the shop counter in my pocket, it makes a difference ethically whether I believe it is mine or yours. At least since Peter Abelard, who wrote an important book on this during the middle ages, appreciation of the key role of intention has been an integral part of Western ethics.[14]

When a person performs an action intentionally, in the view of traditional ethics he is *responsible* for his action. If it is a good action he can be praised for it, and if it is an evil action he can be blamed for it. There can be guilt, and there can be innocence. There can be reward, and there can be punishment. If a person does an action which has the effect of causing harm to someone, but that was not his intention, then he is not normally considered to be fully responsible for the harm, and is not to be blamed for it. Sometimes the intention alone is sufficient to condemn an action or a person, sometimes in addition we recognize a range of other internal states of mind, such as negligence, inattention, or mistaken belief as relevant to the action's moral status. All of these things the Common law has traditionally taken into consideration, in judging a criminal act, under the concept of *mens rea.* St. Augustine wrote: "Without *mens rea* there is no crime."[15]

Responsibility in the traditional sense presupposes that the person, that is, the sane conscious adult, has *free will,* that he has the power to choose either to do the action or not to do it, that he could have done something else. If an action is not performed freely, it is not a human action. In the traditional view, ethics without free will is nonsense.

Since the person has the power to act freely, he can deserve, by the nature of his action and not because of any undertaking made by some human

institution, to receive from others a certain kind of response. If he deliberately does harm to someone who does not deserve to be harmed, in the
traditional understanding of justice the perpetrator deserves to be punished. Our traditional legal system was built on that principle. The purpose
of legal punishment was not to rehabilitate the criminal, nor to sequester
him from society, but to make him *suffer* in some proportion to the harm he
caused others, to "redress the balance of justice." The just punishment is
not the one that cures or rehabilitates or deters, but that is deserved.
Perhaps we could rehabilitate thieves by providing them with a five-year
fully paid vacation in the Bahamas, but that would not be just because not
deserved.

For all these reasons, in the traditional view *only actions can be directly just
or unjust.* A state of affairs can be good or bad, but it cannot be unjust
except as the result of an unjust action. So, for example, if I have $100 in my
pocket, that will be an unjust state of affairs if I have stolen it from you, but
the real injustice was my action in stealing it. The bare fact that I have $100
in my pocket of itself is neutral. Similarly the situation created by a law can
be unjust because a law is an action. In the traditional view, an injustice
cannot exist unless someone has done something wrong.

This applies also to distributive justice. A just distribution of goods is first
and foremost a just *act* of distribution carried out by some person. Aristotle,
who provides us with the classic description of distributive justice, says it is
the virtue of not giving more to oneself than to others of what is good, and
not giving less to oneself than to others of what is bad (as when, in the kind
of example he may have had in mind, one partner divides up the profits or
losses from the voyage of a trading ship among the other partners). Since
distributive justice is a matter of ethics, the primary focus must be on the
individual doing the distributing.

In the traditional understanding there is an important distinction between
justice and charity, or as it is sometimes called, benevolence or humanity.
An obligation in justice is one that can rightly be enforced by the threat of
punishment, but an obligation in charity or humanity cannot.

The traditional understanding embodies a strong conception of the individual. It presupposes that individuals have free will, that they are responsible for their actions, and if they wrong others they deserve punishment.

"Social Justice"

The theory of "social justice" as currently understood in our society rejects
each of these presuppositions. It denies or at least minimizes the role of

free will, and so of individual responsibility, and of action, and marginalizes likewise the traditional concepts of desert, of guilt and innocence, of praise and blame, and of reward and punishment. From the traditional viewpoint, whatever is unjust is also unfair or unequal, but the proposition cannot be inverted: not everything that is unequal is necessarily unjust. There is a difference between justice and fairness. In the new view, however, justice is identified with fairness. Whatever is unequal or unfair is by that very fact considered unjust. This is so even if the subject matter of judgment is not an action but a state of affairs. And that unequal state of affairs is unjust *no matter how it came about.* So we have the bizarre situation that a state of affairs can be labeled "unjust" even though no one has done anything wrong in producing or permitting it, or indeed done *anything* to produce it.

As the French writer Bertrand de Jouvenel has remarked:

> The justice now recommended is a quality not of a man and a man's actions, but of a certain configuration of things in social geometry, no matter by what means it is brought about. Justice is now something which exists independently of just men.[16]

In the words of Friedrich Hayek, "social justice" "defines a factual state of affairs which may but need not have been brought about by deliberate human decision."[17]

Since it is primarily the state of affairs in society that is unjust, irrespective of how it came about, the injustice of actions recedes in significance or even disappears altogether as a matter of concern. Crime, from being the paramount example of injustice, becomes merely a distraction from it.

Correspondingly, the role of *mens rea* and of what Kant called "the good will" (which he famously regarded as the only absolutely good thing), disappears from the ethical scene. Poverty, economic inequality, or inequality of power are objective relationships in society that are judged without reference to anyone's intention or state of mind.

One fundamental difference between the old theory and the new lies in their views of freedom of the will. The way was prepared for "social justice" by scientific determinism, which has led many people, especially among the intellectual classes, to deny the reality of freedom of the will because of what they take to be the implications of science. The physical sciences reveal to us a world in which causality is apparently universal, in which (making due allowance for quantum theory) every event is the product of the circumstances that preceded it. There do not appear to be any exceptions to this in nature, and so it is concluded that this must apply also to human behavior. It is true that whenever we make a choice, we seem to be conscious of having the innate capacity to act differently from the way we do act, and so we assume that we possess the freedom to choose between alternatives, but for many members of the intellectual classes belief in the universal reign of causality trumps our individual consciousness of freedom, and leads them to conclude that that consciousness is an illusion, and that our actions are in fact predetermined by the influence of the biological forces within us and the societal forces around us. This social determinism tends to be especially emphasized in the theory of "social justice."

Ethics, as the study of what is good, must turn its attention, then, it is felt, away from the idea of individual responsibility, to those biological, psychological, sociological, and historical forces which can be viewed as the causes of the individual's behavior. In studying crime, for example, it becomes a mistake to blame the criminal. Instead we must understand the societal circumstances which have made him what he is, and we must remedy those. The same analysis applies to terrorism. In some "progressive" circles at the present time, including some of our schools, the very use of the phrase "individual responsibility" has been reported to mark one as retrograde. The purpose of imprisonment is not, as in the traditional theory, to redress the balance of justice by inflicting punishment on the criminal, because on the most fundamental level he could not really help doing what he did. That is now viewed as mere vengeance. The purpose is to rehabilitate him.

But this acceptance of universal determinism would not have been enough by itself to produce the concept of "social justice," without a factor which has been even more influential, namely a negative view of markets. Adam Smith argued already in 1776, in the first chapter of his classic work, *The Wealth of Nations*, that the chief factor raising the standard of living of a society is its productivity, and that productivity grows in proportion to the division of labor, which in turn grows in proportion to the size of the market. The best remedy for poverty, he argued, is what he called "the obvious and simple system of natural liberty," the system of free or voluntary exchanges, for this maximizes production across the society. The whole tendency of the science of economics has been to support that argument. But from the beginning, the proponents of "social justice" have rejected it. They have rejected especially the exposure of the poor or the disadvantaged to competition, which they view as an affliction to those who do not succeed and the real cause of disadvantage. Anything which advantages one person, they believe, must disadvantage the rest.

This view was carried to its furthest lengths in the communist political systems of the twentieth century. Their collapse since 1989 has raised widespread practical doubts about socialism. But even the free nations of Europe imbibed the gospel of "social justice" deeply, and are currently engaged in a great and historic struggle over it. At the time of writing, the government of France, presiding over 10 percent unemployment (20 percent among the young) produced (if the Austrian economists are to be believed) by the gospel of fairness, is trying to convince its people of the benefits of the free market in creating jobs, but is facing revolt from its labor unions and its university students. In Germany, with unemployment even higher as a result of the "social market economy," the *Sozialmarktwirtschaft*, the chancellor, Angela Merkel, likewise wished to take her country down the path of market freedom, but was not able to succeed in convincing a majority of her people, and was forced into a coalition government with the Socialist party. Similar developments have taken place in Britain, Italy, and Spain.

In the United States the problem of massive unemployment did not develop nationally until the Great Depression of the 1930s. The response of President Roosevelt was in accordance with the theory of "social justice," condemning the factory system and the employers. He has gone down in legend as the hero of the working classes, and it is true that he lifted the morale of the nation by inspiring it with confidence in his ability to overcome the problem, but the measures he introduced were not of such a nature as to increase employment. The problem persisted till the outbreak of the Second World War in 1939, and there is good reason to believe this was mainly the result of his policies.[18] (Subsequent research suggests that the severity and duration of the Depression were mainly the result of mismanagement of the money supply by the Federal Reserve.)[19]

Civil Rights

The concept of "social justice" took on added force with the Civil Rights Act of 1964, especially its Title VII on employment. All together there have been some dozen civil rights acts, six of them passed before 1964. In the earlier legislation, the idea of civil rights was understood very differently. The term referred originally to what would be called today "liberties" or "freedoms," such as the freedom to vote, the freedom to travel, to work, to marry, to make contracts, and to give evidence in court. These liberties are what since Isaiah Berlin have been called "negative" rights, meaning that they do not confer a right to a "positive" performance by other persons.[20]

They are rights to be let alone, not to be impeded in their performance of an action. A "positive" right, by contrast, in this terminology, is a right to receive a performance from other persons. The "right to life, liberty and the pursuit of happiness" mentioned in the Declaration of Independence, despite its positive appearance, is a negative right because it is not a right to receive life when you don't have it, but a right not to be killed.

To understand what happened in 1964 we need to distinguish between two different kinds of discrimination: coercive or forcible and non-coercive or peaceful. Forcible discrimination is the use of force to discriminate. This is the proper meaning of the term "segregation." That was what the Ku Klux Klan practiced, and the governments of the Southern states, with their Black Codes and the Jim Crow laws. The primary form of it, of course, was slavery. Peaceful discrimination, by contrast, consists in refusing to do business in some way or to some extent with a member of a particular group. Forcible discrimination was always contrary to the ordinary and traditional concept of justice. But peaceful discrimination was not, for the same reason that boycotts were not. The basic principle was that a refusal to do business could not be construed as causing harm. In a free society everyone had the right not to do business with anyone else.

The original Civil Rights Movement, from the beginning of the NAACP in 1910, was aimed mainly at eliminating segregation and other forms of coercive discrimination, and that was the purpose of the first six Civil Rights Acts. But in 1964 something very significant happened. The concept of civil rights was expanded from the prohibition of forcible to that of peaceful discrimination, or from the Ku Klux Klan and the Jim Crow laws to the peaceful actions of private individuals. Another way of saying this is that the original negative rights were transformed into positive ones. The effect of the 1964 law is to compel persons to do business with the members of certain groups, if they do business at all. Unlike the earlier civil rights laws, from the viewpoint of economics the new law was a form of protectionism. But from the viewpoint of the new theory of justice, it was fair and therefore just. Significantly, however, the 1964 Act makes a special exception for communists: it is lawful to discriminate against them.[21]

Something else happened in 1964. The civil rights movement of the 1960s, led by Martin Luther King, Jr., was concerned solely with the question of race, and this was also true of the first version of the Civil Rights bill. At that stage, the proposed bill was thought of as a particular remedy for a particular problem in a particular country with a particular history. But the chairman of the House Rules Committee, one Howard W. Smith of Virginia, was strongly opposed to the bill and was determined to kill it.

For this purpose he succeeded in having an amendment added to the bill which prohibited discrimination on the ground of sex as well as race. His reasoning was apparently that no one would vote for a bill containing that provision. But he had reckoned without President Lyndon Johnson, who used the weight of his office to persuade Congress to pass the bill despite the added amendment.[22]

The effect of this legislation was to absolutize and universalize the moral condemnation of all discrimination. For once discrimination on the ground of sex was prohibited, every other ground of discrimination came to be considered illegitimate (except, of course, for affirmative action). For there is no aspect of human life where discrimination has traditionally been viewed as more necessary and more justified than in the distinction between the sexes. If it was illegitimate there, it could not well be legitimate anywhere, it has been felt. And this condemnation of discrimination was soon exported to other countries around the globe. More detail about this is given on page 101 below.

In the course of discussing with my class at Temple University Locke's *Second Treatise of Government*, which among other topics discusses crime, I asked what was the worst of all possible crimes. I expected to be told, genocide, or at least murder, or suchlike. But the first answer I received was "discrimination."

Affirmative Action

Perhaps in the light of this the reader may be inclined to respond that the question then is about discrimination, which is an action, after all, rather than about equality, which is a state of affairs. But to see that this is not so, but that the real question is about equality, you have only to consider the question of affirmative action. Affirmative action, or reverse discrimination, is a policy of deliberate discrimination in favor of the minority or the powerless, rather than in favor of the majority or the powerful as it is usually understood to be. Affirmative action is clearly a form of discrimination. There can be no doubt about that whatever. But it is discrimination for the purpose of creating equality, and so from the viewpoint of "social justice" it is not only permissible but necessary. New Zealand law makes an explicit exception for affirmative action, which it terms a legitimate form of discrimination. This is why the proponents of "social justice" have condemned the moves to eliminate affirmative action as destructive of the very purpose of the civil rights law.

Is Inequality Inherently Unjust?

Equality and inequality are not actions, but states of affairs. If justice consists in equality, and if inequality is inherently unjust, no matter how it came about, then the most fundamental conception of traditional ethics, the basis on which its entire structure is built, has to be abandoned. Ethics is then no longer primarily a matter of what is done, but of the way things are. States of affairs which are considered desirable are by that fact ethical and right, while states of affairs which are considered regrettable and undesirable are also ethically unjust. Individual actions may still be unjust, but this injustice is derivative from and subsidiary to the states of affairs to which they lead.

"Disparate Impact"

An example of this from our current legal system is the concept of "disparate impact." In 1971 the Supreme Court interpreted the 1964 Civil Rights Act to mean that in order to prove discrimination it was not necessary to show that discrimination was intentional, but only that an unequal state of affairs followed from some action. Thus in 1996 a certain Martha Sandoval sued the state of Alabama over a regulation that driving tests be conducted only in English. She could read enough English to cope with street signs but not enough to pass the written test. She sued on the grounds that the law *inadvertently* discriminated against her because of her national origin. The Obama administration has recently announced its intention to enforce the prohibition of disparate impact more stringently.

Redistribution of Liability

In the traditional view, liability for harm was a function of causation: only those who caused the harm in a particular case could be held liable for it. But "social justice" severs the link between causation and liability in the interests of bringing about greater economic equality in society, and makes, not the person who caused the harm, but the one who has the ability to pay for it ("deep pockets"), responsible and liable for it. Liability is assigned, not according to natural justice, but according to public policy. A chief means of doing that is by employing the legal doctrine of "joint and several liability." This means that, in cases where more than one party can be held liable, a plaintiff has the right to collect the entire damage award from any defendant individually or from the defendants as a whole, depending on the plaintiff's preference. In this way the plaintiff is more likely to be compensated, it is argued, and it is left up to the defendants to sort out the responsibility among themselves. But if one defendant is wealthy and the others have no assets, a defendant who has very slight or even no responsibility in the traditional sense for the harm can be held liable for all of it, irrespective of the proportion of his causation.

Since 1960 there have been hundreds if not thousands of cases in the United States adjudicated on this basis. The following, chosen almost at random, are typical. In 2005 a drunk driver speeding at 60 m.p.h. crashed into the back of a Ford Escort stopped at an intersection, killing the driver. His family sued the Ford Motor Co., for $27 million, and won, even though the court accepted that the car was built to higher standards than required by federal law. (*Mikolajczyk v. Ford Motor Co.*, No. 00 L 3342 (Cook County, Ill).) The driver of a car with faulty brakes struck and killed a 6-year-old boy at a school crossing, despite a stop sign and a crossing guard. The plaintiff argued that the accident might have been avoided if the crossing guard, instead of signaling the car to stop, had attempted to get the child out of the car's path. The city, as the crossing guard's employer, was found to be only one percent at fault. Yet because it was the only solvent party, the city had to pay 100 percent, the full amount of damages (*Zimmer v. City of Milwaukee*).

Expansion of Strict Liability

The legal doctrine of strict liability means that one is liable for damages regardless of fault. The question of how careful a defendant was or should have been is irrelevant. Even if a defendant's actions were entirely reasonable, strict liability makes him liable for the plaintiff's injury.

Historically, strict liability was only used in very unusual cases, for example where a wild animal caused an injury. But since 1963 strict liability has become the standard way of assigning responsibility to manufacturers for defective products. A legal authority writes:

> One reason for applying strict liability to defective product cases is that manufacturers (often large corporations) are in a better position to incur the costs of the injuries caused by their products than the individuals who are injured. Moreover, by requiring manufacturers to pay damages for

injuries caused by their products, regardless of fault, the law encourages manufacturers to produce safe and dependable products.[23]

Praise and Blame

In the traditional theory, individuals, provided they are adult, sane, and conscious, are responsible for their actions. It follows from this, as we have noted, that there is such a thing as innocence, and there is such a thing as guilt, and these deserve praise on the one hand, and blame on the other. Those who have done good deserve recognition and reward, and those who have deliberately injured others deserve condemnation and punishment. In the new theory, however, things are very different. There is, strictly speaking, no room for genuine individual responsibility, since injustice consists in the mere fact of poverty or inequality, without regard for how it came about. The poor cannot be held responsible for their poverty, for that would be to "blame the victim." Also, it is assumed they cannot do anything to rectify their situation. The wealthy or powerful are automatically considered responsible for the condition of the poor, presumably because they *can do* something to bring equality about, namely by relinquishing their wealth and power.[24] But in proper social-justice theory even the powerful are "responsible" only in a weak or relative sense, for ultimately their actions too are predetermined by their place in the societal structure.

From the fact that we do not deserve our natural endowments, John Rawls concludes that we do not deserve anything we gain by using them. This applies even to our moral character, for a person's "character depends in large part on fortunate family and social circumstances for which he can claim no credit."[25] If an institution explicitly promises us something on condition that we fulfill some requirement, and if we fulfill the requirement, then can we be said to have a "legitimate expectation" of receiving what is promised, and in this sense, and only in this sense, to "deserve" it. If you enter a race where it has been announced that the first past the post wins the prize, and if you are the first past the post, then you "deserve" the prize. The implication Rawls seems to intend is that we have no exclusive right to what we gain by using the gifts of fortune.

But if a person does not deserve his good character, he also does not deserve his bad one. From which it must follow that a murderer does not deserve punishment unless there is some law which has threatened him with punishment antecedently. And this is in fact now the view of many criminologists. Outside of institutions and their promises, "social justice" allows no room for desert.

Interior and Exterior

In traditional ethics, as we have noted, one's interior intention plays a key role, since it can decide whether an action is just or unjust. The interior dimension of the ethical life is its most crucial dimension. In the tradition of moral thought stemming from Socrates and Plato, as in that of Christianity, ethics is a question about the state of our soul. But in the theory of "social justice," since poverty or equality are external facts in relation to the individual, our soul is irrelevant.

"Social justice" raises a question about our inner identity. One of the great achievements of Western civilization has been what has been called "the discovery of the individual." This happened especially during the Middle Ages, when people became more conscious of the depth of the interior emotional life, beginning with St. Augustine's Confessions, which created the literary form of the autobiography. This interior individuality we possess is fashioned by our choices, by our freedom. We live in a dialogue with ourselves, in which the demands of justice play a basic role. But from the viewpoint of "social justice," what counts is not our individuality, what we choose to do as individuals, or what is done to us: what counts is the group we belong to. Justice means "getting ours" as a group. The effect of the focus on "social justice" is to dry up the deepest sources of the interior life.

Animals

On the traditional view, the concepts of justice and injustice apply only to human or rational beings, since only they have free will and a conscience. Rights go together with duties, and only a being that is capable by its species-nature of having duties can have rights. But in the new theory animals can have rights even though they do not have duties, because the concept of equality can be applied to them. Thus Peter Singer argues that the suffering of animals should be counted equally with that of human beings. In the traditional view, causing unnecessary pain to animals was considered, not an injustice, but a form of inhumanity.

"Capabilities"

Martha Nussbaum has proposed a very expansive version of "social justice" based on "capabilities." These are considered core abilities human beings have to fulfill their human nature. As she treats them, they are similar to provisions of the United Nations Universal Declaration of Human Rights,[26] but go far beyond them in their societal implications. She gives a list of ten, which must be provided by government, such as: not dying prematurely; having good health and adequate nourishment and shelter; having opportunities for sexual satisfaction; not having one's emotional development blighted by fear and anxiety; being able to laugh, play, and enjoy recreational activities; and so on. She describes the list as "open-ended." Nussbaum views all such capabilities as demanded by human dignity, and as entitlement rights against "society," so that a society that does not provide them is unjust. This entitlement is not restricted to human beings, however: it applies in her view also to animals, especially the higher mammals: they have dignity, which demands that they also have the right in "social justice" against human society and government to fulfill their natures.[27]

Economics

The economic implications of "social justice" are vastly different from those of ordinary justice. If the market is allowed to function according to the norms of ordinary justice, with what Adam Smith called "natural liberty," it is capable of bringing transformative wealth to a society, according to the arguments of economists. The reason for this, Smith argued, is the principle of mutual benefit, the fact that both parties to any free exchange engage in it in the belief they will profit from it; otherwise they would not engage in it. Thus, without necessarily intending to, each one benefits the other, and this benefit, though not directly intended, spreads throughout the society through every further transaction they engage in, by what Smith called an "invisible hand." A regime of ordinary justice maximizes employment and production, therefore, for example, and minimizes prices, economists argue. But if the market is regulated in accordance with the norms of "social justice," which demands economic equality, the opposite happens: market activity is reduced, prices are artificially increased, and employment and production are artificially decreased. When the law imposes a minimum wage, for example, the intention no doubt is to help employees by increasing their income, protecting them against excessive competition, and at the expense of their employers, who are felt to be in a stronger economic situation. But the cost is paid by other workers who are now priced out of the labor market, and the net effect is to reduce employment below what it otherwise would have been. The remarkable thing is that such economic arguments carry *no weight* with the advocates of "social justice." It is as if we were dealing with a religious faith rather than an ordinary political conviction. It is a consequence of this that in the twentieth century the principal opponents of "social justice" have been outstanding economists, such as Ludwig von Mises, Friedrich Hayek, and Milton Friedman. Hayek wrote: "I have come to feel strongly that the greatest service I can still render to my fellow men would be that I could make the speakers and writers among them thoroughly ashamed ever again to employ the term 'social justice.' "[28] And, "the prevailing belief in 'social justice' is at present probably the gravest threat to most other values of a free civilization."[29]

Viewed from the perspective of the science of economics, "economic justice" is a form of protectionism. The harmful effects of protectionism in general have been closely studied and are well understood by economists. Unlike protection from coercion, which makes it possible to compete freely, economic "protection" from the voluntary actions of the market has the effect of rendering the "protected" persons less economically productive and less capable of competing. Supporters of "social justice" tend to downplay the significance of the discipline of economics, and even to reject it altogether as immoral. But the basic concepts of economic science, such as the law of supply and demand or the concept of marginal utility, are neither morally good nor bad but simply express the logic of human interaction, as Ludwig von Mises among others has demonstrated. Over the last hundred years "social justice" has arguably caused a truly immense amount of economic harm among the peoples of the world. No doubt, hostility to commerce and its values has been an important motive for "social justice." But those who deliberately inflict this harm have a great deal to answer for.

Although protectionism in general has been well studied by economists, this is not true of the specific forms of protectionism occasioned by social justice. The protectionism embodied in the principle of nondiscrimination and the current understanding of civil rights has not, so far as I can discover, been studied at all.

Institutions

Civil society is made up of institutions. An institution is an organized form of cooperation. The family we grow up in, the language we use, the country in which we live, the school or church we attend, the stores where we shop are all institutions. We rely on them by the myriads, often unconsciously, for things we could not do by ourselves. But "social justice" changes all of them. For every institution is created initially by its founders to serve a particular purpose. Schools are created to give children knowledge, businesses to make a profit, the military to defend the nation, police forces to enforce the law, churches to cultivate the spiritual dimension of human existence, symphony orchestras to offer music, universities to hand on and to increase the store of knowledge, language in order to communicate with one another, and so on. Ordinary justice respects those purposes and helps to attain them. But under "social justice" every institution acquires a new and additional purpose: to help create societal equality. This additional purpose changes every institution because it makes it serve two masters. It is no longer enough for schools to teach knowledge, but they must in addition serve the cause of equality through their hiring practices, their curriculum, through social promotion and other measures. It is not enough for business to benefit its customers, its employees, and its owners, as every successful business does, but it must also help to create equality by paying minimum wages, hiring certain classes of people whether that is in the interests of the business or not, as well as protecting the interests of its "stakeholders," all those in any way affected by its decisions. It is not enough for the military to defend the nation, but it must increase society's equality by recruiting and promoting particular groups of people, even though the military authorities may not consider them desirable for that purpose; it is not enough for the churches to care for the spiritual needs of their members by following their ancient traditions of faith and order, but they must rewrite their scriptures and redefine the requirements for being a member of the clergy; and so on for every institution. It is not enough for universities to teach and do research: the former president of a university said on television recently that the social purpose of universities, the socializing of their students, was more important than their teaching purpose.[30] It is not enough for our language to serve as a means of communication, but it must be reformed and made "inclusive" in order to foster equality. Even the institution of marriage, traditionally the quintessential institution of heterosexuality, must be redefined to permit the "marriage" of homosexuals.

"Social justice" not only changes all institutions, it also weakens them, because it deprives them of authority. No institution can function without authority. But under "social justice" and its demand of equality the authority of parents is diminished in the family, the authority of teachers is reduced in the school, the authority of business owners to run their business is diminished, wherever there is authority, in the military, the police, the church, or even in the realm of literature, it is enfeebled, because now there is always a second master it must serve. Under "social justice" all authority tends to be regarded with hostility as a potential source of exploitation and oppression.

Standards

Another effect of "social justice" is on the concept of standards. Every civilization has defined itself through certain standards of performance. Education consists largely in imparting standards of knowledge and behavior. Without standards there is no civilization. But the very concept of a standard is discriminatory. For in any area of performance, the standard is set by the best. This implies the judgment that some activities are better than others, and that those who do not perform up to the standard are inferior in that respect to those who do. Standards create inequality, it is felt. From the viewpoint of ordinary justice this is natural. But from that of "social justice" and its accompanying idea of civil rights, standards have regrettable consequences and should so far as possible be downplayed and even abandoned, except perhaps for experts in particular circumstances.

There is, therefore, a heavy price to pay for "social justice." If "social justice" is genuine justice and its demands are genuine demands of justice, that price must be paid. For nothing can be more important for any society than that the demands of justice should be satisfied. But if "social justice" is not genuine justice and its demands are not demands of justice, then it is not merely a neutral or indifferent idea, but one whose adoption legitimizes injustice.

Supporters of "social justice" often identify justice with fairness. This has an intrinsic appeal, because an unjust action from the viewpoint of ordinary justice is always an unfair action. The criminal who robs you is scarcely treating you fairly. But, as we mentioned above, the proposition cannot be reversed: not everything that is unfair is necessarily unjust in the ordinary sense. For an unjust act as ordinarily understood must inflict injury of some kind, and not everything that is unfair causes injury. The concept of fairness will be treated more fully below, and is in any case controversial.

Genuine Justice

In the following pages we will argue that justice and injustice, as traditionally understood from time immemorial, possess four distinguishing features, which follow from the simple fact that they are categories of ethical judgment. First, justice and injustice are primarily qualities, not of states of affairs in society, but of the *actions* of individuals ("action" taken in the broad sense explained above, Preface and p. 11, as an umbrella term standing for all those ways in which the individual will has an effect on the world, including such things as willful inaction, negligence, weakness of will, and

so forth, for which the individual can therefore be held directly accountable). Justice is a quality of states of affairs only in so far as those states are
the product of actions. A state of affairs can be good or bad, but it cannot
of itself be either ethical or unethical. Only persons and their actions can
be unethical. To speak of a state of affairs as unethical, independently of
any unethical action that produced it, is to commit a fallacy.

But when it is said, as "social justice" insists on saying, that poverty or
inequality of power, which are incontestably states of affairs and not actions,
are unjust, it is committing precisely that fallacy, of predicating an ethical
quality of a matter that cannot possibly be ethical. Poverty of itself is neither
moral nor immoral, and neither is wealth. It is true that poverty often results
from human actions. But in the ordinary course of events it is not a result
that is intended. It is true that the at least temporary poverty of one group
in society can be caused by another group's selfish pursuit of its own interests. When consumers refuse to buy products that are more expensive and
at the same time of lower quality, and instead buy those that are cheaper
and of better quality, this may well deprive the producers of the former of
their livelihood. But is this unjust? This question leads to our next point.

Second, justice and injustice hinge crucially on the *will*. Human action is
never merely an external or physical event, but is always accompanied by a
subjective, internal, or mental causal force which we call will, and the moral
value of the action depends on the moral quality of that will. The first
requisite for an action to possess moral value is that it be done with a good
will. Similarly with justice. There can be no true injustice unless the subjective will of the agent (if only through negligence or culpable inaction)
makes it unjust. For this reason justice can be described as a *relationship
between wills*.

Now ordinary justice always includes a reference to this interior will. The
necessity of an evil will for an action to be evil is captured by the Common
law in the concept of *mens rea*.[31] But "social justice" has no reference to the
will, and has no equivalent to *mens rea*. What counts for it is purely the objective and material condition of poverty or inequality. As the U.S. Supreme
Court has demonstrated with the concept of "disparate impact," it is possible to be guilty of the crime of "discrimination" without any intention to
discriminate. The absence of this reference to the will removes "social
justice" from the realm of ethics.

Third, justice and injustice necessarily entail *individual accountability
and responsibility*. This follows from the two preceding truths. If there
has been an injustice, this was because some individual performed some
unjust action, and performed it knowingly and willingly. And whoever has

performed an unjust action knowingly and willingly is personally the cause of the harm his action has done. He is responsible for it, which means he can and must be held accountable for it. Not only can but must, for if he is not held accountable, justice is not done.

From this fact of individual responsibility flows the possibility of individual desert, of innocence and guilt, of praise and blame, and reward and punishment, all of which are directly associated with the ordinary concept of justice, and all of which make it possible to use that concept in regulating human affairs, resolving conflicts, and establishing peace.

While ordinary justice rests in this way on personal responsibility and accountability, however, "social justice" does not, but rather replaces the responsibility of the individual with the responsibility of society. As remarked above, "social justice" is a demand addressed to society as a whole and not to the individual; and as such it is a demand that can be met only by the state. This transference of responsibility, however, has two extremely serious effects. For one, it eliminates the possibility of individual desert, innocence and guilt, praise and blame, and reward and punishment. This is a step with incalculable consequences for society.

For another, it condemns the individual to helplessness. If only society has the responsibility to remedy poverty, the individual who suffers from it has no responsibility to do so. This is a message of dependency and despair. Hope arises in an individual heart in a difficult situation because one sees one has oneself the possibility of taking action against it. Supporters of "social justice" condemn ordinary justice because it places the burden of responsibility for removing poverty on the shoulders of the poor themselves. But though this burden of responsibility may not yet by itself be sufficient to create the possibility of hope, it is necessary, since hope involves the belief that I am free to act on my own behalf.

Fourth, justice and injustice presuppose that individuals possess *freedom of will*. This follows of itself from the three preceding truths. If action, will, and responsibility are key elements of justice, this can only be so on condition that the will is free. For a will that was predetermined by extraneous forces might indeed perform an action (though it would not be what we would be disposed to call a human action); and could also indeed be *held* extrinsically accountable by authority for harm that it caused, in the way we hold an animal accountable, but it could not possibly be a source of moral value, and could not be genuinely and interiorly responsible for its actions, unless it were free. Moral value belongs only to a free will.

Now the ordinary conception of justice is built upon this reverence for a free will, and all sorts of allowances are made in its courts of law for the various degrees in which it may be thought that the freedom of the will of the agent was limited or restricted in some way. But "social justice" does not require any doctrine of free will. For the concepts of poverty or inequality in society do not entail any such belief.

These four qualities we have here outlined are necessary features of any genuine conception of justice, but they are not features of "social justice." We are not, therefore, merely arguing that ordinary justice and "social justice" are different, but that they are in conflict with one another, and that of the two only ordinary justice is genuine justice. "Social justice" is not justice at all.

Our aim in these first two chapters has been to show the profound and in fact irreconcilable contradiction that exists between ordinary justice and "social" justice. It is a natural question to ask: how did this state of things come about? We investigate this question in the next three chapters and find ourselves coming to some surprising conclusions. In three further chapters we then develop a positive theory of justice, which we offer as an alternative to "social justice" as currently understood, by examining the four features mentioned above that have traditionally been understood to mark the ordinary concept of justice.

Part Two

Social Justice

Chapter 3

The Origins of Social Justice

"Social justice" has been mainly a religious conception, in the sense that it originated in religious circles, underwent a large part of its conceptual development in official statements of religious authorities, and has been adopted most enthusiastically by the members of religious organizations. Since 1931 it has been part of the official teaching of the Roman Catholic Church. Philosophers seem to have come to it late: only since the publication of John Rawls's *Theory of Justice* in 1971 does it appear to have received much explicit attention from them.[32] Rawls's theory, though it has occupied the center of the philosophical stage since that time, represents only one version of the idea, however, and an idiosyncratic one. In studying the origins of the idea, it will be necessary to make a distinction between the *term* and its *meaning*. The term was coined in Italy, but with a very different meaning from what it now possesses. The meaning it now possesses can be said to have emerged first in a certain sense in England, but (so far as I have been able to discover) originally without the term. In both, however, it was far closer to ordinary justice than it has now become, for initially it was, as ordinary justice is, a formal concept rather than the material one it is now. The course of its history has been notable for the role played by misunderstandings.

Concerns similar to those which came to expression in the concept of social justice can be found in earlier times. They played a decisive role in the French Revolution of 1789, and in some respects even many centuries before that. But what we focus on here is the application to them of the idea of "justice." For this was new.

Italy

The *term* "social justice" owes its origin as a distinct usage (*giustizia sociale*) to the Italian *Risorgimento* of the nineteenth century.[33] It was first used, to our knowledge, by the Jesuit writer Luigi Taparelli d'Azeglio in 1840 in the debates that accompanied that bloody movement to abolish the existing feudal regimes and bring political unity to the Italian peninsula.[34] Despite its many local dialects and political divisions the peninsula had long been recognized as a cultural unity, a fact attested to, among other things, by the founding of the Accademia della Crusca in Florence in 1583, whose mission was to study the vocabulary of the whole of Italy. But by 1840 the territory was carved up politically between a number of different states, among them Austria, which held the north, Piedmont in the northwest, the Papal States across the middle, and the kingdom of Naples. Napoleon, however, had occupied the entire mainland, and divided it up among a number of republics, which he subsequently converted into "kingdoms." He named one of them the "Kingdom of Italy" (roughly Venice), and treated the peninsula in some respects as an administrative unity. For example, the Code Napoleon was introduced everywhere. After his fall, the Congress of Vienna in 1816 largely restored the earlier political powers that had preceded Napoleon. But Napoleon had left behind him the vision of a unified Italy, which in the wave of romantic nationalism that swept Europe in the nineteenth century possessed great inspirational power, especially for the educated and liberal middle classes (liberal in the original European sense, favoring personal liberty and free trade and typically anticlerical because of the church's opposition to both). It was not long before agitation began with the aim of bringing the unification about. Revolutionary movements such as the *Carbonari* sprang up throughout the territory around 1820, though without immediate success. In 1830 violent insurrections inspired by the July Revolution in France broke out in several places, but were soon crushed by the Austrian army. In January 1848 revolution broke out in Sicily, leading to war between Piedmont, which aimed at unification, and Austria, which resisted it, but which Austria won. The pope of the time, Pius IX, ruler of the Papal States, ascended the throne as a liberal, but when his prime minister was murdered took a more favorable view of conservatism. Eventually, through the efforts of Cavour in Piedmont, Garibaldi in the south and others, the unified Kingdom of Italy was achieved in 1870.

This project of unifying Italy, which was thus drawn out over some 50 years, produced not only violence and bloodshed but also fierce debate about fundamental questions of political and philosophical theory. On what foundation does the state rest? What is the origin of its power? By what right does anyone possess the authority to govern others? Is political authority created simply by military power and received by subsequent generations of rulers as an inheritance, or conferred by a contract between the people and the ruler, as Locke had argued? The great aim of the reformers was to replace the existing absolute powers ruling the several states, the monarchies, the aristocracies, and the Catholic Church, with a secular constitutional national government that would guarantee individual liberties. Conservatives were skeptical about the ultimate outcome of this and generally wished to keep as much of the old order as possible. This was the immediate context that gave birth to the concept of "social justice."

Luigi Taparelli d'Azeglio, S.J. (1793–1862)

It is one of the ironies of history that the quintessentially "liberal" idea (in the American sense) of "social justice," as it was to become, should have been originated by an ardent conservative. Prospero (his baptismal name) Taparelli was born in Turin into an aristocratic but nationalistic family which was to play a prominent role in the *Risorgimento*. His father, Cesare, Marquis of Azeglio in the Piedmont, was a soldier and a devout and active Catholic who took his family to Tuscany to escape Napoleon's armies and published there the nationalistic newspaper *Amico d'Italia* (Friend of Italy); his mother, Cristina, the Countess Morozzo, was the sister of Cardinal Giuseppe Morozzo. His younger brother Massimo, after writing a series of nationalistic novels, turned to politics as a pamphleteer in the national cause and became premier of Piedmont; to this day he remains an honored name in the public life of Italy. Luigi's cousin, Count Cesare Balbo, published a book *Delle speranze d'Italia* (On the Hopes of Italy), which aroused a strong sense of Italian nationalism.[35]

The young Prospero studied at first the secular thinkers prominent at the time, such as Condillac, famous for his sensationism, a form of extreme empiricism, and also for his advocacy of free trade, but then discovered the French traditionalists, Lamennais, de Bonald and de Maistre. When Pope Pius VII summoned the Jesuit order back into existence in 1814 (it had been dissolved by Clement XIV in 1773), Prospero joined it without delay, taking the name of Luigi in honor of Saint Aloysius (Luigi in Italian) Gonzaga. He was ordained a priest in 1820, made rector of the novitiate in Novara in 1822, then in 1824 of the Jesuit house of studies in Rome, the *Collegio Romano*, later to become the Gregorian University.

As a thinker Taparelli's chief concern from the first was with the state of political society, which he wished to influence in a conservative direction, toward the preservation of the existing aristocratic and feudal order, and of papal authority, which as we have seen was then not only spiritual but also temporal. But he realized that the intellectual reputation of the church at the time left much to be desired and was a serious obstacle to its effective influence. The church needed a philosophical renewal. In Novara his attention had been directed to the mediaeval scholastics, and in particular to the works of St. Thomas Aquinas. In Rome he now seized on Thomas as the key to intellectual reform, and in 1827 and 1828 laid down a curriculum for the Collegio Romano on Thomistic lines.[36] Through these writings Taparelli became one of the originators of neo-scholasticism and neo-Thomism (though he does not seem to have studied Thomas very intensely).

In 1850 he was appointed to the staff of the Vatican's new journal *Civiltà Cattolica*, where one of his collaborators, on whom he had much influence, was Gioacchino Pecci, a former student of his, who became Pope Leo XIII and in 1879, in the encyclical *Aeterni Patris*, canonized Thomism as the official philosophy of the Catholic church.

Taparelli's aim, however, to which neo-Thomism was meant to contribute, was to develop a conservative and specifically Catholic theory of society that would be an alternative to the liberal and *laissez-faire* theory of writers such as Locke and Adam Smith. In 1833 he was transferred to Palermo and remained there for 16 years, during which he wrote his principal work, *Saggio teoretico di dritto naturale appoggiato sul fatto* ("*A Theoretical Treatise on Natural Law Resting on Fact*"), in five volumes, published from 1840 to 1843. The phrase "*sul fatto*" gives perhaps the most distinctive feature of his approach. The Lockean idea that political authority arises out of some kind of "contract" is absurd, he argues, for such a thing has never actually happened. The facts of history are that the right to govern has been obtained through the "natural superiority" of the ruler and of the ruling class: through their superior valor, knowledge, and wealth. This is the actual system created by divine providence. Whoever brings order into a society has the right to rule it. By "order," which he also refers to as "harmony," he seems to have in mind mainly the administration of criminal justice.

The same rule of natural superiority holds true, according to Taparelli, even between nations: empires and hegemonies are created, not in virtue of any contract, but through the natural superiority of a race or a people over others. This natural superiority establishes its power directly or indirectly, creating, whether by fact or by right, a hierarchy of relationships between the different nations. It is a power independent of particular wills, and imposes itself on individuals and on peoples. In speaking of a "natural superiority," Taparelli means, not "nature" in a species sense, for he considers that "all men are equal in nature," but that superiority of character, knowledge, and wealth mentioned in the previous paragraph. Men are "unequal in their persons." The *Saggio teoretico* seems never to have been translated into English.

The Creator has implanted in all men by nature a tendency to seek the supreme good, and therefore to seek the lesser goods that lead to it. Men do this more effectively by cooperating with one another, and therefore it is God's will that they should live together in societies. But no society can survive without some authority that establishes order in it. This has been true since the beginning of human history. Therefore it is God's will that there should exist "natural authority," the authority that naturally arises in human society by the fact that some men are naturally braver, more competent, more intelligent, more wealthy, or more endowed with the qualities of leadership than others. Taparelli's viewpoint about the origins of governmental authority is not far from Hume's, that the first rulers attained their position through their personal qualities of valor, force, integrity, or prudence which commanded the respect and confidence of the people.[37] It also resembles de Maistre's idea of "legitimate usurpation," that all legitimacy is invariably built on a foundation of illegitimacy, from which it emerges seamlessly.[38]

When a particular authority grows so strong that it has no superior, argues Taparelli, it attains to sovereignty, and if it exists in a stable territory it becomes a state. The right to govern the state belongs to the person who has established order in it. This right is not given to him directly by nature, but is the result of his personal qualities and achievements. No one else has a true right to govern, and all others in the society are therefore subject to his rule.

> Here in a few words is the theory of social existence based upon the facts of history, and likewise confirmed by those facts. The existence of associations of men united by nature, equal to one another in their nature, unequal in their persons, free in their power of choice and therefore in need of a principle of unity: these are the chief facts of history to which we have applied the universal principle of duty. The results of this application are that man needs always to be governed, and so he is, in point of fact; that he who governs is stronger and at the same time possesses authority, and so he actually is; that subjects are not sovereigns, and in point of fact they are not . . . [39]

Compare this theory of the facts of history with the hypotheses of the social contract where man is by nature free but in fact is in chains; by right is sovereign but in fact is a subject; creates the society, but in fact is created by it; confers authority, but in fact has no part of that authority; has made a pact, but did no negotiating; did it to secure all his rights, and meanwhile gave them away; believes every state to be a republic, yet sees there are monarchies; believes all men are equal, yet sees everywhere a hierarchy of classes; believes it gives consent, yet sees things happen despite it; believes it gives laws, yet sees that it receives them; . . . Compare these two doctrines, I say, and judge which of them is truer![40]

The liberal theories of society are nothing more than theories, mere speculation. They are not drawn from history and they are not sufficient to explain the realities of history.

Taparelli makes a distinction, which was to become influential in Catholicism, between "the large society," the State, and "the small societies," the family and the local organizations and authorities that men create to further their local purposes. The foundation of society is not the large society but the small ones. The large society is built, not from the top down, but from the bottom up, out of the small ones. Therefore the large society is in an important sense subordinate to the small ones. Each of these smaller societies has its own end, its own authority, its own principles of action, and its own rights. Like individuals generally, they have an obligation to work together for the common good. Each lesser society must preserve its own inner unity without threatening that of the whole; and every larger society must maintain its unity without destroying the unity of the lesser societies.

This teaching was eventually to give rise to the Catholic doctrine of subsidiarity, that social functions that can be performed adequately by local authorities, such as the family or the town, should be assigned to them and not to higher or more remote authorities such as the national government. It should be noted that this principle is distinctly conservative, though it is often not recognized as such.

Taparelli's Conception of Social Justice

Taparelli discusses justice and social justice against the background of the revolutionary movements which had been aiming since the fall of Napoleon to overthrow the restored feudal and absolutistic political regimes in Italy, including the religious government of the Papal States, and replace them with regimes of political equality. The question at issue for him can be formulated thus: does distributive or social justice require the creation of political equality as the liberal revolutionaries insist, or does it demand the preservation of the existing, traditional order, in which political power is necessarily unequal? Is the existence of an absolute ruler and an aristocracy unjust? His answer is that social justice requires us to accept *inequality*.

Justice, he argues, is the habitual inclination to level or balance accounts. Distributive justice equalizes proportions in the common good. Social justice is justice between man and man. But what proportions exist between man and man? Considering man in the abstract, that is, man endowed solely with the qualities of human nature, man considered simply as a rational animal, between man and man the relationship that exists is one of complete equality, for "man and man" signifies here nothing other than humanity replicated twice. What proportionate equality could be greater? Social justice should therefore level all men in regard to the rights given with their humanity, since the Creator has equalized them by nature; and man fulfills the intentions of his maker by acting according to the norm of this justice.[41]

But this is only half the picture, in Taparelli's view. Actually existing men are not simply instances of abstract human nature but concrete individuals with particular qualities, and on the level of their individuality they are unequal. For social justice, their social rights and duties, that fact is decisive.

But slow. Where is this abstract man, this replicated humanity, the notion of which has suggested to me the first lineaments of social justice? If there exist men associated with other men, they always exist in the *concrete*, always individuated, always endowed with forces possessing definite qualities. But when I consider men from this new perspective, where is the equality? Compare age with age, intelligence with intelligence, strength with strength, etc., everything is disparity between men: a disparity, furthermore, that derives from nature, since it is nature that forms the individual as it does the species; or rather, let us say nature forms individuals, man perceives species. I conclude correctly, then, that all individual human beings are *naturally unequal* among themselves in everything that pertains to their *individuality*, just as they are naturally *equal* in all that pertains to the *species*. And so the activity of man will be just when it is appropriate to the different rights of those with whom one is dealing. Everything in individuals is inequality, even though the likeness of their natures be total.[42]

This individual inequality does not contradict the equality of species-nature, for the qualities of the individual are something added on, over and above, to the species-nature. If unequal quantities are added to equal ones, the sums are unequal. For example, if to the species-property of *man* is added the individuality of *son*, this individual stands to his father in the relationship of a debtor. For to be a son means to have received one's existence, and to be a father means to have given it. If the giver and the receiver considered themselves only as endowed with humanity, they would be equal and they would not owe one another anything reciprocally; but if their accounts are to be in balance in light of the fact that one of the two in becoming an *individual* has received his existence from the other, this other has a right to a repayment. Justice demands, then, that the son render to the father an equivalent of the existence he has received from him.[43]

Not only does individual inequality not contradict species-equality, but it is a product of it. The demand that accounts be balanced, and therefore that individual differences be taken into account, comes from their species-equality.

But why does justice demand that the accounts be balanced? Precisely because the equal humanity in both of them requires the equalization as its right. The inequality between the rights of the father and son just considered, far from standing in contrast to their species-equality, is rather a necessary consequence of it. The species-equality is the basis of all their inequalities as individuals, just as the one nature is the basis of all the different individualities.[44]

The consequence is that justice has very different requirements for private goods and common or social goods. In the one case it requires a quantitative equality, but not in the other.[45]

On the basis of this natural equality and natural inequality, which represent in his view indubitable facts of our historical experience (the "*fatto*" of the subtitle of the book), Taparelli considers it is possible to give a valid account of the particular social rights and duties that apply in particular societies, in a way that will show they arise equally from human nature and the facts of historical experience. The first principle of morality applied to social existence commands us to procure the good of others, and therefore to abstain from impeding it. This implies a correlative right on the other's part to procure his own good without being impeded by us, so long as he does not pose an obstacle to ours.

Social justice as Taparelli discusses it has little or nothing to do with the economy; it is the justice of the constitutional arrangements of a society. This is not a new or revolutionary conception of justice. It does nothing to reduce or eliminate individual responsibility. It is a species of ordinary distributive justice, as that virtue was described by Aristotle, St. Thomas, and Kant. "For distributive justice" is what "governs public administrators in the distribution of the offices of the society." Far from requiring equality, it requires the acceptance of inequality.

Taparelli's conception of social justice has been forgotten, together with the feudal order it defended. But it, and indeed his entire political philosophy, is a serious contribution to conservative thought which ought to be better known than it is. Instead, he was to exert an influence on history through something entirely different, which he never labeled "social justice," and which scarcely corresponds in substance to anything that might be known under that name today, but which would nevertheless come to be known by that name: his conception of morality in economics.

Taparelli on the Economy

Taparelli began writing on the economy after he joined the *Civiltà Cattolica* in 1850. At that time the industrial revolution, which had begun in England around 1770, had not yet reached Italy. Indeed, it is a common opinion among economic historians that properly speaking it never did, at least not until after the Second World War. Rather, Italy experienced only something "analogous" to an industrial revolution. Until the country was unified in 1870, the methods of production in the various separate states were uniformly still very labor-intensive, and trade was governed by guilds and restricted by heavy regulation and high tariffs. Protectionism reigned. The dominant industry remained agriculture. Until the end of the century, when the banking system was reformed, there was little or no indigenous capital. However, the free trade doctrines of Adam Smith and David Ricardo were known, as were the beginnings of the industrial revolution in France.

Taparelli opposed in principle the entire liberal project, both political and economic, which he sometimes summarized under the two names, Locke and Adam Smith. A later collection of his essays bears the appropriate title *Tyrannous Liberty.*[46]

The reason for this opposition was that he saw liberalism as a product of the Protestant Reformation which exalted individual judgment over the divine authority of the church and thereby replaced the Catholic sense of community with an emphasis on the self-interest of the isolated individual. He distinguishes between the "heterodox" or non-Catholic economy, then in the process of being introduced throughout Europe as the free-trade doctrines of Adam Smith took hold, and the Catholic or ideal economy.

The theory of the secular economists such as Smith elevates the self-centered search for utility as the governing force of human life, he argues. The consequence of this individualism is that "society is in a perpetual antagonism where each one offers the minimum in order to obtain the maximum."[47] Because of competition, "society is a war of all against all: war between the producers, war of the producers against the buyers, war of one nation against another in order to absorb its wealth by means of customs duties."[48] Since the wealth of the government depends on the wealth of its citizens, which it takes through taxes, "the government must inject itself into all private enterprises, in order to press all its citizens to work for the public wealth."[49] This injection of itself by government into private enterprises is not something Taparelli welcomes at all. Nor does he welcome taxes. The logical outcome of the society created by individualism is a demand for redistribution, and so communism. At bottom the individualistic economy is just anarchy.

By contrast, the Christian or Catholic economy represents order. It is founded on belief in God, it submits to divine revelation, maintains respect for the human person and for the Christian ideal of charity and self-sacrifice, and is alone capable of explaining what actually happens in economic life. As against the "iron law of wages," for example, Taparelli argues that in practice an employer must as a practical matter pay wages sufficient to support not only the individual worker but his family, and furthermore that this is the right and Catholic thing to do – an argument that, as we shall see, was to become subsequently a founding doctrine of official Catholic social teaching. But the Catholic economy as Taparelli understands it is by no means one that pursues economic equality. Taparelli does not believe in societal equality, either in political life or the economy. He believes, as we have seen, that there is a natural hierarchy among men, and leadership in all spheres goes rightly to those who create order. " . . . there is a big difference between the broom wielded by the humblest workers and the pen held by the higher employees" of the divine master.[50] What distinguishes the Catholic economy is not laws restricting trade, but a spirit of cooperation. The Catholic spirit of cooperation in place of competition in the economy "adds to the sentiment of civic equality respect for the hierarchical subordination which is so natural between those who serve the same master."[51] In the Catholic economy, the highest value will be given, not to the search for money and pleasure, but to honorable and honest conduct. "Hobbes's war of all against all will give way to the universal cooperation of individuals, who are equal in regard to their species-nature, but hierarchically coordinated in their labours under the supreme Master."[52] In a true

Catholic economy, those who carry out the functions of government will do so at their own expense, as a public service performed out of love for their country; they will not be paid salaries out of the public purse.

Taparelli quarrels not only with the secular economy animated by the spirit of competition, but also with the secular science of economics as developed by Adam Smith and his followers. As a science describing human activity, economics cannot be separated from issues of morality and conscience. Economics in his view is essentially a moral science, that is one subordinated to moral considerations. But the difference between the Catholic economy, together with its Catholic discipline of economics focusing on morality, on the one hand and the secular economy with its purely scientific economics on the other is mainly a difference in motivation. It is not a difference in public policy. In the Catholic economy legal restraints on the economy will be minimal. ". . . many of Bastiat's observations in favor of liberty of commerce square with the teachings of Catholic economics."[53]

> We should not judge that it is useless for a Catholic government to investigate the doctrine of the heterodox economists on the production and distribution of wealth. This science of production will always be necessary as an auxiliary to the Catholic science of ordering.[54]

"So a treatise on the Catholic economy is only a treatise on just economic liberty."[55] "An honourable liberty is the goal and utility is merely the means for every good administration."[56] It does not impose restrictions on the liberty of its citizens in order to enrich the government, for it is the freest economy that produces the wealthiest government. The role of justice and charity is not to restrict liberty but to perfect it. "Liberty is more perfect in a state where crime is repressed and honest people are protected than in one" dominated by the Camorra.[57] In regard to public policy Taparelli is essentially a liberal, in the European sense of that word.

In the Catholic economy taxes will be minimal, and government will be careful not to adopt measures that injure capital. Government should know what kinds of taxes will weigh the least heavily on capital, what are the cheapest kinds of tax, how to make the best use of capital not invested, and how to use wisely the money necessary to buy the instruments of commerce. The poor will find themselves free to lift themselves up to riches.[58] He does not place care for the poor among the duties of government, but of individuals. It is the duty of those who have the goods of this world to care for those who lack them, and this should be reflected in the theoretical account of how an economy works successfully.

> If economic science . . . wants to show us how, through the power of self-interest, wealth distributes itself between the proprietor, the capitalist, the worker and the tax collector, it ought also to show us that where Catholic charity reigns, the shares of the capitalist and the proprietor return to a large extent into the hands of the worker as a balm, levelling through generosity the inequalities of fortune.[59]

The role of government, for its part, is the traditional one of bringing moral order, or justice. It is "to protect weakness against force."[60] Justice, together with humane feeling ("tenderness"), is called to protect the order of society both against the cruelty of the powerful who crush the poor and also against the communism of the poor who rise up against the powerful.

Just as there is nothing in Taparelli's doctrine of social justice to undermine individual responsibility, neither is there anything in his conception of a Catholic economy and economics that would do that. What characterizes these is a higher esteem for humane cooperation rather than rigorous competition. Personal accountability for one's actions and inactions is not threatened.

So far as I have been able to discover, Taparelli never used the term "social justice" in reference to economic questions. As we have seen, social justice for him is the constitutional justice of a society, the justice which defends right order in the constitutional arrangements of the society. Its task at that juncture of history, he believed, was to defend the inherited rights of the existing feudal powers, the church and the aristocracy, against the rising tide of democratic equality. But many of those who read him, including Pope Pius XI, leaving Taparelli's constitutional views and his doctrine of inequality entirely aside, focused instead on his economic doctrine, and applied his term "social justice" to that. Under that name, a concept of economic equality which he did not espouse, and which has been far more damaging to individual responsibility, was to be his paradoxical legacy to his church and the world.

Taparelli's Reach

Taparelli has some claim to be considered the father of Catholic social teaching. One of his students was the Jesuit, Matteo Liberatore, who wrote the first draft of Pope Leo XIII's encyclical *Rerum Novarum*, "On the Condition of the Working Classes," published in 1891, the first papal statement on "the social question." Leo himself, as we have noted, had been a student of Taparelli's and collaborator at the *Civiltà Cattolica* and seems clearly to have been influenced by him. Pius XI used to recommend the study of Taparelli's works in private conversations with his friends and colleagues. One of Liberatore's students was Oswald von Nell-Breuning, S.J., who wrote Pius's encyclical *Quadragesimo Anno*, published in 1931, which adopted "social justice" officially as part of Catholic doctrine, but as an economic doctrine and one far stronger than Taparelli's: " . . . the right ordering of economic life cannot be left to a free competition of forces. For from this source, as from a poisoned spring, have originated and spread all the errors of individualist economic teaching."[61] In 1932 Franklin Delano Roosevelt quoted this encyclical in a campaign speech before a large crowd in Detroit, saying it was "just as radical as I am," and "one of the greatest documents of modern times."[62]

Antonio Rosmini-Serbati (1797–1855)

Although Taparelli introduced the term "social justice" in his book of 1840, it seems to have attracted little attention till it was publicized by Rosmini in his work *La Costituzione secondo la Giustizia Sociale* in 1848. While Taparelli was a patent conservative, however, Rosmini was that rare beast in nineteenth century Europe, a Catholic liberal – in the European sense of the term, or what is now referred to sometimes in the English-speaking world as "classical liberal" to distinguish it from the Wilsonian, Rooseveltian, progressive or "modern" liberal.

He was born into a wealthy and modestly noble family in Rovereto in the north of Italy, not far from Trent, then part of the Austro-Hungarian Empire and governed from Vienna.[63] (His *Panegyric for Pius VII*, 1823, was censored by the Austrian government and refused publication till 1831.) From an early age he led an intense spiritual life, both studious and devout, and in 1821 was ordained a priest. He read well beyond the confines of Italian theology, however, becoming familiar with the works both of French *philosophes* such as Condillac, conservatives such as Chateaubriand, de Bonald and de Maistre, and also the British writers David Hume, Reid, Dugald Stewart, Adam Smith, and Malthus, about most of whom he was subsequently to write.[64] After studying at the University of Padua, a center of Aristotelian philosophy, he moved to Milan, where he became lifelong friends with Alessandro Manzoni, author of what was to become the great Italian novel, *I Promessi Sposi*. He was apparently responsible for persuading Manzoni to rewrite his edition of 1840 in the language of Tuscany. In 1828 he founded a religious order, the Institute of Charity, which is still active in several countries including the United Kingdom and the United States.

From the beginning Rosmini evinced what one writer has called "a profound love of individual freedom."[65] He welcomed the revolutionary uprisings of the time, seeing in them "the hand of God."[66] In his philosophy, however, he takes a middle, liberal path between the intense conservatism that largely characterized the Catholic world and the new redistributionist spirit unleashed by the French Revolution. This liberal stance called down on his head determined opposition from conservatives, especially the Jesuits. *La Costituzione* and another work, *The Five Wounds of Holy Church*, supporting reform of the clergy, were placed on the Vatican's Index of Forbidden Books, which was deeply painful to him. He was attacked in the pages of *Civiltà Cattolica* by Taparelli and his fellow Jesuit Matteo Liberatore, even though he had earlier had a long correspondence with Taparelli, Taparelli knew he had worked with his father Cesare in Turin, and it was partly Rosmini's enthusiasm for Aquinas that had initially led Taparelli to that thinker.[67] Not long before his death, however, the books were removed from the Index, to his immense relief. In 1889 40 propositions taken from his books were condemned by Pope Leo XIII as implying an identity of man with God, but in 2001 this was acknowledged to be a misinterpretation. His saintly personal character was always recognized, however, and in November 2007 he was formally declared beatified.

Like Taparelli, Rosmini was concerned from the beginning with the condition of society. Like Taparelli, he concluded that before he could address social questions usefully he needed to lay a prior philosophical foundation. Whereas Taparelli turned to Aquinas and the scholastics, however, Rosmini, though a great admirer of Aquinas, proceeded to develop his own original approach, and first to the modern problem of knowledge. In 1830 he published *A New Essay Concerning the Origin of Ideas*, the title implying a reference to Locke. In this work he develops the theory that from the beginning the mind has knowledge of the non-mental world through the concept of being, which is innate. He went on to publish many further books in which he applies these ideas to various areas of philosophy, and as the knowledge of his works has spread, his philosophical reputation has steadily grown.

At the center of his philosophy, including his philosophy of society, is the individual person. It is the individual who has knowledge of being, and who also has feeling, to which Rosmini pays a good deal of attention, analyzing it in terms of the feeler (the mind) and the felt (body). Within the individual is an active principle, the will, by which it reacts to what it knows and which constitutes it a person. His treatment of the will reflects

Kant's, which we will see more of in the following pages. Because of the will, and the will's power of free choice, more precisely *in* the will, each person has an incommunicable individuality and an inviolable dignity. Unlike Kant, however, and in our judgment correctly, Rosmini accepts the existence of free will because "interior observation shows that such a faculty does indeed exist."[68] Confronted with truth, the will has the power to deny it, but must acknowledge it as truth: to deny what one knows is to step into non-being. This is the first dictate both of reason and of morality, and the source of all further moral principle, which, founded on the principle of non-contradiction, has an objective reality. The good, therefore, exists in an objective "order of being," and moral good occurs when the individual desires the good according to its place in the order of being, rather than solely as a utilitarian good for the individual himself.

The inherent dignity of each person founded on the freedom of the will and the consequent power of moral choice gives rise to the concept of "right." Since each individual is bound to acknowledge as truth what he knows to be truth, each must respect the same obligation in others, and the same dignity. Each therefore has the moral ability to act freely so long as he does not injure the dignity of others. "Right is a moral governance or authority to act, or: right is a faculty to do what we please, protected by the moral law which obliges others to respect that faculty."[69] In the sense of Isaiah Berlin's distinction between positive and negative rights, right for Rosmini is negative: it represents, in Berlin's words, " . . . the area within which the subject (of the right) . . . is or should be left to do or be what he is able to do or be, without interference by other persons."[70]

All rights are at bottom rights of individuals. Society as such does not have rights.

> If we are going to disentangle the intricacies of human rights, it is indispensable to abandon useless abstractions and fictitious entities, which result from the way we conceive things mentally, in order to establish the principle that "the subject of every right is always the individual." We have to reduce to individual rights even those rights which we call, for the sake of abbreviation, "social rights."[71]

As Denis Cleary remarks, "For Rosmini, every society is simply the union of two or more people undertaken with the intention of obtaining a common advantage."[72]

Rosmini makes a useful distinction between the common good and the public good. The former consists of the good of all the individuals who make up the social body and are subjects of rights. The latter is the good of the social body taken as a whole or considered as an organization. If there is a conflict between these two, it is the common good that must take precedence, for the public good is subordinated as a means to the common good. ". . . not a single right of the individual citizen . . . can be sacrificed for the sake of the public good."[73]

The idea of right gives rise to the concept of property, which occupies a central place in Rosmini's thought. Already in 1823, in the *Panegyric*, Rosmini defended the right to private property against the redistributionist policies spawned by the French Revolution. The tradition of thought endorsed by Pius, he stated, holds that property must be considered sacred. Property is rendered inviolable not by the physical force that protects it, but by the human dignity of the owner. It is the equal right to own property that constitutes human equality. God has placed on everyone's property a seal which must not be broken. In his essays on political science Rosmini states as the first principle of justice: "Everyone's property must be so sacred as not to be violated for any reason."[74]

In a fragment also dating from 1823 he in effect defines justice in terms of property. There are three fundamental rules of justice, he states:

1. Always respect others' property, even if by aggressing upon it you could gain something.
2. If someone else deliberately aggresses on your property and you do not have any way to rescue it other than by responding in kind, you can do this.
3. You are entitled to be indemnified at the expense of the people who offended against your legitimate right.[75]

In his *Philosophy of Right* Rosmini identifies the acquisition of property as a defining quality of persons. Property represents

an entirely personal principle, involving consciousness and therefore presupposing an intelligent principle capable of reflecting upon itself and seeing itself objectively . . . The personal principle, therefore, is the principle of property, Self is the principle of what is Proper to Oneself, of what is owned by the self. "Self" must exist before "his" can exist. But self cannot exist except in an intellective being. Consequently, there can be no true property, nothing that is proper to oneself . . . except in an intellective being.[76]

Rosmini rejects the view, assumed by Locke and others including several popes, that originally all the goods of the earth belonged to the human community in common, a view which could serve as premise of an argument for redistribution. Before things are appropriated by individuals, they belong to no one. After appropriation they belong to the person who has first appropriated them.[77] It is not immoral for an individual to accumulate property in material goods. On the contrary, the accumulation of property leads to the increase of productivity.[78]

The ability to own property is the defining power of liberty. "Juridical freedom means nothing but the power that the person-proprietor has over his own thing, with which he can morally do what he pleases."[79] The "concept of freedom does not exist if completely deprived of property."[80]

Property is so much at the center of Rosmini's moral philosophy that he uses it as a replacement for Kant's categorical imperative. The Kantian imperative, "act only according to the maxim by which you can at the same time will that it should become a universal law," is unsatisfactory because, although it establishes an equal freedom of action for all men, it does not specify substantially or materially but only formally where the limits of that freedom are. That means for Rosmini that the calculation of the limits of freedom in practice would have to be, unrealistically, left up to each individual. In place of the formal Kantian rule Rosmini proposes the substantial principle: "Respect that which belongs to others." This, he argues, has the advantage that the quantity of free activity that each person can have is assigned and definite: it is all the freedom that can be exercised without damaging someone else's property. Our freedom to act ends at the boundary of other persons' property. This limitation of each one's freedom is just, because the universal ethical principle of justice is not to harm one's neighbor, and to harm someone else's property in any way is to harm him personally. "Thus, the activity of each person finds in someone else's property the moral limit that cannot be trespassed."[81]

The defining power of the right to property is the "right to exclude." This means that others have a moral obligation to allow themselves to be excluded.[82] "It is the moral law which forbids others from impeding the free disposal of what a person owns."[83]

Social Justice

Although Taparelli was a conservative and Rosmini a liberal, with many and serious disagreements between them about the legitimate extent of liberty, they share the view that justice demands not equality but rather inequality in society. For in Rosmini's view, justice in society means that each should receive from society in proportion to what he gives to it.

If civil society must have as its object the common good of all its individual members, he asks, how is this good to be distributed among them? The view that it should be distributed equally he dismisses as "obviously mistaken," for justice consists not in simple equality, but in proportionate equality. The basis of a just distribution can only be the contribution each individual makes to the capital of the society. Those who shoulder more of the burdens of society consequently must obtain greater advantage from the protection it provides. The goal of society must be to equalize the "share-quota of utility" that its members can derive from the society; it does not consist in equalizing utility among the members. This is the "equitable distribution of the common good to which . . . the government of civil society should constantly tend if it wishes to walk in the way of law."[84]

In *The Constitution Under Social Justice*, which as we have noted was responsible for publicizing the term, Rosmini's purpose was to propose a new kind of constitution for the nations of Europe to adopt in place of the French model they had been following. The French model, resulting from the Revolution of 1789, has been a catastrophic failure, he argues. It has shown time and again, in the experience of all the countries that have tried it, that it is inherently unstable, with the consequence that one revolution inevitably leads to another. The reason for this fatal instability is that it offends against social justice. Namely, it suffers from two radical vices: it does not guarantee political justice, and it does not protect all property equally. It does not provide political justice, because it offers no means by which citizens can obtain redress against the unjust actions of government; and it does not protect all property equally, because it favors some kinds of property over others: namely, smaller property over larger.

Every society has two basic needs: justice and material well-being; and every government has the corresponding task of providing these. The perfect government is one organized in such a way that it renders justice to all, at the same time that it promotes the material well-being of all its citizens. All the rights of men can be reduced to two kinds: liberty rights and property rights. Liberty rights are rights to the free and upright exercise of all one's faculties. Every liberty right should therefore be protected and guaranteed. Similarly all property should be equally protected and guaranteed. In addition, property should be provided with laws designed to foster the development of the nation's wealth. It is the task of government to ensure that the wealth of the nation increases. This is part of social justice.[85] Rosmini does not share Taparelli's aversion to Adam Smith: he holds that government in its legislation must of necessity respect the laws of political economy.

In Rosmini's eyes the constitutions of the nations of Europe in his time were deficient on both the score of justice and also that of utility. They did not render justice to all, because minorities and individuals had no juridical recourse against the political authorities, there was no tribunal to which they could have recourse if political justice was violated. For "the legislative power supposes itself infallible and so gives itself omnipotence." But in fact the contrary was the case: justice toward minorities could be violated even in the formulation of the laws. For the same reason, he argued, the existing republican constitutions infringed on the liberty and rights of the Church as much as, if not more than, the most absolute governments did.[86]

These minorities whose rights were violated, in Rosmini's view, in the very formulation of the laws were not, as might be supposed at the present time, the poor, but just the opposite: the wealthy or those who own large properties, and who, in a system of one-man-one-vote, can be regularly outvoted in parliament by those who own little.

Constitutions of the French type, he writes,

> . . . do not guarantee sufficiently, and do not develop equally, the properties of their citizens, the totality of which forms the wealth of the nation and needs a political-economic administration. In this political power which presides over utility not all properties are represented equally: those that are not represented remain neglected, overpowered by those that alone obtain representation and which dispose of their advantage in legislation.[87]

The properties that are overpowered and neglected are the larger ones, "because smaller properties enjoy the same representation as larger ones."[88]

> How can the property of citizens be inviolable when those who have nothing or a few things can arbitrarily dispossess those who have a lot?[89]
>
> If those who make the laws do not possess anything, it is certain that they will make use of the legislative power they have in their hands to obtain possession of property by robbing those who have it: property will have no defense.[90]

The universal vote is the same in its consequences as the equalization of property; it is the agrarian law (of ancient Rome) which in our times ends up in communism. And the equal vote accorded to all who pay a particular amount has the same vice as the universal vote in regard to the larger property-owners.[91]

Socialism and communism are but the logical consequence of universal franchise in the election of deputies. If this electoral universal right to vote is just, then we must say that it is just that he who does not have anything puts his hand in the pocket of one who possesses something and steals what he wants.[92]

The basic problem with the French constitution, for Rosmini, is that, unlike England's, it is written, which means it is a work of theory rather than practice. "There are two kinds of political constitution: those formed piece by piece without a premeditated design, patched together continuously according to the contrast between social forces and the urgency of the people's instincts and needs; and those created in a single stroke, emerging fine and finished like a theory from the mind, like Minerva from the head of Zeus. The former are put into execution before they are written, the latter written before put into execution."

> The constitutions in existence before 1789 belonged for the most part to the first kind. Such was the constitution of Venice, such is still the constitution of England. The France of the Revolution, hostile to its past, excluded that past's accomplishments, looked upon its constitution as a clean slate, wrote a constitution on it and commanded the nation to give it obedience. The English constitution was undoubtedly a model for it, but there remained the immense difference of origin: the one a product of events, and so itself an event, whatever way it is considered; the other a work of speculative thought, and so written.[93]

However, the people everywhere now demand written constitutions, so Rosmini offers one.

The constitution he puts forward is designed to be in accord with social justice. He proposes two chief measures for this purpose: citizens should have the right to sue the government, and their voting power in elections should be proportionate to the taxes they pay.

To provide for the first right, his constitution creates a special "court of political justice" which is to be the guardian of an individual's rights against the majority, scrutinizing positive laws in order to ensure their accord with natural law. The members of the court would be elected by the entire citizenry.

> All rights cannot be represented through a majority vote. A majority, by its nature, represents only the greater part of the votes, not all. The nature of law is however such that it must be fully respected in all members individually, not simply in the majority: ninety-nine against one would be no more just than one against ninety-nine. Respect for a right does not depend on the number of persons who possess it or defend it, but rather requires equal respect in any subject whatsoever.[94]

Here Rosmini comes close to the U.S. "Bill of Rights," the first ten amendments to the U.S. Constitution, and would very probably have profited from knowledge of it, but he does not seem to have been familiar with it.

The second distinctive feature of Rosmini's constitution is that voting power is proportionate to taxation. Assuming the only direct taxes are those on property (the traditional system before the introduction of the income tax, which only occurred decades later), Rosmini equates people's tax burden with the amount of property they own. Those who pay no taxes have no vote. Those who do pay taxes are divided into two classes: those who pay more and those who pay less. Each group has its own chamber of deputies. The constitution makes provision for how the two are to function together.

> Part of the concept of social justice is the inviolability of all property. Part of this very same concept is the concurrence of all the citizens in paying taxes in exact proportion to their properties.[95]
>
> To give an equal electoral vote to everyone or almost everyone is exactly the same as to give the legislative power into the hands of the proletarians, and so effectively the men in such a system are counted by heads, and not by the complex of rights they possess and which ought to be guaranteed.[96]

Those who believe in the "sovereignty of the people deduced that every man should have an equal part in the government: as if sovereignty was annexed to the nature of man, and not a consequence of social relations. They confused natural equality with social equality."[97] "Men are equal in respect of natural law, but that never entails they ought to be equal in a society they create among themselves."[98]

The Meaning of Social Justice

It should be clear from this account that social justice as Rosmini understood it is continuous with ordinary justice. Nothing could be more in agreement with ordinary justice than the proposition that property is inviolable, and that the law should protect it. A constitution that gives individuals the political power to take the property of others with impunity he therefore rightly, from the viewpoint of ordinary justice, considers to be unjust. This all fits squarely within the traditional conception of distributive justice, as described, for example, by Aristotle, Aquinas, or Kant. There is nothing whatever in Rosmini's conception of social justice that would detract from or undermine the traditional importance of individual responsibility and accountability.

England: The Christian Socialists

1848 was the "year of revolution" in Europe. In January the first revolution broke out in Sicily. It was followed by a much larger and more successful one in France in February, and then by many others around Europe. Also in February, Marx and Engels published the Communist Manifesto, which the Communist League, meeting in London the previous November, had commissioned them to write. (The text was in German, since the members of the League were German. The English translation was published in 1850.)

On Monday, the 10th of April, the English Chartists, a workingman's movement, planned to march on the House of Commons to deliver their third petition for changes in the British constitution, especially the extension of the franchise to those who did not own property, their first two petitions having been rejected. Some of the Chartists believed in using peaceful means to achieve their aims, but others were ready to use force. Their plans led many to believe a revolution was under way like those taking place on the continent. Queen Victoria and Prince Albert secretly fled to the Isle of Wight. But the renowned English weather saved the day: a heavy rainstorm turned the march into a fiasco. In the evening a group consisting mostly of "Broad-church" Anglican clergymen who supported the Chartists met in London to decide what to do. They agreed to launch the movement known as "Christian Socialism." It was among the members of this group that the earliest expression of the idea of "social justice" in English, which is also the earliest in its current equalizing sense, seems to have developed.

The instigation for the foundation of the new movement came from a layman, John Malcolm Ludlow, who had been educated in Paris by a radical widow and had written in French, at the age of twenty, a tract arguing that Christianity was the fulfillment of socialism. This was to become the theme of the movement. Other members were the theologian, Frederick Denison Maurice, already well known for his book *The Kingdom of Christ* (1838), which supported socialism, Charles Kingsley, the novelist, soon to write *Alton Locke*, and Thomas Hughes, future author of *Tom Brown's Schooldays*. The historian Owen Chadwick describes the group as follows:

> Ludlow proffered the social ideas, Kingsley the prophetic fire, Maurice the anchorage in Christian doctrine. In this unusual crew Ludlow stood at the helm, Kingsley flew the flags and sounded the horns, Maurice poked round the engine-room to see that the engines were of authentic Christian manufacture.[99]

They proceeded to publish two journals, *Politics for the People*, which lasted about 18 months, and *The Christian Socialist*, similarly. The group also produced a series of pamphlets under the title *Tracts on Christian Socialism*. Individual members of the movement went on to publish many books and other writings in the course of the century. In 1866 Maurice became Professor of Moral Philosophy at Cambridge University, writing two influential books, *Social Morality* (1869) and *Moral and Metaphysical Philosophy* (1871). But the organized movement of Christian Socialism fell apart within a few years because of disagreements on the direction the movement should take.

Quite apart from the changes the Chartists wished to see in the constitution, the Christian Socialists were deeply distressed by the desperate poverty of the workers who labored in the factories. This had been a concern among the Anglican clergy for a long time, but had grown much worse in the preceding couple of years. In point of historical fact, the wretched economic condition of the workers in England at this time seems mainly to have been caused by the general crisis that had afflicted all the economies of Western Europe in 1846 and 1847, originating in the failure of the wheat and potato crops. The price of food rose sharply, purchasing power declined, and the agricultural depression was soon followed by an industrial one, which led to heavy unemployment. Similar conditions occurred in France, calling forth the revolution of 1848 and the creation of the Second Republic there.[100] The Christian Socialists, however, did not stop to analyze the actual economic forces at work. Instead, they blamed the plight of the workers on "the thralldom of individual labor under the competitive system."[101]

The problem was the general fact of competition between workers for jobs. In their view the wages of workers were, and in principle always would be, inevitably depressed below the level where they could sustain life by the competition from other workers who were willing to work for less. The entire system of the organization of labor was unfair and unjust, as well as unchristian.

> . . . we are of opinion that the rights of a man in the eyes of the law, and his functions, if any, in the business of government, are not the only questions of politics; but that the rate of his wages, and the interest he gets for his money, and the state of his dwelling, and the cut of his coat, and the print he stops to look at, and the tune he hums, and the books he reads, and the talk he has with his neighbours, and the love he bears to his wife and children and friends, and the blessing he asks of his God – ay, and still more the love which he does *not* bear to others, and the blessing he does *not* ask of God – are all political matters. Political, not in the case of one individual, but of all; of the pinched artisan who struggles to keep himself and his old mother on ten shillings a week, or of the poorest tramp who drags her foot-sore child by the hand through dust or sludge, as well as in that of the Queen in her palace.[102]

The goal was "A fair day's wages for a fair day's work." The way to achieve this, the Christian Socialists believed, was to replace worker-competition with worker-cooperation.

> "Is it true," we rejoined, "that many of you work eighteen or twenty hours out of the four-and-twenty?"
>
> "Ay, that we do; and many of us more than that. In the shops of what are called under-priced bakers . . . I know many journeymen who work upwards of twenty hours out of the twenty-four, besides working from the Thursday night to the Sunday morning, without having their clothes off, or so much as once lying down."
>
> "Why, that is worse than negro slavery!" we exclaimed.
>
> "Yes, Sir," was his rejoinder; "but the slaves had the advantage of black faces, and lived a great way off, and therefore people felt for them, and got up meetings in their favour, till they made freemen of them. But somehow or other we are forgotten . . . What we want is to get rid of night-work . . . They say Parliament does not like to interfere, because we are grown-up men, and can make our own bargains."
>
> "But can you do so?"

"No, Sir; we are as powerless in that matter as children. The trade is so overstocked, what with men thrown out of work by sickness, and eager to be employed on any terms, and what with men from Scotland, discharged because they have served their time, and always flocking up to London, that the under-priced bakers can get hands to work any number of hours a day, at almost any wages."[103]

What the Christian Socialists wanted was in reality nothing less than a reorganization and transformation of society. Yet they were not revolutionaries. "We are peaceable, and we would, if we could, be contented; but all these things are against us; we don't want any violent changes, but we do want fair play – fair wages for fair work."[104] Their main efforts in practice were limited to organizing cooperative associations of workers, and businesses owned by the workers. They supported also the cooperative and educational reforms proposed by Robert Owen.

So far as I have been able to discover, the Christian Socialists made little if any use of the term "social justice." They emphasized a conception of justice as fairness, and the fairness of social organization, especially the organization of labor, yet this conception remained still within, or at least very close to, the boundaries of the ordinary, traditional conception of justice.

The initial movement of Christian Socialism in England lasted only a few years; by 1860 it had run its course. Toward the end of the century, however, the movement came back to life, producing among other things a Socialist Quaker Society, the Roman Catholic Socialist Society, and the Christian Social Union. Christian Socialists dominated the leadership of the British Labour Party formed in 1893. The Christian Socialist movement also influenced many of the leaders of the American Socialist Party such as Norman Thomas and Upton Sinclair. But in the intervening years a radical change took place in the movement's underlying philosophy, under the impact of Marxist and communist ideas. The ordinary conception of justice was largely replaced by the new conception of "social justice."

The Concept of Social Justice

It will be evident from this chapter that originally social justice was a formal or procedural concept rather than a material one. By this I mean the term was taken to signify simply a branch of the ordinary concept of justice, analogous to "commutative justice" or "criminal justice," and did not imply any particular content, philosophy, or view of the world. There could be a conservative conception of social justice, a liberal conception of it, and a socialist conception of it, as we have just seen, all equally entitled to call themselves "social justice," though one might argue, of course, about which one was right. In other words, the concept of social justice was simply an extension of the existing, traditional idea of justice, which is formal or procedural, into a new area, that of society as a whole, so that it did not require developing any new content to the idea, but just new conditions for its application.

These three possible theories can be seen, accordingly, as based on three different conceptions of where injustice, in the ordinary sense of the term, primarily arises in society: through the rejection of legitimate authority (conservative), through interference with liberty and property (liberal), or through the exploitation of the propertyless (socialist). For conservatives, for example, authority plays an indispensable role in society, and tends to be derived from inheritance, history, and tradition; and a revolution in which legitimate authority is deposed by force and replaced by a regime of "tyrannous liberty," of the sort that Taparelli witnessed and protested against, represents a particularly fundamental form of injustice. This was a large part of Burke's argument against the Revolution of 1789 (an argument that, it should be noted, did not require a conception of justice beyond the ordinary).

In Rosmini's liberal view, injustice arises in society principally through interference with liberty and its associated right of property. Government has the task of protecting both, and it is an especially basic and far-reaching kind of injustice to set up a form of government that is incapable of doing that because it gives some the political power to dispossess others.

In the socialist view, the most urgent form of injustice in society is to be found in the economic realm, which, as Marx was to argue, undergirds the other institutions of society and plays such a fundamental role in the lives of ordinary people. Economic injustice consists in the exploitation of the powerless by the powerful, of the poor by the rich, and of workers by their employers.

That these early conceptions of social justice did not represent an exotic new species of justice but were forms of ordinary, traditional justice, albeit in a new area, can be seen from the fact that they satisfy the formal criteria for a valid concept of justice mentioned in Chapter 2, criteria which, we shall argue at some length in the chapters to come, are necessitated by the nature of ethics. The first of these criteria, as stated on (p. 25f), is that justice and injustice should be primarily qualities, not of states of affairs in society, but of the actions of individuals.[105] And according to all three of these conceptions we have just discussed, social justice and injustice were indeed primarily qualities, not of states of affairs in society, such as the equality or inequality of wealth or power, which could occur by accident of history, but of the free actions of particular persons who could be held accountable for them. For the conservative Taparelli, as we have just noted, social justice demanded acceptance of the existing constitutional arrangements of society, the inherited and established rights, and powers of the existing authorities, including the church; and injustice consisted in the forcible rejection of those rights and powers by persons who attempted to set up alternative forms of government. The social injustice was caused and brought about by particular individuals, who deserved punishment.

For Rosmini, social justice was a quality of the constitutional arrangements of society in so far as they governed the distribution of the common good, and the basic principle of that distribution was that it should be proportionate to the contribution each one makes to the society. For justice, as he observes, is not a question of simple equality, but of proportionate equality. This is not a new species of justice, but one that Aristotle would immediately recognize. The great test of social justice for Rosmini was the inviolability of property, the protection given by the laws to individual ownership, such that no political majority could use its power to dispossess the minority. In other words, social justice was a quality of the laws, which of course are actions of persons, for which they can be held accountable, even if they act collectively.

For the Christian Socialists, again, social justice consisted in "a fair day's wages for a fair day's work," and the source of injustice, as we have just mentioned, was the exploitation of workers by employers, their deliberate willingness to pay the minimum possible wages while extracting the maximum amount of labor. Obviously this was a human action for which the individual employer could be considered accountable.

The original concept of social justice, therefore, was simply an extension of ordinary justice into the new arena of society as a whole. During the twentieth century, however, that view of "social justice" changed dramatically, and it became instead the name of a particular philosophical viewpoint; and one, as we shall see, intrinsically incompatible with ordinary justice. In the next two chapters we will investigate something of the process by which that change took place, and what viewpoint the term now designates.

Chapter 4

The Socialistic Conception of Social Justice

During the latter half of the nineteenth century the conservative conception of social justice developed by Taparelli and the liberal one employed by Rosmini both fell by the wayside, being overtaken, as it seemed, by the course of events. The socialistic one that emerged with the Christian Socialists, however, gathered strength, and was transformed from a peaceful doctrine, that remained within the ambit of ordinary justice and was even doubtful about the usefulness of requesting the help of the law in carrying out its program, into a revolutionary one that had no hesitation in appealing to coercion and the law, and even coercion beyond the law. In the process it was transformed from the purely formal concept that it originally was, as part of the ordinary and traditional concept of justice, into the material concept, defined by its content, that it now is. As part of that transformation, it changed from being a quality of actions for which people can be accountable, like the ordinary concept of justice, to a quality of impersonal states of affairs which can occur without anyone having done anything to produce them.

The aim of this chapter is to show how, when, and why that threefold transformation took place. It occurred primarily in religious writings: namely in certain papal documents, which will be the main focus of our interest. The key document is the encyclical letter *Quadragesimo anno* issued by Pope Pius XI in 1931. Before our story leaves the nineteenth century, however, we must take note of the *eminence grise* whose silent shadow will lie over all the subsequent discussions, and of a brief but important comment by John Stuart Mill.

Marx (1818–1883)

Marx does not discuss social justice. He scarcely even discusses justice. Not only that, but he scarcely considers ethics at all.[106] Nonetheless, his ideas lie at the origin of the fate that was to overtake these ideas in the twentieth century. For Marx, ethics, and especially justice, are part of bourgeois ideology. They are conceptual tools that help to maintain the system of "exploitation" in being. This is a modern version of the skeptical thesis of Thrasymachus in Plato's *Republic*, that justice is the power of the strong to dominate the weak.

Marx's ultimate goal was a society where no individual had power over another individual. It made no difference that one person should willingly give another such power. Since the family can be a means, among other things, of acquiring power and handing it on, Marx held the family should be abolished. And since property and the exchanges of the marketplace can give one person the power to accumulate economic power over others, Marx wished also to abolish both property and the market.

Marx's substitute for justice was the force of history, both the past, as he understood it, and also the future, as he predicted it. The forces of history have produced capitalism, but they will also eradicate it, as the workers, who already outnumber their employers, will in future do so more and more, and will eventually dispossess and eliminate them, creating the classless society. Whatever actions will assist the coming of the revolution are good, and whatever actions resist it are bad. The traditional idea of justice had offered an alternative to force in the settlement of disputes. Ironically, Marx's desire to eliminate force resulted in its apotheosis.

Despite his dismissal of justice, most people influenced by Marx have not abandoned the idea of it. But since Marx, many have reinterpreted it as the ideal of the classless society in which all have equal power.

John Stuart Mill (1806–1873)

Mill possesses the distinction of having introduced explicitly into the (socialistic) concept of social justice the idea of equality. This is still not equality as a state of affairs in society, which was destined to have so profound an effect on the sense of individual responsibility, but only equality of *treatment*, and so of actions by and toward individuals. Also, it is not yet an unqualified right to this equality of treatment, but only a presumption of such a right, which can yield to other considerations. Still, he formulated what many today will regard as the basic principle of "social justice" and even as an obvious principle of ethics: "All persons are deemed to have a *right* to equality of treatment, except when some recognised social expediency requires the reverse."[107] This is "the highest abstract standard of social and distributive justice."[108]

What is the foundation or origin of this presumption? It cannot be our common human nature, or any principle of natural moral law, for Mill rules absolutely out the possibility of deriving moral principles from nature. Nature is purely a realm of fact and can never be a source of value.[109] It also cannot be any Kantian principle of *a priori* reason that can provide Mill with his equality, for Mill is a utilitarian, who explicitly rejects any appeal to "abstract right, as a thing independent of utility,"[110] a viewpoint Kant despised in moral questions and went to great pains to demonstrate was incompatible with his own theory. Mill, however, considers that utilitarianism supplies the answer: equality of treatment is a necessary consequence of the very concept of utility. The Greatest Happiness principle, he asserts, demands that each person's happiness count equally with that of every other person, and consequently it demands that *all* persons have an *equal* claim to *all* the means of happiness.[111] He recognizes, however, that this equal claim is limited by the conditions of human life, and by the interests of society at large, and so can only be a presumption.

Mill's argument for this presumption, however, is not very obviously valid. What the Greatest Happiness principle directly and obviously demands is that the total happiness of a society should be maximized. But it is not difficult to imagine that that could happen as a result of *inequality*, of some people being happier than others, and even of some people having a greater *claim* to happiness than others. The presumption is not saved by adding that the equal claim is sometimes limited by circumstances or the larger interests of society, because that still leaves the question as to why there should be such a presumption in the first place. The explanation, though scarcely the philosophical justification, of Mill's devotion to equality as a utilitarian lies in his avowed conversion to socialism, a result he attributes to the influence of his wife Harriet.[112]

The socialism to which Mill converted was not that of Marx, whom he appears never to mention, but of Saint-Simon and Fourier, or at least of that style which Marx described as "utopian" as if his own were not. His progress toward this is evident in the *Autobiography*, written during the mid-1850s before Harriet's death, though published only after his own in 1873. Here the notion of injustice is already broadened to include the fact that some are born into wealth but others into poverty.[113]

Harriet died in 1858. In 1869 Mill set to work on a book which he intended to be an even-handed examination of socialism that would be recognized as objective and unbiased. He died before he could finish it, however, and the unfinished text was published after his death by his step-daughter Helen Taylor under the title *Chapters on Socialism*. His verdict on socialism there is that in the existing condition of the human race it "is not available as a present resource," that is it is unworkable, for it requires a new kind of human being that does not yet exist. Yet he persists in believing it is valuable as an ideal.[114]

Leonard Trelawny Hobhouse (1864–1929)

In 1889 the German Chancellor, Bismarck, introduced the first old-age pension. This was not the product of any theoretical argument, at least directly, but a purely political ploy to gain an electoral advantage over his opponents – a fulfillment of Rosmini's predictions. It was copied by the Liberal government of the United Kingdom in 1908. Hobhouse, who described himself as a "liberal socialist," aimed to provide a justification of such measures in his book *The Elements of Social Justice*, published in 1922. His work represents a further development of the line of thought begun by J.S. Mill.

Hobhouse made two principal contributions to the concept of social justice. First, he introduced the idea of need as morally equivalent to desert as a ground of distributive justice. Hobhouse begins from Aristotle's analysis of distributive justice, which emphasizes the role of desert while acknowledging that this concept is understood differently under different forms of government, such as aristocracy and democracy. Aristotle allows that in democracies every citizen is considered to deserve an equal share in distributions. Hobhouse adds that need must also be considered, alongside of desert, as a just ground of distribution. It cannot be said, however, that he makes any very extensive argument for this thesis. The common good consists in harmony, he asserts, and that requires the satisfaction of at least basic needs.[115] The problem is that, at least in regard to adult human beings, need is not an objective concept but a subjective one. Hobhouse recognizes this to some extent, but considers it only a superficial objection, whereas in truth it strikes at the root of need as a criterion of justice. We shall return to this point below (pp. 170, 175), where we argue that need cannot create a right.

In addition, Hobhouse makes a distinction in the concept of individual property between that property which is the product of the individual's efforts and that which is due to the contribution of society. He argues that while the individual has a right to the former, the latter may justly be redistributed. How this distinction could be calculated in practice, however, has proved an intractable question. For the true situation would seem to be that *everything* an individual achieves is due *both* to the contribution made by society *and also* to the contribution made by his own personal will. Whatever the achievements of society may be, nothing whatever would be produced without the will of the individual agent.

The Liberal party had once, of course, in the nineteenth century, been the defender of property and the standard-bearer of free trade. But arguments such as these led it in the twentieth century to take a fairly large step in the direction of socialism without actually becoming socialist. Hobhouse is viewed as an important thinker in their tradition, now represented by the Liberal Democratic party, which has officially committed itself to "upholding the value of social justice."[116]

The Popes

The major statements of the socialistic idea of social justice are contained in writings of the popes. Since it is going to be necessary for me, while supporting some of their views, to point to serious problems with others, I wish to explain briefly my attitude about this in order to avoid misunderstanding. There is more to Catholic social teaching than the concept of social justice. The basic concern of the popes in regard to economic questions has been the praiseworthy one of defending human dignity in the labor market, where it is continually under threat. In an age when many governments abandoned this concern, or tried to fulfill it by the paradoxical means of destroying it, this should be welcomed. This consistent papal concern with human dignity should be borne in mind in reading the following pages. It has led the popes to propose certain very general ideals for social existence such as solidarity, subsidiarity, and devotion to the common good which can play a valuable role as ideals. Since they are all susceptible of a wide range of interpretations, much hinges on how they are concretely understood. My focus here, however, is on an idea and an ideal which is quite different and in a separate class from these, "social justice."[117]

The standpoint of the first papal statement on "the social question," Leo XIII's encyclical letter[118] *Rerum novarum*, issued in 1891, was essentially liberal, in the European sense of the term. But the next, *Quadragesimo anno*, by his successor Pius XI, issued in 1931, crossed the momentous threshold into the territory of revolution. To appreciate the extent of the changes wrought by this letter, we must first have studied its predecessor. Subsequent letters by John XXIII (*Mater et magistra*, 1961; *Pacem in terris*, 1963), a statement of the Second Vatican Council (*Gaudium et spes*, 1965) and Paul VI (*Populorum progressio*, 1967) became even more radical.

These papal statements have had an influence far beyond the boundaries of Catholicism. Almost all the varieties of Christianity have adopted their teachings in some measure, if only by default because no other Christian leaders have spoken on the topic so consistently and in such detail. Even beyond the borders of organized religion their effects can be traced widely. Leo's *Rerum novarum* inspired the creation of the Christian Democratic political parties in Europe and Latin America. Pius's *Quadragesimo anno* gave the stamp of papal approval to Mussolini's economic policies and to those of the Roosevelt administration during the Great Depression in the 1930s, and led to the United Nations' *Universal Declaration of Human Rights* of 1948. The letters of John XXIII led to the U.S. Civil Rights Act of 1964 and to the movement of "Liberation Theology" with its many thousands of "base communities" in Latin America. Paul VI's letter carried similar ideas out beyond national boundaries into international efforts for the economic development of the Third World. In 1971 the socialistic conception of social justice received an elaborate philosophical development in the celebrated theory of John Rawls, followed by the work of Ronald Dworkin and others, in particular, for our purposes, Brian Barry. With John Paul II the papal pendulum began to swing back. I should stress that what follows here is by no means intended as a full history of papal or Roman Catholic views on social justice; my aim is merely to point to the highlights.

Leo XIII (1878–1903) Gioacchino Pecci

Leo's celebrated encyclical letter, *Rerum novarum* (usually Englished as "On the Condition of the Working Classes"), 1891, is generally considered the foundational statement of official Catholic social teaching and of the Catholic doctrine of social justice, though it does not explicitly use that term. Its purpose is to point out what, according to Christian teaching, can and should be done to help the new working classes arising out of Europe's growing industrialization. Its conception of justice in society is very different from what later popes would teach, and from what is current at the present time. If it has a clear affinity with the views of the earlier Christian Socialists, it also owes a great deal (as they did) to liberalism, about which a few words need to be said.

Liberalism was at that time before the First World War the reigning public philosophy throughout the Western world. In the United States, and in areas influenced by American usage, the word "liberal" has come to have a quite different meaning as a result of the success of President Franklin D.

Roosevelt in appropriating the term for his own philosophy, which would more accurately be considered a form of "progressivism" or moderate socialism. But on the continent of Europe it still preserves its original significance, though it has lost all the power once associated with it.

In regard to economics, liberalism meant free trade, both abroad and at home. The transactions of the market should observe all the ordinary rules of justice, but should otherwise be kept entirely free of government intervention. The acceptance of this doctrine of Adam Smith's, replacing the conservative mercantilism that preceded it, led to the industrialization of many of the nations of Europe in the course of the nineteenth century, some earlier but most later, and with it to the mass production of consumer goods at lower prices and a corresponding improvement in the overall standard of living. It also led to the emergence of a new and initially very poor laboring class that is the focus of Leo's attention in this encyclical. Poverty was not new in Europe: the peasantry had lived in it since time immemorial, but they were dispersed across the land and their poverty did not stand out, given the level of economic development at the time. But the new factory workers tended to live congregated together in industrial towns, whose poverty was very visible.

Liberalism was not just an economic doctrine; it was a broad philosophical movement aiming at greater freedom and rationality in most aspects of social life. In politics it stood for constitutional and representative government, as contrasted with the absolute monarchies that were traditional on the continent. As part of its belief in free trade, it held an absolute respect for private property, without which, it rightly believed, there could be no freedom. It stood for the freedom of scientific investigation, which included Darwin. In religion it wished to diminish the political power of the church and so was often described as anticlerical. In Italy it replaced the authoritarian and clerical government of the Papal States with an elected parliament, which led to the pope's voluntary isolation as "prisoner of the Vatican." "Liberal Christianity" meant a focus on the ethical teachings of the church rather than a deep faith in its doctrines, and an openness to the new science of biblical criticism. To devout Catholics liberalism generally appeared as an archenemy. The doctrines of Adam Smith were cast under the same shadow as the guns of Garibaldi.

Because of the encyclical letter's pivotal position in Catholic social teaching, and because of the wide influence of that teaching outside the Catholic realm, it is important that the letter's doctrine should be properly understood. It is true that it retains certain elements from the economic thinking of the middle ages, especially the concept of a "fair price" and "fair wage."[119]

But it is also deeply impregnated with liberalism. Its doctrine can be summed up under three main points:

– There is an absolute natural right to own private property, and forcible redistribution by government in the name of equality is unjust and absurd;[120]
– Certain wages and working conditions are unjust, independently of any agreement between employer and employee; in particular, justice requires that a married man's wage be sufficient to support a frugal family;
– The right way to overcome unjust wages and working conditions is not through governmental intervention but through private, voluntary associations of workers, or workers together with owners, to reduce competition among workers for jobs.

Apart from that the letter recommends only that government "watch over" (*curam gerit*) the interests of the working classes, for example by encouraging them to own property.[121]

Private Property

The first and in some sense the main thesis of the encyclical, occupying roughly the first third of its length, is a strong defense of private property against socialism in the name of justice. "The first and most fundamental principle," Leo writes, "if one would undertake to alleviate the condition of the masses, must be the inviolability of private property." This is a viewpoint reminiscent of Rosmini, even down to the use of the term "sacred" to describe the moral status of property. ". . . the whole question under consideration [of helping the working classes] cannot be settled effectually unless it is assumed and established as a principle, that the right of private property must be regarded as sacred."[122] This sacredness is reinforced by the Decalogue, which forbids us in the severest terms even to *covet* what belongs to another.[123] In Catholic writing in the twenty-first century this powerful defense of private property is typically ignored.

The right to own property, including productive property, is given by the natural moral law, says Leo. The ground of this right is the fact that man is endowed with reason, which enables him to take thought for the morrow.

> . . . it must be within his right to possess things not merely for temporary and momentary use, as other living things do, but to have and to hold

> them in stable and permanent possession; he must have not only things
> that perish in the use, but those also which, though they have been
> reduced into use, continue for further use in after time.[124]

Man needs a stable foundation for his life, for his needs do not die out, but
forever recur; although satisfied today, they demand fresh supplies for
tomorrow. Hence man should not only possess the fruits of the earth, but
also the soil itself, since he has to make provision for the future. The right
to provide for his own existence, and so the right to own land, is antecedent
to the state and independent of it. "There is no need to bring in the state.
Man precedes the state, and possesses, prior to the formation of any state,
the right of providing for the substance of his body."[125]

Leo also uses a Lockean argument: the universal human right to own
private property follows from man's labor, which transforms the products of
nature into resources for human use. The earth can produce fruits in abun-
dance, but this does not happen until man has brought it into cultivation
and expended his labor on it. By his labor he makes his own that portion
which he cultivates, and it is only just that he should have the right to hold
it without anyone else violating that ownership.

> For the soil which is tilled and cultivated with toil and skill utterly changes
> its condition; it was wild before, now it is fruitful; was barren, but now
> brings forth in abundance. That which has thus altered and improved the
> land becomes so truly part of itself as to be in great measure indistin-
> guishable and inseparable from it. Is it just that the fruit of a man's own
> sweat and labor should be possessed and enjoyed by any one else? As
> effects follow their cause, so is it just and right that the results of labor
> should belong to those who have bestowed their labor.[126]

If this right holds good for the individual man, Leo argues, it holds
a fortiori for man as head of a family. The family is a true society, antecedent to the state and having its own independent rights, and it is governed
by its own authority, the authority of the father. The child belongs to the
father, and the father therefore has a sacred duty to provide food and
other necessities for the children he has begotten. The only way he can do
this is by owning productive property, which he can transmit to them by
inheritance.[127]

By this universal right to property Leo does not mean a right to obtain
property through redistribution. It is not a right *for* redistribution but
against it. It is a right not to be dispossessed of property that one has acquired

by just means. Socialist redistribution "violates the rights of lawful owners, perverts the functions of the State, and throws governments into utter confusion."[128] The idea of economic equality, far from being required by justice, is nothing less than absurd. Redistribution does not serve the common good. The appeal to the common good is an important argument for Leo and for the Catholic tradition, since it is an axiom of Catholic philosophy that the specific task of government is to secure the common good, and whatever measures serve that purpose are just. (We will see a little more of this below in the section on St. Thomas Aquinas's conception of general or legal justice.) There is a natural inequality which can never be eliminated by human measures, and which is ultimately for the good of the human race. ". . . for to carry on its affairs community life requires varied aptitudes and diverse services, and to perform these diverse services men are impelled most by differences in individual property holdings."[129] There will never be a utopia, where all tribulation has been banished from human life; utopian promises are fraudulent.[130]

The main reason why people go to work is to obtain the means necessary for their livelihood, and it is a matter of justice that they should be able to dispose of their wages as they see fit. The socialists ". . . make the lot of all wage earners worse, because in abolishing the freedom to dispose of wages they take away from them by this very act the hope and opportunity of increasing their property and of securing advantages for themselves."[131] Divine law (i.e. the Ten Commandments) forbids us most strictly even to desire what belongs to another, let alone to take it. The aim of public policy should be to increase the ownership of property among the masses.

Leo makes a distinction between the ownership of property and its use. Ownership brings with it a moral obligation – one which he stresses obliges only in charity, not in justice, and should not be enforced by the law of the state – to help those in need. God has given the earth for the use and enjoyment of the whole human race. But this is no bar to the private ownership of property, nor does it set limits to the amount of property an individual may own. It means simply that no part of creation was assigned to any one in particular. The limits of private possession have been left to be fixed by man's own industry. Furthermore, the land that is owned by individuals does not cease to benefit others, for it produces fruits that sustain them. Later popes will make much more of this distinction between ownership and use, seeing in it a doctrine of "the universal destination of material goods," transforming it into a question of justice and giving rise to "the option for the poor."

Nothing like Leo's stout defense of private property will be seen again in papal statements, or in any other official explanations of Catholic doctrine. In the course of the twentieth century they move decidedly toward the left.

The Proletariat

But if the defense of private property is one pole around which the encyclical revolves, the other is its insistence that the proletariat or working class[132] and its interests should be cared for. For this to take place properly, there must be a united effort on the part of all in society; "all human agencies must concur" (31). A first question concerns the role of government. As will become clear, Leo does not believe in the "welfare state."

The first duty of the state in caring for the working classes is, *not* to do anything special in regard to them, but to do its ordinary job properly. It is to arrange the ordinary affairs of society in such a way as "to realize public well-being and private prosperity" for all its members. This means

> moral rule, well-regulated family life, respect for religion and justice, moderation and fair imposition of public taxes, the progress of the arts and trade, the abundant yield of the land – through everything, in fact, which makes the citizens better and happier. (32)

Government has the power to benefit every class, and to promote the interests of the poor *among the rest.* (My italics.) For its task is to serve the common good. The best way to help the working classes is through a good general regime. "For in the state, the interests of all, whether high or low, are equal" (33). Government must care for the poor because it must care for everybody. "It would be very absurd (perabsurdum) to neglect one portion of the citizens and favor another" (33). The first and chief duty of rulers is to act with strict justice toward each and every class alike. Leo explains that by strict justice he means distributive justice; there is no indication in the text that he means by this anything other than its ordinary meaning. This view of Leo's has a certain affinity with Adam Smith's conception of the invisible hand, namely that the ordinary free operation of the market brings the maximum benefit to all classes.

Although the state has the obligation to care for all its citizens, this does not mean there are not classes of different importance and rank in society, Leo continues. The foremost place in the state belongs to the class of people who devote themselves to the work of the commonwealth, who make the laws and administer justice, who advise government in time of peace and defend the country in time of war. "Everyone sees" that these are the people who should be held in the highest esteem.

The working classes do not promote the general welfare to the same extent. But nonetheless they are indispensable, for it is their labor that provides the material necessities of life. Leo now continues with a paragraph that requires closer attention.

> Equity, therefore, demands that the interests of the proletariat should be carefully watched over by the administration, so that those who contribute to the advantage of the community may themselves share in the benefits which they create – that being housed, clothed, and bodily fit, they may find their life less hard and more endurable. It follows that whatever shall appear to prove conducive to the well-being of those who work should obtain favorable consideration.[133]

Present-day commentators on this passage routinely leap to the dramatic conclusion that it means government should directly assist the working classes with clothing, housing, health care, and employment.[134] But that places the statement in contradiction to the insistence in the letter's previous paragraph that government should care for all classes equally. It is to be understood simply as an application of that general statement to the particular case. As can be seen from the footnote below, the Latin text translated here as "carefully watched over by the administration" runs: "curam de proletario publice geri," which is quite vague, suggesting that the government should do something, without specifying what. Elsewhere Leo suggests it should encourage them to own property. The text continues,

> This care (for the proletariat) is so far from harming anyone, that it rather is of benefit to everyone, for it is certainly in the interests of the commonwealth that those from whom it receives such necessary benefits should not live in complete misery.

This does not suggest he is recommending special treatment.

Early in the encyclical Leo states that he has been moved to write by the desperate plight of the workers, which in his analysis has been caused by their employers. ". . . by degrees it has come to pass that working men have been surrendered, isolated and helpless, to the hardheartedness of employers and the greed of unchecked competition." ". . . a very few rich and exceedingly rich men have laid a yoke almost of slavery on the unnumbered masses of non-owning workers."[135] This much-quoted passage is certainly a powerful indictment of the employer class. It is almost as strong as Adam Smith's denunciations of capitalists. Yet, like Smith, the remedy Leo will propose consists far more in private action than in actions of government.

Employers and employees have obligations in justice toward one another. Workers must do the work they have agreed to do, which means they *must never go on strike or hold work stoppages.* (My emphasis.) They must respect the person of their employer and never engage in violence (20). This is the first and last encyclical to emphasize the obligations of workers.

Employers must treat their employees properly by respecting them as persons, not defrauding them, paying them just wages and not requiring excessive work from them. "Neither justice nor humanity can countenance the exaction of so much work that the spirit is dulled from excessive toil and that along with it the body sinks crushed from exhaustion." However, Leo does not attempt to suggest there should be any fixed rule in terms of a maximum number of working hours, such as the 40- or now 35-hour week embodied in some modern legislation, but concedes that the length of the appropriate working day is relative to the kind of work done. He does not consider working hours a fit matter for legislation.[136] From the standpoint of the conception of social justice current at the present time in the United States, Leo is guilty of "sexism," for he asserts that the sex of the worker should be taken into consideration. Certain occupations are less fitted for women, who are "intended by nature for the work of the home."[137]

The centerpiece of Leo's response to the plight of the proletariat is his doctrine of the "living wage." It is a matter of "natural justice" that employees should be paid a wage sufficient to support themselves and any family they may have if they live frugally.

> We are told that free consent fixes the amount of a wage; that therefore the employer, after paying the wage agreed to would seem to have discharged his obligation and not to owe anything more; that only then would injustice be done if either the employer should refuse to pay the whole amount of the wage, or the worker should refuse to perform all the work to which he had committed himself; and that in these cases, but in no others, is it proper for the public authority to intervene to safeguard the rights of each party.[138]

But there is a flaw in this argument, Leo maintains, namely that an important element has been left out: the fact that the worker has no choice about working, but necessarily depends on his wage for his livelihood. The worker has a right to those things necessary to secure life. Leo does not argue that the worker has a right to have a job *created* for him by somebody else, whether private persons or government. But he has a right that if he is offered a job, it should be at a certain minimum wage.[139]

Leo now takes a fateful step: he equates an employer's offer of a job at a lesser wage to the use of *force*. It is this step that leads him to declare it an injustice.

> Let it be granted then that worker and employer may enter freely into agreements and, in particular, concerning the amount of the wage; yet there is always underlying such agreements an element of natural justice, and one greater and more ancient than the free consent of contracting parties, namely, that the wage shall not be less than enough to support a worker who is thrifty and upright. If, compelled by necessity or moved by fear of a worse evil, a worker accepts a harder condition, which although against his will he must accept because the employer or contractor imposes it, *he certainly submits to force, against which justice cries out in protest.*[140] (my emphasis)

Having made this strong statement, however, which would warrant strong measures by government, Leo steps back! The remedy for all the various problems workers experience, including those of the hours of labor and the burden of work, should be provided, not by government, but through private, voluntary associations of workers, "in order to avoid unwarranted governmental intervention." These associations are the key to improving the condition of the workers, in Leo's view, and he spends several pages discussing them. While he mentions different kinds of associations, the ones he mainly has in mind would seem to be what used to be called "beneficial" societies. This is a kind of organization that once played a large role in society, but no longer exists today because its functions have been preempted by governments.

Leo will have nothing to do with the idea of what we would call today the welfare state. There is indeed a duty to help the poor, but it is a duty of Christian charity, not one of justice, "except in cases of extreme need," and even then "obviously cannot be enforced by legal action." Government is no substitute for personal concern: ". . . no human devices can ever be found to supplant Christian charity, which gives itself entirely for the benefit of others."

There is one area, however, where government does have a role. The task of government is to preserve peace and good order. "Wherefore, if at any time disorder should threaten . . . the power and authority of the law, but of course within certain limits, manifestly ought to be employed." At the head of his list of such disorders Leo places, as we have just seen, strikes and stoppages of work. Government should prevent these because they not only inflict damage on employers but also on workers, and also injure trade and commerce, and they are "usually not far removed from violence and rioting." But it is better to prevent them by anticipation, by removing the causes of conflict, rather than wait till they occur.

The word "justice" is used 22 times in this document. If we examine the passages in which it occurs, we find three things about the meaning the word has for Leo, corresponding to the three points we made above. First, the concept of justice and injustice here is still formal, not material; it is not defined by any definite content. Second, it is peaceful, not revolutionary; for it does not appeal to coercion as the remedy for what it designates an injustice. Third, it refers to human actions, for which people can be accountable, not to states of affairs that can occur without anyone having done anything wrong. In short, Leo's idea of justice remains well within the limits of our ordinary and traditional idea of justice.

Pius XI (1922–39), Ambrogio Achille Ratti

If there is any single document that can be regarded as the primary source of the conception of social justice prevalent at the present time, it is Pius's encyclical letter *Quadragesimo anno*, published in 1931. It canonized the socialistic conception of "social justice" for the Catholic world, and arguably for the world at large; and at the same time radicalized the concept, abandoning Leo's vigorous defense of private property, and approving of, even demanding, the forcible redistribution of wealth from rich to poor. Pius took the critical step of expanding the idea of injustice so that it no longer needed to refer to the actions or inactions of an individual, for which that individual would be accountable, but could be applied to an impersonal state of affairs, namely inequality in the distribution of this world's goods, that can occur by accident, without anyone having done anything wrong. That is, from being a formal concept, as it was originally when considered part of ordinary justice, it has been transformed into a material concept having for content a particular ideology. With Pius, "social justice," and often simple "justice" by itself, *means* economic equality, and those phenomena that are associated with economic equality.

On the other hand, the kind of society that would embody the equality of social justice to the fullest was for him one whose economic life was organized into guilds like those of the middle ages: an ideal reminiscent of Mussolini's.

The initial draft was written by Oswald von Nell-Breuning, S.J., professor of moral theology at a Jesuit school in Frankfurt and a member of the German nobility. He appears to have been influenced by the writings of Matteo Liberatore, the Italian Jesuit who we have seen was a disciple of Taparelli. But Taparelli was already also a favorite author of Pius himself, who used to recommend his works to his personal friends. Nell-Breuning, after his work on the encyclical, went on to live an exceptionally long life devoted to the writing of some 1800 books and articles in a similar vein which earned him acknowledgment as the foremost Catholic social thinker of the century, dying only in 1991 at the age of 101.

The ostensible purpose of the papal document was to celebrate the fortieth anniversary of Leo's *Rerum Novarum*. In the intervening years European society had undergone vast changes. Pius observes that capitalism had spread in that interval everywhere around the globe. But much else had happened. Europe and the world had suffered through the Great War (1914 to 1918). For the purpose of winning the war, the nations of both sides were mobilized in command economies which gave their governments immense powers they had never had before; and which they would be very slow to give up. Great multinational empires were dissolved, notably the German, the Austro-Hungarian, and the Ottoman. Russia had undergone a Communist revolution, which it would soon be seeking to export. And no sooner had the war ended than Germany and other countries were struck by ruinous hyperinflation, which impoverished millions. As we saw in the previous section, the ruling philosophy of European governments in roughly the latter third of the nineteenth century until 1914 had been liberalism. But now the verdict on all sides was that liberalism was dead. Some thought, unfairly, it had committed suicide. The question was, what would take its place? The answer came soon. In Italy, Mussolini took power in 1922. At first Pius's relations with him were cordial enough, but by 1931 he had become disenchanted with "the Leader's" dictatorial regime and condemned it in the letter *Non abbiamo bisogno*. In America the Great Depression had begun, and was spreading to the nations of Europe. The Smoot-Hawley Tariff Act, which brought America's international trade almost to a halt, was passed in 1930.

Italy in Pius XI's day was a poor and economically backward country. It had little in the way of natural resources, and labored under an enormous national debt stemming from its participation in the First World War. Its political class was deeply corrupt. There was heavy unemployment throughout the country, a fact alluded to in this encyclical. Runaway inflation had reduced the lira to a fifth of its pre-war value. Although Mussolini undertook large-scale measures to create a vigorous economy, improving transport and developing hydroelectricity in the North, the nation's standard of living did not rise, but rather fell further. It was only after the Second World War that industrialization took hold and serious economic development began.[141]

Inequality as Injustice

Leo's encyclical had focused on the economic condition of the working class. Nell-Breuning's purpose was more ambitious: it was to develop a Catholic theory of society. European society could be considered at this time to be suffering from many serious problems, as we have just noted, but in Nell-Breuning's view, which undoubtedly derived from Marx, whom he quietly held in high esteem, the chief problem was that European society was divided into two economic classes, the rich and the poor. On the one hand there was the small class of the wealthy, the "capitalists," whose political philosophy could still be summed up in terms of liberalism and individualism; on the other hand, there was the vastly more numerous class of the working poor, who were in danger of succumbing to the lure of socialism and collectivism. This division of society into rich and poor Nell-Breuning and Pius judged to be not merely regrettable or tragic, but a "violation of *justice*."[142] Their reason for this view was that the "*inequality* in the distribution of this world's goods" was "*unjust.*"[143] (My emphases.) In other words, poverty itself is an injustice.

In the context of history this was a strong statement. It gave a revolutionary new meaning to the word "justice," for it disconnected justice and injustice from what had always been considered their indispensable bearer: actions[144] of individuals, for which they could be held accountable. Inequality is not an action. Nor is poverty. Nor is a division of society between two classes an action. Nor can these things be considered results of unjust actions. No one need necessarily have done anything wrong to bring them about. In fact, no one need have done anything to bring them about. They are simply facts, states of affairs. *From now on, the simple fact of economic inequality will count as unjust, irrespective of how it came about.*

Pius does not attempt to solve the problem by agreeing with the philosophy of either the one class or the other, but condemns both philosophies.

Liberalism, or what is the same thing for him, individualism, he condemns because, in his judgment, it is incapable of helping the poor, that is, because its doctrines prevent *government* from helping the poor. For according to liberalism, the role of government is merely to be the guardian of law and order; but, states Pius, contradicting his predecessor Leo, "the whole care of supporting the poor is not to be left to charity alone." Furthermore, liberalism believes in free competition. But free competition is fatally destructive of society. It is the great cause of unjust inequality.

> Just as the unity of human society cannot be founded on an opposition of classes, so also the right ordering of economic life cannot be left to a free competition of forces. For from this source, as from a poisoned spring, have originated and spread all the errors of individualist economic teaching. (88)

As we have noted, President Franklin Roosevelt quoted this statement in a campaign speech in Detroit in 1932, claiming that he was just as radical as the pope was.[145]

Economic life must be governed, says Pius, not by "the evil spirit of individualism" or market freedom, but by "a true and effective directing principle," and that principle is social justice. *All* the institutions of social life ought to be penetrated with social justice. He is not at all content with implementing social justice through the private, voluntary associations that Leo recommended, but ominously demands the establishment of a new "juridical order" which will "give form and shape to all economic life."

Socialism, on the other hand, he observes, has split into two distinct movements: communism, which pursues unrelenting class warfare and absolute extermination of private ownership, and is therefore to be absolutely rejected; and democratic socialism, which, though a big improvement over communism, remains materialistic and unchristian in its view of human life, and must ultimately also be rejected.

But to this rejection of democratic socialism, Pius adds a big "however." If socialism becomes genuinely democratic and peaceful, it will gradually change into "an honest discussion of differences" founded on a desire for justice, and that can become the point of departure for launching a societal system which will replace competition with cooperation throughout economic life. This is the system of "Industries and Professions" or guilds which he considers the ideal form of social organization; about which more below. The war that socialism declared on private ownership is being largely abandoned, he remarks, and now it tends to attack no longer the possession itself of the means of production, but only excessive power in society. Pius approves of socialism's attack on the "excessive power" of owners. For ownership, he claims, has usurped, "contrary to all right," a degree of power that rightly should belong only to the state. If socialism continues to undergo this transformation, he asserts, it may no longer differ much from Christian principles.

In the meantime, Pius wishes to propose a third way between liberalism and socialism. This third way in its ideal form consists in nothing less than a return to the mediaeval guild system, the system of "Industries and Professions" just mentioned, which we will discuss further below. Pius recognized reluctantly that it might be difficult (to say the least) to restore the mediaeval system. But at least it would be possible to fight the twin dragons of liberalism and socialism, or individualism and collectivism. One weapon for this struggle was the doctrine of property.

Property

Pius teaches, as did Leo, that individuals have a natural right to own property. However, Pius wishes to weaken this right rather than emphasize it. He emphasizes the fact that the idea of property is not absolute, but has changed in the course of history, from primitive early forms down to feudal and monarchical forms and to various kinds current at the present time (33). For "God has left the limits of private possessions to be fixed by the industry of men and institutions of peoples." He acknowledges that it is "grossly unjust" for the state to impose taxes so high they are confiscatory (36). Yet the State has the right to "bring private ownership into harmony with the needs of the common good," and when it does this the state does not commit a hostile act against private owners but rather does them a friendly service; for it thereby prevents the private possession of goods from causing intolerable evils and so bringing about its own destruction. Pius views juridical restrictions on the power of ownership as necessary to avoid communism.

Pius accepts and repeats Leo's Lockean argument for the original acquisition of property. ". . . ownership is originally acquired both by occupancy of a thing not owned by any one and by labor . . . " For ". . . no injury is done to any person when a thing is occupied that is available to all but belongs to no one . . . " (52). However, he introduces an important restriction which Locke did not make: the labor must be performed by oneself. It does not apply where (as in Locke's example of the servant who digs turf) the work is hired out to others (53). Pius uses this argument to undercut the common liberal principle that a worker has a right only to the salary he agreed to, and that the employer owns the finished product. Instead, Pius argues that the worker's labor confers on him a partial *ownership* right in the finished product. This was Marx's version of Locke's and Adam Smith's labor theory of value.

Locke had argued in support of his theory of ownership that most of the value of any item is due to the human labor that went into producing it, ". . . for it is labour indeed that puts the difference of value on every thing."

> . . . if we will rightly estimate things as they come to our use, and cast up our several expences about them, what in them is purely owing to nature and what to labour, we shall find that in most of them ninety-nine hundredths are wholly to be put on the account of labour. (*Second Treatise*, chapter 5, Par. 40)

Adam Smith had adopted this concept as a consequence of his doctrine of the division of labor.

> . . . after the division of labour has once thoroughly taken place, it is but a very small part of these (necessaries, conveniences and amusements of life) which a man's own labour can supply him. The far greater part of them he must derive from the labour of other people, and he must be rich or poor according to the quantity of that labour which he can command, or afford to purchase . . . Labour, therefore, is the real measure of the exchangeable value of all commodities.

For Marx this meant that the entire profit of a factory should go to its workers.

Pius repeats and emphasizes Leo's teaching that the right to own property is distinct from its use (30). As we see above (p. 67), Leo acknowledged the biblical teaching that God has given the earth for the use and enjoyment of the whole human race. But his purpose in making this statement was to say that this fact was no bar to private ownership and did not set limits to the amount of property any individual could own. Pius uses it for a different purpose. The right to own property, he teaches, is given by God and nature, but it is given for a twofold purpose. While it is given so that men may be able to provide the material necessities of life for themselves and their families, it is also given for a much wider purpose: the benefit of *all mankind.* This view of Pius's was to become the foundation of the later popes' doctrine of "the universal destination of material goods," which serves as foundation for policies of redistribution.

The Just Economy: Guilds

Leo had taught, as we have seen, that wages and working conditions can be unjust even though they are freely agreed to. The remedy he advocated for this injustice, however, was not any intervention of government, but purely private associations of workers, or workers and employers, to reduce competition, especially between workers for the available jobs. Pius expands the scope of social justice beyond this to the whole economy. For example, he teaches that social justice demands full employment, and any measures that would hinder full employment are unjust. Social justice means that neither capital alone nor labor alone owns the whole products of labor, no matter what agreements have been made, and both aspects of the nature of work must be taken into account in calculating just wages.

This calculation of just wages is no simple matter, if Pius's views are to be followed, but requires the employer to walk a fine line between various considerations, not all of which can easily be calculated. Justice requires that a married worker be paid a wage sufficient to support himself and his family. If this is not possible under existing circumstances, social justice demands that changes be introduced in society that will make it possible. But on the other hand, the condition of the business and its owner must also be taken into account (72), for it would be unjust for employees to demand wages which the business cannot afford. But this depends again on the reason why the business cannot afford to pay just wages. If the reason is the employer's lack of energy or lack of initiative or because of his failure to use up-to-date equipment, then the payment of lower wages is unjust. But if the reason why the business cannot afford just wages is because it is forced to sell its product at less than a just price, those who are responsible for this lower price are guilty of injustice. Lastly, the calculation of pay must take account of the public economic good, which demands among other things, as we have just seen, that there should be work available for everyone who is able and willing to work; and if wages are either too high or too low, the effect will be unemployment, as "everyone knows" (74).

The remedy Pius advocates for all the various injustices of the free market is not any private measure, but the introduction of nothing less than a new *juridical* order which will reorganize the entire economic life of the society, to do away with the labor market altogether and to replace competition with cooperation. This is the system of "Industries and Professions" or guilds mentioned above (p. xxx). According to this scheme, each industry and profession would be organized into a guild containing both employers and workers, which would be given monopoly powers to regulate all aspects of that industry or profession, including wages and prices. Since the guilds would combine both employers and workers, they would overcome the hostility and division between the classes, he reasoned. He describes the guilds as self-governing organizations where men will have their place, not according to the position each has in the labor market – for that is to be abolished – but according to the "social functions" which each performs. He considers that while these guilds may not be essential to civil society, they are at least natural to it (83). He foresees from this arrangement a society living and working in harmony, where the various occupations will "coalesce," in effect, "into a single body," and where members of the body will mutually aid and complete one another (75).

This recommendation of a restoration of the guild system did not come out of the blue. The guild was for many centuries the normal method of organizing economic life in the towns and cities of Europe. There is evidence that they existed already in Rome in the 6th century BC.[146] As economic life revived in the Middle Ages they were recreated, reaching a peak in their number and size in the seventeenth century. They are essentially a protectionist and monopolist form of organization, but also serve other purposes such as the maintenance of standards. With the discovery of the power of the free market as a result especially of the writings of Adam Smith, they came under increasing criticism in the late eighteenth century and were abandoned as the industrial revolution gathered strength. In the early twentieth century the movement known as guild socialism developed in certain circles in England around figures such as G. D. H. Cole, which would have been sympathetic to Pius's suggestion. Some guilds still exist and remain powerful in our own day, including those of the professoriate and the medical profession. Pius's proposal was radical, in that it recommended returning, in the name of justice, to the form in which economic activity had been generally organized before the industrial revolution.

Subsidiarity

We saw in the last chapter Taparelli's distinction between "the large society," the state, and "the small societies," the family and other local organizations, the large society being subordinate or subsidiary in important ways to the small ones, which are the true foundation of civil society (p. xxx above). The ethical conclusions he drew from this distinction remained on the level of moral obligation: the state has an obligation not to absorb or destroy the small societies, and these in turn have an obligation to work together for the common good. While one could easily imagine these were to be understood as obligations in justice, he does not say so explicitly. Pius develops the idea more fully: the state should let the smaller societies handle matters of lesser importance. With him, however, the obligations between these levels of society become explicitly duties in justice. For ". . . it is an injustice and at the same time a grave evil and disturbance of right order to assign to a greater and higher association what lesser and subordinate organizations can do" (79).

Pius XI and Mussolini

After describing the fascist system created by *il Duce*, Pius gives it strong praise, but with a caveat. Anyone who gives even slight attention to the matter will easily see fascism's obvious advantages, he remarks. The various classes work together peacefully, socialist organizations and their activities are repressed, and a special magistracy exercises a governing authority (95). He adds, somewhat as an afterthought, that some people fear the fascist state is substituting itself for free activity instead of merely providing assistance to the new organizations, and that "in spite of those more general advantages mentioned above, which are of course fully admitted," the fascist system is aimed more at serving political purposes than genuinely reconstructing the social order. He pointedly does not include himself among those who entertain this fear; but of course the fact that he mentions it might be taken to suggest that.

The Reach of *Quadragesimo Anno*

We have already noted U.S. President Franklin Delano Roosevelt's public adoption of Pius's program in the election campaign of 1932. His New Deal, enacted after his election, gave it concrete form, in such legislation as the National Industrial Recovery Act of 1933, which aimed to replace "destructive competition" with "fair competition" through collective bargaining and trade unions, gave the federal government power to set minimum wages and maximum working hours, and established the Public Works Administration which created millions of make-work jobs; and the

Social Security Act of 1935. Although the Recovery Act of 1933 was unanimously declared unconstitutional by the Supreme Court, many of its provisions reappeared in the Wagner Act, which was passed later in the same year. The New Deal transformed American society to a significant degree from one based on a tradition of self-reliance to one of reliance on the redistributionist powers of government. Economists and historians are generally agreed, however, that it did little if anything to solve the problem of the Depression, which was cured, so far as it was, by the onset of war.

In January 1944, in his State of the Union address to Congress, Roosevelt proclaimed a "Second Bill of Rights" (the first Bill of Rights in the American sense being, not the English one of 1689, but the one appended to the U.S. Constitution in the following century). While the rights given in the Constitution's Bill of Rights are uniformly negative ("Congress shall make no law . . . ; . . . the right of the people . . . shall not be infringed . . . ; No soldier shall . . . ; etc."), the new rights Roosevelt advocated were without exception positive, requiring to be financed from tax monies:

> The right to a useful and remunerative job in the industries or shops or farms or mines of the nation;
>
> The right to earn enough to provide adequate food and clothing and recreation;
>
> The right of farmers to raise and sell their products at a return which will give them and their families a decent living;
>
> The right of every businessman, large and small, to trade in an atmosphere of freedom from unfair competition and domination by monopolies at home or abroad;
>
> The right of every family to a decent home;
>
> The right to adequate medical care and the opportunity to achieve and enjoy good health;
>
> The right to adequate protection from the economic fears of old age, sickness, accident, and unemployment;
>
> The right to a good education.

The president asserted that these rights had already become accepted as "self-evident," and were necessary "to assure us equality in the pursuit of happiness." Although not further enacted into law at the time, these rights have remained an ideal for many down to the present day. We will return to *Quadragesimo anno* and its influence from a slightly different aspect in the next chapter.

Social Justice[147]

We have seen how and when the transformation of "social injustice" from a purely formal concept to a material one meaning poverty and societal inequality took place. But we have still to answer the question: why? For there is a puzzle. Pius was an ardent admirer of Taparelli, who, as we have seen, did not believe in societal equality but rather rejected it vehemently. Taparelli believed in the guilds, as Pius does, which are scarcely embodiments of equality. There is a tension, if not a contradiction, between the two ideals of equality and the guilds. Where does the encyclical's unexpected devotion to the cause of equality come from? I believe there is good reason to suppose that it comes from Nell-Breuning, the admirer of Marx. If so, it would be perhaps something that Pius accepted into the encyclical, not so much because he believed in it personally, as because of Nell-Breuning's acknowledged "expertise" in regard to the social question; since that was the reason why he invited him to take on the work. At the moment this is only a conjecture.

Aquinas's "General Justice"

The sudden appearance of this new term "social justice" in an official document galvanized Catholic commentators to enquire what it meant and where it came from. Searching the theological tradition, some recalled St. Thomas Aquinas's treatment of what he called "general justice" or "legal justice," and identified it with that. Since this is the interpretation given in the authoritative *Catholic Encyclopedia*, we will make a brief detour to discuss it.

Aquinas has, in comparison with modern assumptions, a very broad conception of what constitutes a just law. In general, any law is just in his view if it is intended to serve the common good rather than the private good of the ruler. Aquinas's conception of the common good is positive, rather than solely negative (in the Berlinian sense), but he does not attempt to say what the positive common good of a society consists in substantively, for that will change as circumstances change. It is the task of the ruler to decide what is for the common good at any particular time. So long as the dispositions of the ruler are sincerely intended to serve the common good, then, even if they should in the end prove to be mistaken, they possess "general justice," or (what means the same thing) "legal justice." If the ruler's dispositions are intended, on the contrary, to serve his own personal good rather than that of the society, he is guilty of general or legal injustice.

There are several problems with interpreting Pius XI's encyclical as an expression of these ideas of Aquinas. One is, of course, that Aquinas refers exclusively to human actions and does not include any conception of justice as a state of affairs in society such as inequality. Another is that, even as a theory about human actions, it has reference only to the role of the ruler, not of individual citizens, as "social justice" typically does.

John XXIII (1958–63) Angelo Roncalli

With John XXIII the decisive turn taken by Pius XI was confirmed and carried further toward the conception of social justice that prevails today, a material rather than a formal concept, and a quality that can apply to states of affairs in society irrespective of how they came about. To understand this development it may be helpful to bear in mind the political situation in Italy at that time, and a development in Italian politics known as the "opening to the Left" or "*apertura alla sinistra.*"

After World War II, Europe was divided into a Communist East and a capitalist West kept separate by the Soviets' Iron Curtain. When the newly formed Italian Republic was set up in 1948, its political life was dominated by three large parties, the Socialists, the Communists, and the Christian Democrats, representing the three groups that had led the resistance to Mussolini's Fascists during the war. The Christian Democrats had close ties to the Catholic Church. The Vatican under Pius XII excommunicated the Communists, and prohibited Catholics from collaborating politically with the Socialists. The consequence was that until Pius's death in 1958 neither the Socialists nor the Communists were ever part of the national government, which was controlled from its inception by the Christian Democrats. No party ever obtained an absolute majority of the votes in elections, so that to form a government coalitions of various parties always had to be created; and from these coalitions the Christian Democrats had always been able to exclude the Communists and Socialists. Yet grassroots support for the Communists was very strong, not to mention for the Socialists. Italy possessed the largest Communist party in Western Europe. Within Italy, the Communist party had the largest number of "card-carrying" members, larger than the Christian Democrats. This was all the more surprising in that Italy, as we have noted, did not have the heavy industrialization and large class of factory workers that some other countries had. The Communists were particularly strong in the band of territory across the peninsula that had formerly been the Papal States, and among the peasantry.

Furthermore, in the wake of the Soviet Union's brutal suppression of the Hungarian uprising in 1956 the Italian Left had declared its independence from Moscow, and had taken other steps to liberalize itself. As a result the feeling grew among the other parties that it was time to rethink in more generous terms the role of the Left in the political life of the country, and allow them to take part in a governing coalition. This was the concept of the *apertura alla sinistra.* But what would be the attitude of the church?

Pius XII, Eugenio Pacelli, had been an aristocrat, a member of one of Italy's noble families by birth, and a patrician by temperament; his grandfather had founded the Vatican newspaper, the *Osservatore Romano.* Angelo Roncalli, elected pope as John XXIII in 1958, was, by contrast, the son of a peasant. As a seminarian in Bergamo in northern Italy he had come under the influence of several leaders of the Italian social movement, and after ordination to the priesthood he became secretary of the new bishop of Bergamo, Giacomo Radini-Tedeschi, who took a special interest in the problems of the working class and gave Roncalli practical experience in dealing with them. Once elected pope, he issued two encyclicals on social concerns: *Mater et magistra,* 1961, and *Pacem in Terris,* 1963.

Mater et Magistra, subtitled *On Recent Developments of the Social Question in the Light of Christian Teaching,* is devoted entirely to the question of social justice, and canonizes the broad interpretation of this concept as a feature of states of affairs in society that can exist independently of human action. " . . . [B]oth within individual countries and among nations" there must be "established a judicial order . . . inspired by social justice . . . "[148] It is a "strict demand of social justice . . . that with the growth of the economy there occur a corresponding social development."[149]

> . . . the economic prosperity of any people is to be assessed not so much from the sum total of goods and wealth possessed as from the distribution of goods according to norms of justice, so that everyone in the community can develop and perfect himself. For this, after all, is the end towards which all economic activity of a community is by nature ordered.[150]

It is a "manifest injustice" that "a whole group of citizens" should occupy "an inferior economic and social status, with less purchasing power than required for a decent livelihood."[151] "National income" must be distributed among the citizens "according to the principles of justice and equity."[152] "Unfortunately, in our day, there occur in economic and social affairs many imbalances that militate against justice and humanity." Justice requires that richer countries come to the aid of those in need.[153] Unless workers receive a fair wage, "justice is violated in labor agreements, even though they are entered into freely on both sides."[154] It is a "norm of justice and equity" "that workers receive a wage sufficient to lead a life worthy of man and to fulfill family responsibilities properly."[155] And so on. The word "justice" is used 41 times in the encyclical, often in the sense of "social justice" and implying coercive redistribution.

Pacem in terris, as its name implies, is concerned with the achievement of peace on earth, and sets out a politico-ethical program for this. It first discusses relationships between individual men, then those between individuals and public authorities, thirdly those between states, and fourthly those in the world community. Relationships between men must be governed by respect for man's rights. John's conception of these rights is very expansive – more so even that that of the United Nations Universal Declaration of Human Rights of 1948, of which he approves.

Man has a right not only to life and to bodily integrity, but also to all the means necessary for the proper development of life, such as food, clothing, shelter, medical care, rest, and "the necessary social services."[156] He has the right to be looked after in the event of ill health, of disability stemming from his work, of widowhood and old age, of enforced unemployment, or whenever through no fault of his own he is deprived of the means of liveli-hood.[157] He has a right to be respected, a right to his good name, a right to freedom in investigating the truth, and (here for the first time a qualifica-tion: "within the limits of the moral order and the common good") a right to freedom of speech and publication, and to freedom to pursue whatever profession he may choose. He also has the right to be accurately informed about public events.[158]

Man has a natural right to share in the benefits of culture, and to receive a good education as well as technical or professional training. Gifted mem-bers of society have a right to the opportunity for more advanced studies.[159] Man has the right to worship God in accordance with the dictates of his own conscience, and to profess his religion in private and in public. He has the right to choose for himself the kind of life that appeals to him, whether married or celibate.[160]

"In the economic sphere, it is evident that a man has the inherent right not only to be given the opportunity to work, but also to be allowed the exercise of personal initiative in the work he does."[161]

The conditions in which a man works form a necessary corollary to these rights. They must not be such as to weaken his physical or moral fibre, or militate against the proper development of adolescents to manhood. Women must be accorded such conditions of work as are consistent with their needs and responsibilities as wives and mothers.[162]

Man has a right to engage in economic activities suited to his degree of responsibility. Especially, he has a right to a fair wage, namely, one "sufficient, in proportion to available funds, to allow him and his family a standard of living consistent with human dignity."[163]

Man has a right to the private ownership of property, including that of productive goods.[164] But (here only the second restriction) this right "entails a social obligation as well."[165]

Men have a right to meet together and to form associations, to organize these associations as they wish, and exercise initiative and responsibility in them.[166] They have the right to freedom of movement and of residence, the right to emigrate (a third restriction: "when there are just reasons in favor of it")[167], and the right to take an active part in public life and make their own contribution to the common welfare.[168] They have the right to the effective and unbiased legal protection of their rights.[169]

Countries have a right not to suffer racial discrimination from other countries.[170] With regard to individuals, the pope merely narrates, though with evident approval, that "Today . . . the conviction is widespread that all men are equal in atural dignity; and so, on the doctrinal and theoretical level, at least, no form of approval is being given to racial discrimination."[171] It will be remembered that this is before the U.S. Civil Rights Act of 1964.

Inevitably, such a long list of rights, many of them requiring "positive performance" on another's part, and difficult if not impossible to achieve, must raise a question in the mind of the enquiring reader as to what exactly is meant by the term "rights" here. Are they perhaps to be understood in a weak or merely analogous sense, as desiderata or ideals rather than strict rights? But John insists that each of these rights gives rise to a corresponding duty in other men to recognize and respect them.[172]

In 1963, when this encyclical was published, the nations of the world were divided, as we have just mentioned, into those of the First World, the capitalist West, and those of the Second World, the communist regimes subject to the rule of the Soviet Union behind the Iron Curtain (the Berlin Wall had gone up in 1961), as well as the Third or underdeveloped World outside of these. In neither of these two encyclicals of John XXIII is there any explicit discussion of communism by name, let alone a condemnation of it.[173] The list of rights seems aimed solely at the capitalist world.

Not only do individuals have rights, but also states, as we have just noted, including therefore presumably the communist states, have rights. ". . . all states are by nature equal in dignity."[174] "There are no differences at all between political communities from the point of view of natural dignity."[175] But at the present time people "are living in the grip of constant fear" because of the arms race,[176] which must be brought to a halt. "Nuclear weapons must be banned."[177] "It no longer makes sense to maintain that war is a fit instrument with which to repair the violation of justice."[178] The letter betrays no sense that the Communist states represent a threat of undeserved aggression in regard to the free world, or are in any way specially responsible for the international state of fear.

One effect of these two encyclicals was to give John's blessing to the *apertura alla sinistra* in Italy. The historian Harry Hearder remarks that *Pacem in terris* "clearly implies that communism, though based on a false philosophy, may be the right form of social organization for certain peoples at certain times."[179]

In the Italian context John XXIII clearly approved of the "opening to the left," and although he was equally clearly not trying to increase the Communist vote, his encyclicals had that effect, as did the audience which he gave to Nikita Kruschchev's son-in-law, the editor of *Izvestia*.[180]

The Second Vatican Council *Gaudium et Spes* (1965)

The title often given to this document in English translations is *The Pastoral Constitution on the Church in the Modern World*. Since it was issued by the pope, Paul VI (John XXIII having died in 1963), in conjunction with the Council, it is considered to have more weight than encyclicals issued by the pope alone.

The chief significance of this document in regard to social justice is that it is the first official Catholic statement to clearly condemn "discrimination" against individuals. We have just seen that John XXIII had mentioned discrimination twice in *Pacem in terris* of April 1963, and only on the ground of race, and in one instance only in regard to discrimination by countries against countries. Discrimination against individuals is not a problem to which he devotes much space. *Gaudium et spes* is different. It elevates discrimination against individuals into a major theme. Work on *Gaudium* began in the Council in 1962, but was not completed till December 1965, so that we will not go far wrong if we perceive here the substantial influence of the U.S. Civil Rights Act, which was passed in 1964. (For a further discussion of this, see below, Chapter 5.)

The concept of discrimination developed here is already comprehensive, going far beyond John's statements.

> . . . every type of discrimination, whether social or cultural, whether based on sex, race, color, social condition, language or religion, is to be overcome and eradicated as contrary to God's intent. For in truth it must still be regretted that fundamental personal rights are still not being universally honored.[181]

As the inclusion of "cultural" discrimination makes clear, there is no suggestion here of the distinction we make below in Chapter 5 between coercive and peaceful discrimination. Both are placed in the same category.

Similarly:

> . . . the duty most consonant with our times, especially for Christians, is that of working diligently for fundamental decisions to be taken in economic and political affairs, both on the national and international level which will everywhere recognize and satisfy the right of all to a human and social culture in conformity with the dignity of the human person without any discrimination of race, sex, nation, religion or social condition.[182]

All economic discrimination is an offense against justice and equity:

> To satisfy the demands of justice and equity, strenuous efforts must be made, without disregarding the rights of persons or the natural qualities of each country, to remove as quickly as possible the immense economic inequalities, which now exist and in many cases are growing and which are connected with individual and social discrimination.[183]

There should be no economic discrimination against immigrants:

> When workers come from another country or district and contribute to the economic advancement of a nation or region by their labor, all discrimination as regards wages and working conditions must be carefully avoided.[184]

The prohibition of discrimination is extended beyond the sphere of economics to the political realm. The following statement in its historical context suggests perhaps a reference to the dispute in the U.S. over voting rights. The U.S. Voting Rights Act was signed into law by President Johnson on August 6, 1965, four months before the conciliar document was promulgated by the Vatican.

It is in full conformity with human nature that there should be juridico-political structures providing all citizens in an ever better fashion and without any discrimination the practical possibility of freely and actively taking part in the establishment of the juridical foundations of the political community and in the direction of public affairs, in fixing the terms of reference of the various public bodies and in the election of political leaders.[185]

In our view, discussed more fully in Chapter 5 below, the prohibition of peaceful discrimination is now the main form in which the idea of social justice impinges on Western society. It, more than any other conception, has redefined the concept of justice. In the process it has taken a large step toward undermining every institution of society, because it compels every kind of institution to serve two contradictory masters: the purpose for which it was created, and the additional purpose of increasing societal equality.

Paul VI (1963–1978) Giovanni Battista Montini

In his encyclical *Populorum progressio* (1967) Paul extended the doctrine of social justice, which had originally been applied only within nations, systematically to the international sphere, especially to the problem of the economic development of the poorer countries. The stated purpose of the encyclical was "to encourage social justice between nations . . ."[186] Leo XIII's defense of private property as an absolute right is not only abandoned but contradicted. For Paul, ". . . private property does not constitute for anyone an absolute and unconditioned right. No one is justified in keeping for his exclusive use what he does not need, when others lack necessities."[187] Since in the foreseeable future there will always be others who lack necessities, this seems to imply one is never justified in keeping for his exclusive use what he does not need. The principle of the just wage applies equally to international contracts: "Freedom of trade is fair only if it is subject to the demands of social justice."[188]

In trade between developed and underdeveloped economies, conditions are too disparate and the degrees of genuine freedom available too unequal. In order that international trade be human and moral, social justice requires that it restore to the participants a certain equality of opportunity.[189]

Businessmen should not "return to the inhuman principles of individualism when they operate in less developed countries."[190] Nothing is said in the encyclical about the immense role of corruption in impeding the economic development of the Third World, nor about the inhumanity of communist governments that prevent their citizens from engaging in trade.

With Paul VI the papal development and expansion of social justice theory has come essentially to an end, at least for the time being. John Paul II (1978–2005) Karol Wojtyla, the first non-Italian pope since the 16th century, issued three encyclicals dealing with the social question: *Laborem exercens* (1981), on work, *Sollicitudo rei socialis* (1987), and *Centesimus annus* (1991) commemorating the 100th anniversary of *Rerum novarum.* Between the second and third of these publications the momentous event occurred of the collapse of the Soviet Union and its hegemony over eastern Europe, including the pope's native land of Poland, a collapse to which he was widely credited with having made a contribution through his support for the Polish union Solidarity against the Communist Polish government maintained by the armies of Moscow. *Centesimus annus* takes a more favorable view of capitalism than any papal encyclical preceding it.

In 2009 the current pope, Benedict XVI (2005–), Joseph Ratzinger, published the encyclical letter *Caritas in veritate,* on international economic development. It takes the form of a commemoration of Paul VI's letter *Populorum progressio,* which we have just discussed. Benedict accepts Paul's expanded concept of social justice and explicitly advocates the redistribution of wealth. "[T]he social doctrine of the Church has unceasingly highlighted the importance of distributive justice and social justice for the market economy."[191] "[G]grave imbalances are produced when economic action, conceived merely as an engine for wealth creation, is detached from political action, conceived as a means for pursuing justice through redistribution."[192] "Economic life undoubtedly requires contracts [and therefore, from the previous sentence, commutative justice], in order to regulate relations of exchange between goods of equivalent value. But it also needs just laws and forms of redistribution governed by politics . . . "[193] Having said this, however, it is also noteworthy that he changes the emphasis in Catholic social teaching from social justice to charity. "Charity is at the heart of the Church's social doctrine. Every responsibility and every commitment spelt out by that doctrine is derived from charity which, according to the teaching of Jesus, is the synthesis of the entire Law."[194]

This leads him to envision an "economy of solidarity" which is neither voluntary market nor coercive redistribution. "When both the logic of the market and the logic of the State come to an agreement that each will continue to exercise a monopoly over its respective area of influence, in the long term much is lost: solidarity in relations between citizens, participation and adherence, actions of gratuitousness, all of which stand in contrast with giving in order to acquire (the logic of exchange) and giving through duty (the logic of public obligation, imposed by State law). In order to defeat underdevelopment, action is required not only on improving exchange-based transactions and implanting public welfare structures, but above all on gradually increasing openness, in a world context, to forms of economic activity marked by quotas of gratuitousness and communion. The exclusively binary model of market-plus-State is corrosive of society, while economic forms based on solidarity, which find their natural home in civil society without being restricted to it, build up society."[195] Just what this means, however, is not entirely clear. It seems to imply the giving of free gifts. But is the giving to be unilateral or mutual? If unilateral, this already exists in enormous programs of foreign aid, which have a history of encouraging corruption and subverting the local market. If mutual, that will be hard to distinguish from the market.

A puzzle about Catholic teaching and responsibility

Catholic support for social justice as currently understood is paradoxical. For, as we will see more fully below in Chapter 6, the concept of social justice inherently by its nature marginalizes or eliminates individual responsibility. Social injustice consists primarily not in actions but in states of affairs in society such as inequality which are not necessarily the result of any actions, and so for which no one need be responsible. The classic case is the doctrine of "disparate impact." Yet Catholicism continues to teach that individuals are responsible for their actions and bear responsibility for social injustice, and apparently does not see a conflict between these two positions.

Defining Social Justice

When we view the immense differences that exist between the various conceptions of "social justice" described in the documents we have been examining, it becomes very difficult, I would even say impossible, to offer a single definition that will cover all of them. Quite apart from the differences between the original conceptions, conservative, liberal and socialistic, discussed in Chapter 3, there are also the differences between those and the papal conceptions examined in this chapter, and among these latter themselves. If we regard *Rerum novarum* as a document of social justice, as it generally is regarded, there are first the differences between it and the later papal statements beginning with that of Pius XI that we have just been outlining. But there are also the differences among the later statements; one thing that stands out is the fact that the statements issued since the Second World War completely omit the "industries and professions" or guilds which for Pius XI represented the ideal fulfillment of social justice. Not only this, but we have one more component to add to the mixture, and an especially important one at that: the principle of non-discrimination, which is the subject of the following chapter.

Chapter 5

Non-Discrimination

Since the 1960s, the principle of non-discrimination has come to be widely considered an intrinsic part of our ordinary and traditional idea of justice. On this view, discrimination or preferential treatment on certain grounds and in certain areas of social life is unjust. This conviction has now been enshrined in numerous laws in many countries.

But this simple view of the relationship between justice and discrimination neglects an important distinction. We have drawn attention to this distinction in Chapter 2 above (p. 16), and briefly in Chapter 4 (p. 86), but will repeat it here for further discussion. There are two fundamentally different kinds of discrimination, with very different relationships to the idea of justice. On the one hand there is what we may call forcible or *coercive* discrimination, which discriminates by employing violence, physical force, or the threat of force, for example the power of government, the law, the military or the police, or patently criminal force, and so causes injury to those discriminated against. Examples of coercive discrimination in the history of the United States include slavery, the Black Codes, the Jim Crow laws, the activities of the Ku Klux Klan, voter suppression, the biased implementation of police and judicial procedures, and lynching. In its original meaning, "segregation" suggested coercive separation. Many other examples of coercive discrimination can be found in the history of other countries, such as the "ethnic cleansing" witnessed during the 1990s in the Balkans.

On the other hand there is non-forcible, non-coercive, or what we may call *peaceful* discrimination, which does *not* employ force or the threat of force, and is immune to charges of causing injury as this is customarily understood. Peaceful discrimination is of a totally different order from coercive discrimination, for not only does it not employ coercion, but it proceeds typically by not performing actions at all. Rather, it proceeds by *in*action, by *abstaining* from doing certain things, by *not* employing or *not* doing business with certain persons. For example, the employer who has a policy of hiring only members of a certain ethnic group can do so simply by not employing others. Coercive discrimination was always recognized as incompatible with ordinary justice; the arguments for it were invariably made in terms of some kind of practical necessity. Until the 1960s, however, what I am calling peaceful discrimination was universally and correctly believed to be compatible with ordinary justice. *The condemnation of peaceful discrimination as unjust belongs, not to the ordinary and traditional idea of justice, but to the socialistic conception of social justice.*

Courts have several times made reference to "private discrimination," in the sense of discrimination by persons not associated with government, but there is no special term for discrimination by government; "public" tends to evoke the discussion about discrimination in "public accommodations." To a certain extent the distinction I have made between coercive and peaceful discrimination will coincide with that between governmental and private discrimination, but that leaves out of account the extreme discrimination practiced by such as the Ku Klux Klan, or in lynching, and it is arguably just such forms of discrimination that are private but coercive that lead to confusion in the concept of discrimination unless the distinction between peaceful and coercive is kept in mind.

With regard to non-coercive discrimination, there is also an important distinction to be made between two methods of eliminating it, namely mandatory and voluntary. The early Civil Rights movement in the United States wished to achieve the goal of ending peaceful or non-coercive discrimination in employment, but by voluntary means, not mandatory ones.

Coercion

Different writers have understood the idea of coercion differently. The chief question is whether it should include the actual use of force. Probably the most common understanding of it at the present time does not do so, but includes the threat of force, and also fraud, which is deliberate deception employed to get a person to act against his own interests or desires, for example in market transactions. "Coercion" is used in this sense in contrast to the use of force. Robert Nozick uses it in this sense in his well-known article, "Coercion."[196] Other writers, however, include in the concept of coercion not only the threat of force, and fraud, but also the actual use of force. There are many frameworks where it is helpful to have one term to cover these ideas because they are closely related, and it is in this more comprehensive sense that I use the word here. Otherwise it would be necessary to speak constantly of "force and coercion."

Beyond this mere difference of terminology, however, there is a deep division between the proponents of traditional justice and those of social justice in regard to the types of conduct that are equivalent to the use of force. Proponents of social justice commonly regard inequalities of power, influence, and bargaining power as tantamount to the use of force, and therefore as coercive. For example, because the laborer has to have a job in order to live, and because the employer has no need to employ just this particular person, the inequality of power that results is viewed as equivalent to coercion, so that the wage contract between them is considered not a free contract at all but a form of slavery. The Left tends to see coercion wherever there is inequality. An important reason for this is undoubtedly the fact that those on the Left typically deny or at least minimize the existence of free will. If human actions are invariably the product of circumstances, whether exterior or interior, the difference between force and other kinds of successful influence is only one of degree, not of kind. This view naturally erodes the distinction between coercive and peaceful discrimination.

The sense in which I use the term admittedly reflects my belief in freedom of the will, which I regard as an ineliminable presupposition of ethical judgment. All forms of genuine coercion manifest contempt for another person's will. They are employed in order to bypass the other's will, and to achieve one's purpose regardless of the other, even if the other is critically involved in the result. By their very nature they are forms of injustice unless they are used to prevent or punish injustice.

The principle of non-discrimination has in the course of its history undergone a dramatic transformation: it began in the nineteenth century as a prohibition of coercive discrimination, and has metamorphosed in the twentieth century into a ban on peaceful discrimination. The consequence has been a thorough corruption of the idea of justice.

In the American context, the principle of non-discrimination is usually referred to as "civil rights." Outside of the United States. it is now often considered part of "human rights." In this chapter we will take these concepts in turn, investigating first the origin and development of civil rights in the United States from the perspective of the distinction between coercive and peaceful discrimination, and then the origin and development of human rights from that perspective.

In law, in all the English-speaking nations, the principle of non-discrimination owes its existence to legislation. For reasons we shall see, there has never been a crime of discrimination either in Roman law or in the Common law. We will begin our discussion, therefore, by referring to pieces of legislation.

The American context: civil rights

The United States seems to have been the first country to give the term "civil rights" official legal status. There have been some dozen Acts of Congress passed employing it in their titles, as well as others that treat of the same or similar materials without employing the term.

Our first thesis is that the original concept of civil rights prohibited only coercive discrimination; but that the Civil Rights Act of 1964, adopting the standpoint of the socialistic conception of social justice, took the revolutionary and fateful step of prohibiting peaceful discrimination. Our second, related thesis is that the original civil rights were liberties, which did not require any positive performance from those who respect them, but that the civil rights of 1964 and later require a positive performance from those who respect them.

1. The original civil rights: the prohibition of coercive discrimination

The Thirteenth Amendment to the U.S. Constitution, passed in 1865, freed the slaves but did not give them U.S. citizenship. The white South hastened to create a variety of restrictions on what blacks could do, usually referred to as the Black Codes. They varied from state to state, and even locality to locality, but generally shared certain provisions: they prevented blacks from voting, holding office, or serving on juries, or from serving in state militias; required that poor, unemployed persons (who were almost invariably blacks) should be arrested for vagrancy or bound as apprentices; compelled free blacks to have labor contracts with whites; and prohibited marriage between blacks and whites. In addition they typically provided for the segregation of public facilities and placed strict limits on other rights, such as the right to own real estate or to testify in court. The Black Codes of Mississippi, for example, restricted the rights of freed blacks to keep firearms, ammunition, and knives and also prevented them from leaving the service of their employer before the expiration of their term of service without good cause. Some of these codes had already existed before the Civil War in places in the North. In March 1866 Congress responded to them by passing the first civil rights act.

In order to establish our thesis, it will be necessary to examine each of the civil rights acts before 1964 to show how they understand the term "civil rights." What follows is by no means a comprehensive account of all the actions of Congress, government, and the courts having to do with our topic; its aim is simply to show the meaning attached in federal legislation to the term "civil rights."

As a prefatory note, we observe that in the discussions that took place in the eighteenth century around the adoption of the U.S. Constitution, "civil rights" are distinguished from "religious rights." "In a free government, the security for civil rights must be the same as that for religious rights."[197] These are obviously ordinary rights as guaranteed by ordinary justice, only in the non-religious sphere.

The first paragraph of the Civil Rights Act of 1866 states its purpose, and also defines what is meant in it by the term "civil rights." The purpose of the Act is to confer citizenship on blacks together with the "full and equal benefit of all laws and proceedings for the security of person and property, *as is enjoyed by white citizens.*" (My emphasis.) That is, it does not intend to create any new rights, but only to extend to blacks rights that whites already possess. The term "civil rights" in the title is explained as meaning the right

> to make and enforce contracts, to sue, be parties, and give evidence, to inherit, purchase, lease, sell, hold, and convey real and personal property, and to full and equal benefit of the laws and proceedings for the security of person and property, as is enjoyed by white citizens.

Let us examine these a little more closely. How can a person be *prevented* from making contracts? Only either by physical force or by laws which do not recognize any contracts he makes as legally binding. Both are coercion. Similarly, how can a person be prevented from suing, being party to a lawsuit, giving evidence in court, inheriting property, or buying and selling it? Only by two ways: through physical force, or by laws that withhold legal recognition from these activities. Both of these are coercive. The purpose of the Act is clearly to prohibit certain kinds of coercive discrimination. There is no trace here of any prohibition of peaceful discrimination, for example in hiring, or the purchase and sale of property.

The Supreme Court, however, noted for its almost miraculous power to find in the Constitution provisions otherwise invisible to mortal eyes, has ruled, in 1968, in the wake of the national disturbances that followed the Civil Rights Act of 1964, that this Act can provide the basis for a suit alleging private discrimination. (*Jones v. Alfred H. Mayer Co.*, 1968.) The District Court and the Appeals Court had both ruled to the contrary, but were reversed. This would seem to be possible only because the Court has not grasped the difference between coercion and peaceful discrimination, and assumes, incorrectly, that a prohibition of coercive discrimination, which is what we have in this Act, necessarily implies also a prohibition of peaceful discrimination, which, of course, it does not.

In 1868, the 14th Amendment to the U.S. Constitution was ratified. Section 1 reads:

> No State shall make or enforce any law which shall abridge the privileges or immunities of citizens of the United States; nor shall any State deprive any person of life, liberty, or property, without due process of law; nor deny to any person within its jurisdiction the equal protection of the laws.

According to the text of the law, it is only states that are required to give "equal protection," and therefore not to discriminate in their enforcement of laws. Nothing is said about discrimination by private persons, whether coercive or peaceful.

The Civil Rights Act of 1870 enforced the right of blacks to vote, a right already conferred by citizenship but widely prevented from being exercised. The Act was directed especially against the coercive (to use no stronger word) activities of the Ku Klux Klan. It provides that all citizens of the United States who are qualified by law to vote in any election must be allowed to vote in all elections, without distinction of race, color, or previous condition of servitude. The only way in which people who wish to vote in an election can be prevented by others from doing so is, of course, by some form of coercion, and that is what this Act prohibits.

The Civil Rights Act of 1871, enforcing the previous ones, was likewise directed against the Ku Klux Klan and government officials who might conspire with them to deprive citizens of their rights "by force, intimidation or threat."

In the Civil Rights Act of 1875 we meet for the first time in U.S. law provisions outlawing peaceful discrimination. "Inns, public conveyances on land or water, theaters, and other places of public amusement" must offer "full and equal enjoyment" of their facilities to all persons in the United States. These are new rights, not merely extensions to blacks of rights already possessed by whites. In addition, the Act disallows the coercive practice of rejecting blacks as jurors: all qualified persons have the right to be called as jurors. Citizens are given the right to sue for personal damages those offending against the statute.

In 1883, however, the Supreme Court declared the Act unconstitutional, on the telling ground that the Fourteenth Amendment to the Constitution, which alone could have justified it, was limited in its scope to correcting laws made by the states, and so did not confer on Congress authority to regulate the conduct of individuals. The court acknowledged that the 13th Amendment does apply to private actors, but only to the extent that it prohibits people from owning slaves, not exhibiting discriminatory behavior. The Court said that

> it would be running the slavery argument into the ground to make it apply to every act of discrimination which a person may see fit to make as to guests he will entertain, or as to the people he will take into his coach or cab or car; or admit to his concert or theatre, or deal with in other matters of intercourse or business.

This decision of the Court still stands: the Act has never been rehabilitated.

The Act of 1957 reinforced the right of blacks to vote. In addition, it created the Civil Rights Commission to investigate allegations that citizens are being deprived of their right to vote, or to have that vote counted, by reason of their color, race, religion, or national origin.

The Act of 1960 enabled federal judges to appoint referees to hear persons claiming that state election officials had denied them the right to register and vote.

Our conclusion is well established, then, that in all the civil rights acts recognized as valid by the Supreme Court up to and including 1960, the term "civil rights" refers exclusively to the prohibition of *coercive* discrimination, and not to the prohibition of peaceful discrimination.

Another way of describing the civil rights to be found in these acts is that they are freedoms, such as the freedom to make contracts or to buy and sell land. They were previously often referred to as "civil liberties" rather than civil rights, because they confer a liberty or power to do something. They are "negative" rights, meaning they are rights not to be impeded in the performance of an action. In order to respect these rights it is not necessary to *do* anything; all that is necessary is to *abstain from hindering* their exercise. A positive right, by contrast, is a right to receive a performance from another person.[198] This, as we shall see, applies to the civil rights given in 1964 and later.

2. *Civil rights since 1964: the prohibition of peaceful discrimination*

The Civil Rights Act of 1866 effectively eliminated the Black Codes. In 1877, however, the Reconstruction era that followed the Civil War was brought to a sudden halt and the federal troops that had occupied the South and enforced the law were withdrawn. The response of the white South was to turn to a different species of laws, both state and local, mandating "separate but equal" accommodations and public facilities for whites and blacks, from railroads to schools and water fountains: the "Jim Crow" Laws.[199] The separate-but-equal doctrine was challenged in court in *Plessy v. Ferguson*, 1896, but the Supreme Court upheld its constitutionality. This was segregation in the true sense of the word.

In 1911 the National Association for the Advancement of Colored People was incorporated with the mission

> To promote equality of rights and to eradicate caste or race prejudice among the citizens of the United States; to advance the interest of colored citizens; to secure for them impartial suffrage; and to increase their opportunities for securing justice in the courts, education for the children, employment according to their ability and complete equality before law.

These goals can all be understood in such a way that they would be satisfied by elimination of coercive discrimination, but the distinction between coercive and peaceful discrimination was not made.

The leadership of the new organization was predominantly white and largely Jewish. It proceeded to attack the separate-but-equal doctrine in the courts. Eventually it succeeded in 1954, when the Supreme Court ruled in *Brown v. the Board of Education of Topeka* that *de jure* separate educational facilities violated the "equal protection" clause of the 14th Amendment because, whatever their actual condition, they were "inherently unequal."

In June 1963, the Kennedy administration introduced into Congress a bill to expand the scope of civil rights legislation dramatically. President Kennedy explained its rationale in a public speech on June 11. In August a large political rally took place in Washington, DC, the "March on Washington for Jobs and Freedom," organized by representatives of a number of black organizations, to increase pressure for passage of the bill. Martin Luther King, Jr., delivered an impassioned speech advocating the complete acceptance of blacks by whites into American life. The pressure was successful, and the bill was passed the following year, despite the intervening assassination of the president, as the Civil Rights Act of 1964.

The act is of historic importance because it criminalizes not only coercive discrimination (segregation, voter suppression), which is entirely right and proper, but also non-coercive or peaceful discrimination. The operative section of the act from this perspective is Title VII on employment. The first few paragraphs of the title (given here in its present amended and final form) are sufficient to make this clear.

(a) It shall be an unlawful employment practice for an employer–

(1) to fail or refuse to hire or to discharge any individual, or otherwise to discriminate against any individual with respect to his compensation, terms, conditions, or privileges of employment, because of such individual's race, color, religion, sex, or national origin; or

(2) to limit, segregate, or classify his employees in any way which would deprive or tend to deprive any individual of employment opportunities or otherwise adversely affect his status as an employee, because of such individual's race, color, religion, sex, or national origin.

(b) It shall be an unlawful employment practice for an employment agency to fail or refuse to refer for employment, or otherwise to discriminate against, any individual because of his race, color, religion, sex, or national origin, or to classify or refer for employment any individual on the basis of his race, color, religion, sex, or national origin.

The pressure for passage of the bill came entirely from the Civil Rights movement, whose concern was focused entirely on the question of race. So far, up to this point, it might have been considered simply a particular measure to correct a particular problem in a particular country. But it soon transpired that much more was at stake. The reader will have noted in each clause of the above text the presence of the word "sex." The original text of the bill did not contain this word. As we have noted above (p. xxx, note 46) it was added through an amendment moved by Howard W. Smith, Democratic congressman of Virginia, chairman of the House Rules Committee, which controlled the procedure for passing the bill. By an irony of historic proportions, Smith's motive for moving the amendment, according to the plausible account given later by his colleague, Representative Carl Elliott of Alabama, was not, as one might suppose, to advance the cause of women's rights, but to sink the original bill. For he was adamantly opposed to it, and reasoned that if it included a prohibition of discrimination on the ground of sex, that would prevent it from obtaining the necessary votes.[200] As the reader can see, however, his reasoning was faulty: the pressure was sufficient to ensure the bill did receive the necessary votes.[201] It faced further opposition in the Senate, but President Lyndon Johnson, who was determined to get the bill passed, was able to use the power of his office to persuade enough senators to support it.

Unlike with the question of race, there had been no large, popular movement in the United States to eliminate differential treatment of the sexes. In 1964 the feminist movement was still small. Betty Friedan had just published her "*Feminine Mystique*" (a product of the labor union movement), the year before.[202] Gloria Steinem did not publish *Ms* Magazine till 1972. American society at large generally accepted that men and women had in many respects different desires and different needs, and that there was a natural division of labor between them. There was no political constituency for a law imposing gender equality. It is true that the Equal Pay Act had been enacted some months earlier, but the motive for that was very different: it was put forward by the labor unions in order to ward off "unfair competition" for men from women doing the same job at lower wages. The Civil Rights Act of 1964 had a different motive, was far broader in scope, and its consequences have been much more far-reaching.

To repeat what we have written above (p. 17), by this accident of history discrimination *as such* was absolutized as an evil, and universalized. For once discrimination on the ground of sex was prohibited, every other form of discrimination came to be considered illegitimate in principle (except, of course, for affirmative action). For there is scarcely any aspect of human life where discrimination has traditionally been viewed as more obviously necessary and more completely justified than in the distinction between the sexes. If it was illegitimate there, it could not well be legitimate anywhere, it has been felt. And this condemnation of discrimination was soon exported to other countries around the globe. In remote New Zealand the law now prohibits discrimination on the grounds of sex – which includes pregnancy and childbirth – marital status, religious belief, ethical belief, color, race, ethnic or national origin or citizenship, disability, age, political opinion, employment status, family status, or sexual orientation. In other words, all forms of discrimination are evil.

On p. 15 above we observed that the civil rights recognized before 1964 were liberties, which did not require any positive performance from others, but demanded only that they abstain from hindering the exercise of the right. We can now add that that the civil rights conferred in 1964 and after are something very different: they *do* demand a positive performance from other persons. The right to free speech is just the right not to be prevented from speaking, just as the right to vote is just the right not to be prevented from voting; but the right not to be discriminated against in employment does not mean merely that one should not be prevented from being employed, but that an employer has a legal obligation in certain circumstances to give employment to the members of certain chosen groups.

The global context: human rights

Outside of the United States, the principle of non-discrimination is largely treated now as a question of human rights. Corresponding to the revolution that the idea of civil rights underwent in the United States, the concept of human rights has also undergone a revolution.

"Human rights" is the heir and successor to the earlier concept of "natural rights," as developed during the Enlightenment by writers such as Locke on the foundation of natural law. For Locke, while governments can give legal rights to their citizens, there is another and more fundamental kind of right, a moral right, which is not dependent on government and may or may not be expressed in legislation but is possessed by all men in virtue of the natural moral law. This natural moral law has been placed in the hearts of men by God when he conferred their human nature on them in the act of creation. The main content of this natural moral law is to prohibit men from causing harm, either to themselves or to others. In consequence, men have a natural right not to be harmed by others.

> The state of nature [contrasted with society under government] has a law of nature to govern it, which obliges everyone: and reason, which is that law, teaches all mankind, who will but consult it, that being all equal and independent, no one ought to harm another in his life, liberty or possessions. For men being all the workmanship of one omnipotent and infinitely wise maker, all the servants of one sovereign master, sent into the world by his order and about his business; they are his property, whose workmanship they are, made to last during his, not one another's pleasure: and being furnished with like faculties, sharing all in one community of nature, there cannot be supposed any such subordination among us, that may authorize us to destroy one another, as if we were made for one another's uses, as the inferior ranks of creatures are for ours. Everyone, as he is bound to preserve himself, and not to quit his station wilfully, so by the like reason, when his own preservation comes not in competition, ought he, as much as he can, to preserve the rest of mankind, and may not, unless it be to do justice on an offender, take away or impair the life, or what tends to the preservation of the life, the liberty, health, limb, or goods of another.[203]

This passage is important because it emphasizes the negative character of the natural moral law as Locke conceives of it. It does not command any positive action. It is true Locke says the law commands us "to preserve the rest of mankind," and some have taken this in the sense of a positive command, but the natural sense of the phrase in the context is the one parallel to the statement immediately previous to it in the paragraph, that we are bound to preserve ourselves, which Locke explains in the purely negative sense that we should not commit suicide.

The concept of natural rights was powerful in the debates leading to the secession of the American colonies from the British Empire and the founding of the United States. The *Virginia Declaration of Rights* of June 1776, authored by George Mason, stated (in a document which is still part of the state Constitution)

> That all men are by nature equally free and independent, and have certain inherent rights, of which, when they enter into a state of society, they cannot, by any compact, deprive or divest their posterity; namely, the enjoyment of life and liberty, with the means of acquiring and possessing property, and pursuing and obtaining happiness and safety.

A month later Thomas Jefferson availed himself of the Virginia statement in composing the Declaration of Independence, stating it was a self-evident truth for the Americans that all men, being created equal, were endowed by their Creator with unalienable rights to life, liberty, and the pursuit of happiness. These rights testified to by Mason and Jefferson are negative natural rights, all of them, for the right to pursue happiness is just the right not to be hindered in that pursuit.

The Lockean and American negative conception of natural rights was echoed in the French "Declaration of the Rights of Man and the Citizen" of 1789. This document, drawn up by Lafayette and modeled on the American Bill of Rights, specifies that every man possesses four "rights that are natural, inalienable and sacred," namely the right to liberty, property, security, and resistance to oppression. "Liberty," it explains, "consists in the power to do everything which does not harm others." The right to property is described as "inviolable and sacred."[204]

In the wake of the French Revolution, however, as secularism spread across Europe during the nineteenth century, the link between nature and God highlighted by Locke and Jefferson came to be regarded by some thinkers as an embarrassment. John Stuart Mill argued that "nature" was a purely factual term with no moral weight. The term "natural right" came to be replaced by "human right." This substitution is not entirely a gain, however. Mill misunderstood what the natural law moralists meant by "nature." What he said was true about inanimate nature. But in speaking of nature the natural law moralists meant human nature, or, as they said often enough, the power of reason. In regard to that nature Mill was absurdly wrong. "Natural right" points to a rational foundation for rights in human nature. "Human right," however, points to no foundation at all, and the question remains philosophically acute as to what foundation can be discovered for a right claimed to be possessed by all human beings if that foundation does not somehow lie in their nature as human beings.

The United Nations

Undeterred by such considerations, in the spring of 1946 in the aftermath of the Second World War the nascent United Nations decided to proceed to the issuance of a Declaration of Human Rights. The moving force in this endeavor came from what might seem at first glance a surprising source: the nations of Latin America. Among the 50 nations represented at the creation of the United Nations in San Francisco, 20 were from Latin America – the largest bloc. They were to exert a decisive influence on the idea of human rights. Conservative commentators have sometimes assumed that the expansive definition of human rights to include economic and cultural "rights" such as to education, work, health care, and social security, for which the United Nations Declaration has become famous or notorious, must have derived from a socialist or communist source; but the communist representatives at the United Nations were opposed to making any declaration on human rights, considering it a distraction from the main task of creating arrangements for international security. The actual source of these socialistic "rights" was the delegations from Latin America. For the political elites of these nations operated within a culture heavily imprinted with the values of Roman Catholicism, and even if they did not consider themselves personally Catholic, that tradition provided them with a large part of their intellectual horizon. An important portion of that horizon at this time was the papal encyclical letter *Quadragesimo anno*, 1931, with its particular conception of "social justice." We have referred to this document in the previous chapter. Now we shall follow the trail that led from that papal statement to the United Nations' Declaration of Human Rights.

Already during the 1930s, under the influence of the encyclical, the political elites of Latin American had begun to think about human rights in a way very different from that of the earlier French declaration. In 1938 a "Declaration in Defense of Human Rights" was adopted at a meeting in Lima, Peru, of the Inter-American Conference (predecessor of the Organization of American States). In 1945, before the Commission on Human Rights was established, while the Charter of the UN was being drawn up, several Latin American nations attempted to include in it provisions regarding human rights in the sense of the encyclical. Panama's Foreign Minister, Ricardo Alfaro, supported by the delegations from Chile, Cuba, and Mexico, submitted a draft declaration of human rights which included "rights" to education, work, health care, and social security. This immediate effort failed, but together with a number of other delegations they succeeded in having the Charter "reaffirm faith in fundamental human rights, in the dignity and worth of the human person, in the equal rights of men and women and of nations large and small . . . " References to human rights were incorporated in several places in the document, and a provision was included to establish a commission on human rights.

The UN Human Rights Commission was created in 1946. Its 18 members included the representatives of Panama, Chile, and Uruguay, under the chairmanship of Eleanor Roosevelt, a tireless campaigner for her deceased husband's redistributionist New Deal policies (supported by *Quadragesimo anno*, see above p. xxx) and the developing Civil Rights movement in the United States, who had been appointed to the UN by her deceased husband's Vice President, now President Truman. The Commission entrusted to four of its members[205] the task of preparing a "bill of human rights." They began by asking the Canadian, John Humphrey, professor of law at McGill University, to prepare a first draft. The first three governments to submit proposals to him were Panama, Chile, and Cuba. He accepted the proposals of Panama and Chile as the foundation of his draft. The Panamanian document was the same proposal that Ricardo Alfaro had unsuccessfully put forward in San Francisco for inclusion in the UN Charter. The Chilean draft was a version of a document called "The American Declaration of the Rights and Duties of Man," which had been commissioned by the Inter-American Conference meeting in Mexico City in 1945. This document was adopted at Bogotá, Colombia, on April 30, 1948, becoming known as the Bogotá Declaration. The commentator Johannes Morsink has concluded that "Humphrey took much of the wording and almost all of the ideas for the social, economic, and cultural rights of his first draft" from those two proposals.[206] When Humphrey finished his initial draft of the Declaration, he turned it over to the Human Rights Commission, which appointed an eight-member drafting committee to continue the work. A key member of that subcommittee was Hernán Santa Cruz, Chile's representative on the Commission. As the commentator Mary Ann Glendon writes, "Contrary to what many suppose today, it was Santa Cruz, far more than any Soviet bloc representative, who was the Commission's most zealous promoter of social and economic rights."[207]

As we saw in the last chapter, Pius XI's conception of "social justice" owed much to socialist ideas. Yet there are important differences between the approaches of Socialism and Catholicism to the question of social rights. The Catholic documents, taking their basis in *Quadragesimo anno*, emphasize the importance of the family, of religion, and especially the dignity of the human person. As Mary Ann Glendon comments,

> One feature that set most twentieth-century Latin American rights documents apart from Marxist models was their resemblance to two influential papal encyclicals that grounded social justice in respect for human dignity: the 1891 encyclical *Rerum Novarum*, and *Quadragesimo Anno*, published on the fortieth anniversary of Rerum Novarum.[208]

We have seen, of course, that *Rerum novarum* does not specifically mention "social justice"; but Catholic commentators such as Miss Glendon commonly pass over the differences between the two documents.

Hernán Santa Cruz was the principal advocate of social and economic rights on the Human Rights Commission, and, though a member of the Chilean aristocracy, his views reflected the left wing of the Catholic tradition.[209] His vision of human rights melded freedom, dignity, and social justice.[210] He had been a member of the Chilean Popular Front, an alliance of the Communist Party with several socialist and left-wing parties, and was a close friend from boyhood of Salvador Allende. "Particularly in the drafting stages, Santa Cruz was vigilant in his defense of these rights and stepped in with persuasive arguments when North Atlantic nations sought to trim them back."[211]

In the autumn of 1948, the Human Rights Commission presented its draft declaration to the UN's Committee on Social, Humanitarian, and Cultural Affairs, a large body composed of representatives from each of the then 58 member nations, for review. Approval by that group was a necessary step before the Declaration could be presented for a final vote in the General Assembly. The Latin American countries were still the largest single group in the UN.[212] In the course of the debates, which stretched out over October and November 1948, the Latin American delegations succeeded in adding further clauses to the draft. On the motion of Minerva

Bernardino of the Dominican Republic the preamble was amended to emphasize that the Declaration's rights belong to women as well as men. At the instance of Pérez Cisneros, the Cuban delegate, the reference to the needs of families was inserted into what would become Article 23(3) on the right to a just wage.[213]

John Humphrey later published a memoir of these events in which he remarks that

> Pérez Cisneros used every procedural device to reach his end. His speeches were laced with Roman Catholic social philosophy, and it seemed at times that the chief protagonists in the conference room were the Roman Catholics and the communists, with the latter a poor second.[214]

In his private diaries, published after his death, Humphrey describes Pérez Cisneros as a man who "combines demagogy with Roman Catholic social philosophy," remarking that the Cuban "should burn in hell, but he will probably go down in history as a great defender of freedom."[215]

On December 9, 1948, Charles Malik, Rapporteur of the Human Rights Commission, presented the draft Universal Declaration of Human Rights to the General Assembly for its vote. Significantly, he described the document, not as an attempt to state a fundamental or agreed truth, but as a *synthesis of all existing rights traditions.* He recognized especially the work of the various Latin American delegates, commending Hernán Santa Cruz for having "kept alive in our mind the great humane outlook of his Latin American world." On the following day, the Universal Declaration was adopted by the General Assembly without any dissenting votes (the Soviet bloc, Saudi Arabia, and South Africa recorded abstentions).

Let us look now at the text itself. Several passages proclaim that all human beings have equal rights (Preamble, Articles 1, 2, 7). The main sections for the discussion of non-discrimination are Articles 2 and 7. Article 2 states that

> Everyone is entitled to all the rights and freedoms *set forth in this Declaration*, without distinction of any kind, such as race, colour, sex, language, religion, political or other opinion, national or social origin, property, birth or other status. (My emphasis)

This is limited to the particular rights included in the Declaration – which are, however, pretty extensive.

Article 7 is more to our purpose, however:

All are equal before the law and are entitled without any discrimination to equal protection of the law. All are entitled to equal protection against any discrimination in violation of this Declaration and against any incitement to such discrimination.

What everyone is entitled to according to this passage is not non-discrimination in general, but non-discrimination *in the protection they receive from the law.* No distinction is made here between forcible or coercive discrimination and non-forcible or peaceful discrimination. But by the general sense of these passages, the discrimination that is prohibited would seem certainly to be forcible or coercive, since it would consist in failure to provide legal protection.

Otherwise, from the Preamble up to Article 21, the provisions of the Declaration reflect those of the classic declarations of rights, such as the French, in recognizing only negative rights and the procedural rights associated with them. But beginning in Article 22, these restrictions are abandoned and the field of rights is extended almost without limit, to utopian benefits that lie beyond the power of any human being to grant, and that could only be implemented by depriving individuals of rights that the document has just declared inalienable. Now "everyone . . . has the *right* to social security," and "is entitled to . . . the economic, social and cultural *rights* indispensable for his dignity and the free development of his personality." This is very close to saying everyone has a right not to be poor. Of course, it would be very good indeed if no one was poor, and everyone had economic security and everything necessary for the free development of his personality. But conceptually there is a significant gap between the concepts of "the good" and "the right." Mrs. Roosevelt and her Latin American associates have committed the fallacy of confusing the two.

According to Article 23, "Everyone has the *right* to work . . . and to just and favourable conditions of work and to protection against unemployment." Furthermore, "Everyone, without any discrimination, has the *right* to equal pay for equal work." Nothing is said about equal productivity, or about the rights of employers.

Everyone who works has the *right* to just and favourable remuneration ensuring for himself and his family an existence worthy of human dignity, and supplemented, if necessary, by other means of social protection.

In Article 24, "Everyone" is given "the *right* to rest and leisure, including reasonable limitation of working hours and periodic holidays with pay."

Article 25:

Everyone has the *right* to a standard of living adequate for the health and
well-being of himself and of his family, including food, clothing, housing
and medical care and necessary social services, and the right to security
in the event of unemployment, sickness, disability, widowhood, old age or
other lack of livelihood in circumstances beyond his control.

According to Article 26:

Everyone has the *right* to education. Education shall be free, at least in
the elementary and fundamental stages. Elementary education shall be
compulsory. Technical and professional education shall be made generally available and higher education shall be equally accessible to all on
the basis of merit.

The article goes on even to mandate a curriculum:

Education shall be directed to the full development of the human
personality and to the strengthening of respect for human rights
and fundamental freedoms. It shall promote understanding, tolerance
and friendship among all nations, racial or religious groups, and shall
further the activities of the United Nations for the maintenance of
peace.

Curiously, amid this plethora of rights, the praiseworthy attempt of the
Latin Americans to include protection of the rights of the unborn was
unsuccessful.

What is the meaning of the word "right" in these later clauses?

The least that can be said is that it is very different from its meaning in the
earlier ones. In the earlier clauses, where it refers to negative rights, the
right has a defined object, and entails defined duties corresponding to it.
When the Declaration states that "Everyone has the right to leave any country, including his own, and to return to his country," this is something definite and identifiable, which it is well within the powers of any government
to give. It entails a definite duty: not to hinder such travel. But when the
Declaration goes on to say that "everyone has the right to rest and leisure,"
this is not something definite. It is not at all clear what would satisfy it and
what would not. Does the "everyone" include entrepreneurs who must work

60 or 70 hours a week to get their new company up and running success-fully? Who has the duty to provide employees with this rest and leisure? If the employer, should he bear the cost?

Considerations such as these led Jeane Kirkpatrick, U.S. Ambassador to the United Nations, to call the Declaration "a letter to Santa Claus."[216] She also pointed out that economic rights cannot be human rights, for they must be provided by others through forceful extraction, for example taxa-tion, and that they negate other peoples' inalienable rights.

If we take the word "right" in the strict sense it usually has in English-speaking countries, therefore, in virtue of our heritage of the Common law, namely a claim that can be directly enforced by a court of law, these state-ments make no sense, since so many of them are impossible.

I believe, however, that this puzzle can be solved, and that the solution lies in the fact that these "rights" were sponsored by delegates from Latin America. The word needs to be taken in the somewhat looser sense it often is understood to bear in Latin countries. Not only in Latin America, but also in France, Spain, and Italy, it is possible to speak of a "right" in the sense of an aspiration, an ideal, a *bon sentiment*. Statements of rights in this sense are testimonies to the good character of those making them.

Of course, in the English-speaking countries, the use of the word "right" to designate a mere wish or ideal, however attractive, is parasitic on the traditional usage and suggests improperly that the use of coercion to realize these wishes is justifiable.

In short, these Latin American contributions to the document, for all their good intentions, betray to the English-speaker, and perhaps to many others, an astonishing and irresponsible looseness of conceptuality.

There can be little doubt that this expansion of "rights" was aided by the switch in terminology from "natural rights" to "human rights." It would be more difficult to defend the positive "rights" bestowed so universally by the Declaration if they were claimed to possess an objective reality in nature, that is, in reason, as natural rights were understood to do. What could it mean, to declare that there was a natural "right to social security," and "to . . . the economic, social and cultural rights indispensable for his dignity and the free development of his personality" among the Bushmen of the Kalahari or the aboriginal inhabitants of Australia? These rights are obviously creations of the Western, economically advanced societies of the twentieth century. There is no such difficulty in assigning to those popula-tions of human beings, however, the negative natural rights specified by Locke and Jefferson.

The Long Arm of *Quadragesimo Anno*: The European Convention on Human Rights

The idea of "social justice" developed in *Quadragesimo anno* was decisive for the development of the expansive, socialistic idea of "human rights" at the United Nations. But the prohibition of peaceful discrimination as unjust is contained at most only implicitly in the Declaration. Explicit prohibition came only after passage of the American Civil Rights Act of 1964. Non-peaceful discrimination was converted into a human right for the nations of Europe mainly when Protocol 12 was added in 2005 to the European Convention on Human Rights.

Article 14 of the Convention prohibited discrimination in regard to the rights and freedoms set forth in the Convention, such as the right of free thought and free speech, but this was still far from the general prohibition of peaceful discrimination brought about by the U.S. Civil Rights Act. Protocol 12 institutes a "general prohibition of discrimination."

> The enjoyment of any right set forth by law shall be secured without discrimination on any ground such as sex, race, colour, language, religion, political or other opinion, national or social origin, association with a national minority, property, birth or other status.

As we have already noted, no distinction is made between forcible or coercive discrimination and peaceful discrimination. Both are tarred with the same brush.

What Kind of Injustice is Peaceful Discrimination?

In the societies of the West, peaceful discrimination is now condemned in the name of civil rights and in that of human rights. This condemnation does not follow from the ordinary and traditional conception of justice, however, but from the socialistic conception of social justice.

Our ordinary conception of justice condemns forcible or coercive discrimination, as it condemns all coercion that is not justified on appropriate moral grounds, for example by the necessity of preventing or punishing unjust coercion. But it does not condemn peaceful discrimination; just as it does not condemn boycott, which is undoubtedly a form of discrimination. Neither boycott nor peaceful discrimination was ever a crime in Roman law or the Common law. To constitute an injustice according to our ordinary conception of justice, an action must cause some *injury*, and peaceful discrimination, though no doubt a blow to one's self-esteem, does not necessarily inflict an injury. For first, there may be good and rational grounds for it. A business may wish to practice discrimination in regard to the persons it hires because of the preferences of its customers, just as it seeks to satisfy its customers' preferences in regard to the goods it sells or the services it provides. This is not an injury to the individuals who are not hired, for they are not deprived of any good they possess. But second and more important, in order to practice discrimination, it is not necessary to perform any action in regard to the individual discriminated against. All that is necessary is to give a benefit to someone else. At the time of writing, a large penalty has been inflicted by a New York court on the Swiss pharmaceutical company Novartis for discriminating against women on the ground that the firm paid men doing the same work $75 a month more (see above, p. 6). It is hard to see how the women's resentment is not mere envy. This recalls the parable of Jesus in the New Testament, Matthew chapter 20, of the householder who went out at various times during the day to hire laborers for his vineyard, and at the end of the day paid the last-comers first and generously. When it was the turn of the first-comers to receive their wages, they complain, for though they had agreed to receive only one denarius, and that was what they were paid, they expected more because they had worked longer. But the householder replies:

> Friend, I am doing you no wrong. Did you not agree with me for a denarius? Take what belongs to you and go. I choose to give to this last as I give to you. Am I not allowed to do what I choose with what belongs to me? Or do you begrudge me my generosity?

This is an apt response to all complaints of peaceful "discrimination." And from its source it has an authority that should make all Christians pause.

The condemnation of peaceful discrimination is not aimed at individuals. Defenders of the Civil Rights Acts rarely argue that the solitary individual act of discrimination is unjust. Rather, the concern is with the state of society that follows from a multitude of discriminatory actions. It is the "imbalance" in society that is viewed as "unjust." This view derives, not from ordinary justice, but from social justice, and specifically from the socialistic conception of social justice that, as we have seen in the last chapter, developed during the twentieth century. For the goal of prohibiting peaceful discrimination is the promotion of greater equality in society, especially economic equality.

As mentioned above, President John Kennedy explained the rationale of the civil rights bill he was introducing into Congress in a public speech on June 11, 1963. This speech is where we should be able to find the arguments intended to justify the bill's prohibition of peaceful discrimination, contained in Title VII on employment. But the crucial distinction between peaceful and coercive discrimination was not made. Consequently, while the speech contains numerous arguments against coercive discrimination or segregation, there are none whatever made specifically to justify the bill's prohibition of peaceful discrimination, which is what gives the Act its historic significance. For to prohibit forcible or coercive discrimination, nothing further was needed than enforcement of the existing Common law.

The Conception of Social Justice to be Opposed

At the end of the previous chapter we noted the difficulty, if not impossibility, of arriving at a single satisfactory definition of social justice. There have been too many, and too varied, conceptions of it. What we can offer here, however, is a description of the view we will argue against in the remainder of this book. This is the view that *there is a particular state of affairs in society, namely inequality of power or economic inequality, which is* ipso facto *unjust, irrespective of how it came about.* And correspondingly, it is the view that *there is a particular state of affairs in society, namely equality of power or economic equality, which is* ipso facto *just, irrespective of how it came about.* Our argument will be that this view, the modern socialistic conception of social justice, which among other things lies at the heart of current U.S. Civil Rights law, is mere pseudo-justice, a false imitation, and not justice at all.

There is, however, a very different conception of social justice that we will defend later in this book. It will be one that owes much to Immanuel Kant and Antonio Rosmini. It will entail the conclusion that peaceful discrimination is a human right.

Part Three

Justice

Chapter 6

The Concept of Ethics

The concept of social justice implies that there is a justice for society which is different from, and takes precedence over, justice for individuals. This view derives its initial support from a particular feeling, namely that extreme inequality in a society presents, by itself, and without any causation of actual injury, a moral problem. The problem consists in the humiliation, the offense against human dignity, implied in the fact of inequality. Since human beings naturally measure themselves against others, it is not to be wondered at, I suppose, that some people will find the experience of being unequal extremely unpleasant. Let us call this the psychological problem of inequality. Rousseau calls it pride. It has no doubt been with us *ab origine mundi*. But the feeling we are talking about here goes beyond that. It is a feeling that the problem is moral. Being unequal is not merely a blow to one's pride, as so many misfortunes are, but morally wrong. This feeling seems to be modern. To my knowledge, no expressions of such feeling have been handed down from the ancient or mediaeval world. It is not a feeling that the Christian gospels do anything to endorse – on the contrary, the admiration for poverty, humility, meekness, and forgiveness which everywhere informs the gospels would imply a deep suspicion of the resentments which underlie the demand for equality.

Around 1752 the Academy of Dijon announced it would give a prize for the best essay on the following question: What is the origin of inequality among men, and is it authorized by the natural law? So far as I have been able to discover, this was the first expression in history of the new spirit.[217] The natural law in question here was the natural moral law. That is, is inequality immoral? The very question gave its own answer. Much hinged, of course, on what was understood by "inequality," which the Academy did not trouble to elucidate. It could, and probably did, mean political inequality, a characteristic of the feudal system. But if so, it was swiftly to come to mean economic inequality, as it so widely does today. Rousseau won the prize by arguing that inequality is the product of civilization and artifice, but nature is a state of equality. Curiously he does not mention either morality or the natural law.

Wherever they occur, and whatever object they are applied to, justice and injustice are categories of thought that belong to the realm of moral judgment. If we wish to understand what justice is and what it is not, it will help if we can first attain some clarity about the nature and meaning of moral judgments in general. There are many different kinds of value; what is it that distinguishes moral values from the others? There are many different principles of action; what are the features that separate ethical principles from non-ethical ones? In this chapter we wish to argue that ethical judgments are distinguished from other kinds of judgment by three qualities: they apply primarily only to the will and its products and not to states that exist independently of the will; they rest on the assumption that the will is free and do not apply wherever it is clear the will is not free; and they depend on the supposition that the person acting is responsible for his actions and answerable for them to others. Of equality and inequality in society in the current sense of "social justice" none of these propositions is true.

Will

The concept of ethics can be stated initially in this way, that as adult human beings we are conscious of a mysterious interior rule that tells us some actions are absolutely to be avoided, even though they might bring us personally substantial benefit, and other actions are good to do, even though they do not bring us any obvious or direct personal benefit and may even cause us harm. Our consciousness of this twofold rule is accompanied by a sense of "oughtness" or obligation, which recognizes on the one hand that we have the power to do something else, namely to be guided by our natural concern for our personal well-being, but which gives us a special kind of reason not to do that something else which we could do, but to be guided instead by concern for the well-being of others, even though to our own detriment.

Almost everyone seems to acknowledge that moral goodness is the supreme kind of goodness, which trumps every other kind. All other forms of goodness, even that of life and existence, pale into insignificance beside it, and it is considered praiseworthy to sacrifice them for it. It is to universal approval that Dickens's Sydney Carton takes the place of Charles Darnay in the queue waiting for the guillotine, "It is a far, far better thing I do than I have ever done." What is the distinctive quality that makes the ethical goodness of other people so attractive to us? For even those who themselves are not models of ethical conduct usually rejoice when they make the acquaintance of someone who is upright, honest, kind, and generous. We find these qualities admirable even when we do not personally benefit from them, when they are not directed or exercised toward us but toward some-one else. We regard them as worthy to be imitated, even if we do not imitate them.

This mysterious interior rule is not addressed in the first place to our intellect, like a rule of mathematics or logic, but to our will. It is a matter of doing or not doing something, not a matter merely of understanding. It seems to have been one of the mistakes of Socrates to believe otherwise, a mistake that Plato himself recognized.[218] Being morally good no doubt has a cognitive element, but it is more than that. It involves having a particular kind of motivation – what Kant called a "good will," and no armchair moralist can possibly acquire a reputation for moral goodness simply by making moral judgments and doing nothing to act in accordance with them. Furthermore the moral motive is not a form of self-interest, but is indeed expressly opposed to it. Moral goodness is not something envis-aged as good for me, but for someone else, or as good *simpliciter.* "Justice is another's good," as Plato's Thrasymachus points out. It may be our harm. Yet even though it be for our harm, we consider it good. This is the mystery of the moral life.

We have just said that the ethical rule is addressed to the will. All ethical values are values of the will. A judgment that something is ethical or unethi-cal – kind or unkind, generous or selfish, just or unjust – always implies a judgment about a will. It is in the will that ethical goodness resides, and ethical badness. An accidental event cannot, of itself, in any literal sense of the term, be either ethical or unethical. Accidental justice is never more than poetical. Accidental kindness is merely good fortune. The events produced by the causality of nature, while they may or may not accord with human desire, lie inherently outside the realm of moral judgment. A moral judgment is always a verdict on the quality of a person. Not about his native gifts or abilities, his intelligence or skill, his knowledge or appearance, or any other aspect of his existence, however these may distinguish him, but in his quality as a person. That quality resides in his will. For it is in his will that a person takes up his most fundamental, definite, and decisive attitude toward reality: toward the objective world, toward the human world of other persons, and toward his own reality both subjective and objective. A person is good or evil, selfish or unselfish, kind or unkind, generous or grasping, just or unjust, depending entirely on his will.

Virtue may be a habit, as Aristotle rightly says, but it is not a mere unthinking habit, as it were out of laziness, but the habit of a will. Courage is will; temperance is will; prudence is will; charity is will; and justice is will. Equally, vice is will: cowardice, intemperance, imprudence, unkindness, and injustice are will. Not only will is will, but also negligence is will, weakness of will is will, and failure of will is will.

This is what Aristotle is saying when he restricts ethical judgments only to the realm of the voluntary (το 'εκούσιον), not to the involuntary (το 'ακούσιον).[219] This is a fundamental truth. Whatever is involuntary, whether it be a thought or an action[220] or an omission or a state of affairs in society, does not belong in the category of the ethical. In every ethical or unethical action there is a choice (Aristotle speaks of προαίρεσις, a decision). An action done in ignorance is not done willfully and is involuntary – unless of course it is willful ignorance. It is not enough for what is done to possess a certain objective quality, but the action itself must be done with knowledge and must be willingly chosen, or in some other way the result of a person's "practical reason."

Interiority

By "will" we do not mean a mere velleity but always something that expresses itself in exterior action. This does not mean, however, that the full reality of the will is manifest in its exterior and observable action. Some important aspects of the will are not of themselves manifest. Intention, motive, strength or weakness of the will, and relation to other wills are among such aspects. The fundamental reality of the will which includes these aspects is not exterior but interior. If it is in the will that ethical virtues and vices reside, it follows that the decisive element in every moral judgment will be an interior one which is not directly open to observation by others. This is the foundation of the legal doctrine of *mens rea*. For an action to incur guilt it is not sufficient that the external action should contravene some law. The interior *mind* must be guilty. This holds not only for legal guilt but also, and even more, for moral, since it cannot be morally right to condemn someone's character for an action that was no part of his intention and for which he therefore cannot be regarded as morally responsible.

To judge from early laws and literatures, it has taken the human race many centuries and much reflection to arrive at this realization. Primitive society generally confines itself to judging exterior actions. Even in such an advanced product of moral consciousness as the ancient Greek tragedy, as with Oedipus, the external action was everything. It was therefore a significant step in the development of moral awareness when, as reported by Plato and Xenophon, Socrates described justice as first and foremost a quality of the *soul.* Justice, he says, or moral virtue in general, constitutes the health of the soul. For the soul is in a healthy condition when it is rightly ordered, and this occurs only when its faculties or powers, such as its desires, are under the control of its reason.[221] It is true he does not speak of moral virtue as a quality of the will specifically, since he considers that the will always aims at what is good, as it were by definition, and therefore immoral action is always the product of mistaken belief. "Virtue is knowledge." But, that said, the whole point of the statement that justice is a quality of the soul is to recognize that moral virtue and vice are qualities of the deepest part of human personality, that which gives the person his most fundamental orientation. And Plato lets it be known he has doubts about Socrates's identification of crime with mistaken belief.[222]

In the socialistic conception of social justice, however, this dimension of interiority is entirely lacking. For this conception identifies justice and injustice with objective states of affairs in society such as economic equality and inequality which are by no means necessarily the product of anybody's will.

Will and states of affairs

If any state of affairs in society is claimed to have an ethical status, to be ethically good or ethically bad, a first question to ask, then, is whether that state of affairs is voluntary or involuntary. Is it the product of a will? Was it, in some genuine sense of the word, chosen? If not, can it at least be imputed to a will, so that someone can be held to account for it? If none of those questions can be answered in the affirmative, then ethical predicates cannot apply to the state of affairs. Just as it cannot be described as kind or compassionate or thoughtful, it cannot meaningfully be described as either just or unjust.

In *The Concept of Mind,* published in 1949, Gilbert Ryle identified an error of thought, a logical fallacy, which he named a "category mistake." The mistake as he described it consists in confusing the logical type of a concept, treating a concept which belongs in one category as if it belonged in a different one, or attributing a predicate to an object which is of such a kind that it cannot possibly have that kind of predicate. Noam Chomsky composed a sentence often considered a good example, though perhaps not the most realistic one: "colorless green ideas sleep furiously." Ideas are a kind of thing that can neither be green nor sleep, and so the sentence, though perfectly in accord with the rules of surface grammar, is nonsense.

Similarly, to attribute a moral or mental predicate to a nonmoral or nonmental object is to speak nonsense. For example, if someone were crazy enough to speak of a brick as "thoughtful," intending to speak literally and not with poetic license.

It is our contention that the idea of "social justice" as it is currently understood involves just such a fallacy. For it applies the moral concept of injustice to something that cannot possibly have moral qualities, namely a state of affairs in society, such as poverty, economic inequality, or inequality of societal power, which is involuntary, which is not the result of any design or intention on the part of anyone and for which, as a result, no one need be considered responsible or accountable.

From the viewpoint of ethics, nothing can take the place of a good will. It is the core of the moral life. Kant was right to hold that it and it alone is unconditionally good. No objective aspect of the individual or of society is always and under all circumstances good. Nor is any other subjective aspect of them always and under all circumstances good. If we are to speak of ethics and ethical values in regard to society, we must show the relationship, not only of external (and objective) realities, but of the internal (and subjective) reality of will and good will, to society.

The fact that moral judgment is a judgment of the will does not contradict, but entails, that an individual's morality consists in how he acts. As we mentioned above, a will is not a mere wish or velleity. The will expresses itself in action, and action is always the expression of will. In action the will projects itself into the world. That is what we mean by "action." A mere bodily movement that is not the expression of a will, such as the involuntary motion of a limb, is not action, nor is one done by mistake. In speaking of action in these pages, we understand it in the broad sense of how will projects itself into the world. This includes not only the particular actions that individual persons do, but also the failures of will and action mentioned above, such as negligence or the willful omission of action.

If it is alleged that a state of affairs is unjust, therefore, the first requirement that must be satisfied in order to establish that is to show how it is the product of will. There is a very big difference indeed between an outcome that is deliberately intended and one that is the unintended by-product of willing something else. To show that a case of inequality is unethical, it must be shown that will has been exercised in such a way that there is some person who is responsible for bringing the inequality about. It is not enough to argue that the items themselves that are judged unequal are the products of a will. If A pays B's salary, and independently X pays Y's salary, and the two salaries are unequal, this disparity cannot be the object of any ethical judgment because it is not the product of a will.

The diagnosis of ordinary injustice always refers to a will, that of the perpetrator who is responsible for it. And the remedy for ordinary injustice also always therefore refers to a will, that of the legislator and judge who condemn and punish it. In the case of social justice in the socialistic modern sense, however, there is a paradoxical discrepancy. The diagnosis of social injustice does not refer to a will. For societal inequality, economic inequality, or inequality of power, as we have observed, can occur entirely by accident, without the relevant contribution of any will. Yet the remedy proposed for societal inequality is addressed to the will. The remedy for social injustice is invariably thought to be an action, a policy of equalization, to be undertaken by those in government who make the law, by those in society who vote for them, and by those who are to carry out the programs of equalization. The message of "social justice" is addressed to the conscience of individuals and to that extent claims to support and to be supported by the traditional conception of ethics. Yet it is deeply wrong, not to say absurd, that free persons should be declared responsible in conscience for something they have had no hand in causing, and which they had neither the duty nor the power to avoid, but which they are to be coerced nevertheless into rectifying.

Will and persons

Moral value, then, is always a quality of the will and a quality of actions in the sense described. But what quality? Not one, but two. For will or action regarded from the point of view of ethics has two sides. On one side is a negative test that any action must pass in order to be ethical, for an action can be ethical in the minimal sense that it is not unethical. And in addition to that every virtuous action has its own particular positive ethical quality that makes it attractive and constitutes the reason why it is good and desirable.

This positive quality is captured by the terms made famous by Kant, who saw the ethical will as a will in regard to persons. It is a will to treat persons in a certain way, namely, in a way that recognizes the unique dignity that they have as persons and that sets them apart from other beings. Dignity is a worthiness to be respected. Persons have this worthiness from a fact about them that we have still to investigate, but which we can state in a preliminary way here as their freedom of will. For it is this freedom that confers on them by their very nature the dignity of moral beings, subject to the moral law and capable of choosing between good and evil. Even when they commit the worst crimes, their inherent dignity places limitations on how we may treat them. As Kant puts it, in the second formulation of the Categorical

Imperative, persons are to be treated always as ends, and never as means only. I leave aside here the question whether Kant's notion of the ethical captures all that we might wish to include under that idea. But in all that concerns the concept of justice, I claim, Kant is right in identifying the core of moral judgment in the "respect for persons," as this is expressed in his theory of the Categorical Imperative. By "respect" is meant here not in the first instance an emotion, as it were akin to a feeling of reverence, but the steadfast will to perform or especially to avoid performing certain actions.

An action of such a kind that it respects the dignity of persons is a rational action. Consequently it will possess another quality that is implicit in that: it will be universalizable. If it is permissible for me under certain circumstances, it must be equally permissible for other persons under those same circumstances. If it is obligatory for me, it will be obligatory for all other persons in the same circumstances. Every ethical action constitutes a standard for all rational beings.[223]

Will and reason

Ethical behavior is therefore an expression of reason: not theoretical but practical reason. Theoretical reason is concerned with concepts, practical reason with purposes. For reason can be employed not only to arrive at propositions to be believed, but also to discover actions to be performed. And this in two ways. One way is instrumental. This consists in discovering, from the nature of a purpose we wish to achieve, what will be the most effective means to achieve it. If we wish to put a screw in the wall to hang a painting, we can try to use our fingernail, but practical reason will tell us to use a screwdriver if we have one. This is not merely a proposition, but, in its own mild way, a command. We should use a screwdriver rather than our fingernail because it is the sensible thing to do, it is rational. A person who insisted on using his fingernail when a screwdriver lay at hand would incur a charge of foolishness.[224] Rationality in a certain minimal sense is an obligation. Hobbes, in *Leviathan*, attempts to give an entire account of morality in terms of practical reason in this instrumental sense. Utilitarian reason commands us to preserve ourselves, he argues, and the best means to preserve ourselves is to seek peace with our fellow human beings. Therefore this is our first ethical duty. It must be granted that Hobbes is ingenious in arguing that this duty, once accepted, can provide a satisfactory foundation for social and political life. Much that he says strikes home. He has built, as it were, a beautiful castle of rational thought. Yet morally this castle seems to be built on sand, because self-interest and more broadly instrumental practical reason is not what we mean by morality, but is rather the opposite of it. It is true this objection might not keep him awake at night.

But there is another form of practical reason which is not concerned with the production of effects. The moral motive commands us to do certain things that are harmful to us and not to do other things that could benefit us. This is obviously not of that utilitarian nature. The voice of conscience does not tell us to do good so that we may live long and prosper. If our only reason for giving up our time and comfort in order to help a sick neighbor is to improve our reputation in our community, we may have done an objectively good deed in providing help, but the true realm of ethics is that of the subjective will, our purpose or intention, and there we have failed. (It should be noted, however, that there is an important difference between the intention to gain some material end in this world and the intention to gain a transcendent goal such as salvation in a possible future life. Philosophers often confuse these two. While the latter may, no doubt, be understood in a crassly self-centered way, that is not necessarily the case. Its subtext may be and often is a desire to be worthy of the promises of God and therefore to become more moral.)

There is a kind of practical reason or rationality that applies to unselfish actions which are not done for any self-serving purpose but because they are ethically commendable. This has to do with the internal consistency of a course of action. For it is possible for an action to conflict with itself or undermine itself. This is invariably what unethical actions do. The act of stealing another person's property is done in order to possess the item as one's own property. But the act of stealing it negates the very concept of property. For property means that one has the exclusive right to use it. The thief should logically accept that anyone else has the right to steal from him. But he does not accept this, and will become indignant if it should happen. Theft is irrational, not only in the sense that it fails to serve a utilitarian purpose, though ultimately and in general that is true, but also in the sense that it is in conflict with the assumptions on which it itself rests, and is therefore internally incoherent. Ethical actions do not do this; they are internally coherent.

It should not be imagined, however, that the incoherence of an unjust action is mere or simple incoherence, as if we were explaining the moral in terms of the nonmoral. It is not my view that the moral can be explained in terms of the nonmoral, for that would mean reducing it to the nonmoral. I hold that the moral is a primitive or fundamental notion, present immediately whenever there is freedom of the will. The incoherence of the unjust action is always a specifically moral kind of incoherence. This is even the way people themselves report it, by saying, for example, that if they did a certain kind of wrong they "could not live with themselves." Mere or ordinary incoherence does not have that drastic kind of effect.

This is why the special kind of coherence that moral action possesses is reflected in the term so often used to describe persons of character: integrity. A person who has integrity is not merely one whose actions are consistent among themselves. In that case a Hitler would have integrity because he did not waver from his unspeakable policy of genocide. Integrity means the subordination of appetite to moral will, and of self-interest to moral principle. And this means adopting the imperative of reason, which tells us to treat people as ends and not as means only – an imperative that had no weight whatsoever for Hitler.

The voice of conscience that utters the internal rule of moral practical reason or ethics may speak in response to the events of our experience. Experience may in this sense give rise to our consciousness of moral principle. But moral principle, the voice of conscience, cannot depend on our experience of life for its validation. For if it did it would present itself as changing when our experience of life changes. But in fact it presents itself at bottom as a simple unqualified and even, as Cicero says, eternal command.[225] The historical origin within our consciousness of a moral principle is not identical with the source of the principle's validity or authority. It is important not to confuse the two. For the effect of confusing them is to convert all moral principle into a form of utilitarianism.

Our conclusion so far is that the hallmark of an ethical action is that it treats persons with the respect due to their dignity as free agents. It becomes possible on this basis to imagine the perfect society. It is one where everybody treats, and is treated by, everybody else with due respect. Respecting persons as beings possessing reason and conscience means in the first place respecting the *freedom* of their individual wills. This does not necessarily mean respecting the particular objects of their wills, that is, the directedness of their wills to particular purposes, for those purposes, though freely chosen, may be foolish or immoral. But where we have no ground for rejecting them, it will be right and generous not to hinder them, and even to help and further them so far as we can, all things else being equal. This vision of the perfect society, which we owe especially to Christianity and to Kant, is a very far cry indeed from the socialistic vision. It is a vision of individuals voluntarily respecting the will of others and thereby attaining their own moral fulfillment. It is a society filled with a sense of individual responsibility and accountability. It is the free society. It bears a strong resemblance to what Christians have called the kingdom of God, and to what Kant, consciously echoing the gospels in the language of the Enlightenment, called the Kingdom of Ends.

Will and emotion

So far we have been occupied with one particular facet of ethics, the minimum requirement for something to be describable as ethical or moral. We have seen that only a will can be moral, together, of course, with the actions in which the will is expressed and the character or habitual attitude of will that results from them. And we have seen that to be moral a will must respect the dignity of persons as persons. This is in the first instance negative and formal: it consists in not doing certain kinds of action which constitute disrespect. But, as we mentioned, there is another side of every ethical virtue, which goes beyond the mere fact that it is not unethical, and constitutes its positive moral attractiveness and desirability. The realm of ethical value is not exhausted by rational principle. It also contains as part of its essential nature an affective or emotional dimension. A kind or generous action is not merely one that meets the minimum requirement of being universalizable and rational, but is fully grasped in its nature as kind or generous only in the emotional response of admiration, and if the generosity is directed toward oneself, gratitude. The action of stealing not only contravenes the rationality required of any action that is to be ethically acceptable, but is properly grasped only in the emotional response of revulsion and anger (so long as the person stolen from is not oneself, for then anger may be merely a natural inclination). The affective response to an ethical or unethical action is also in part cognitive: it is essential for grasping the moral qualities of the action.

This feature of morality points to something remarkable in the human condition, which is the cognitive function of affective states. Phenomenologists like Husserl and Scheler have pointed to the way in which truths about each other remain unperceived and unperceivable to the person who is devoid of interpersonal emotion: the person who looks impassively and without anger or joy on the conduct of his fellows is one who cannot perceive a whole range of truths about human beings. The point has been made in other terms by Sartre in his *Esquisse d'une théorie des émotions*, and has been the topic of extensive research among psychologists, particularly those striving to fathom the deep mystery of autism. However we analyze the matter, however, it seems undeniable that perceiving people correctly in many areas involves responding to them rightly. And in no area is this more obviously true than in the area of morality and moral judgment.

Moral emotions are responses to the will of another. What we admire when we admire a generous action is the will of the generous person, and what we detest when we detest a theft is the will of the thief.

The Old Testament (II Samuel, chapters 11 and 12) tells the story of David and Nathan. David had fallen in love with Bathsheba, wife of Uriah the Hittite, and had given orders that Uriah should be placed alone in the forefront of the battle so that he would be killed, but in a manner not likely to arouse suspicion. After the due death of Uriah in this fashion God sent to David the prophet Nathan, who told him of a rich man who, despite having many sheep of his own, took the one lamb of his poor neighbor in order to feed a guest. David's reaction to the story of this robbery was anger.

Then David's anger was greatly kindled against the man; and he said to Nathan, "As the Lord lives, the man who has done this deserves to die; and he shall restore the lamb fourfold, because he did this thing, and because he had no pity." And Nathan said to David, "You are the man."

Why did David get angry about the injustice done to the poor man – before he discovered the irony of his own role, and so at a time when it appeared that the fate of the poor man did not particularly touch him personally? Why do we get angry, not only when injustice is done to ourselves, but when we see it done to others? The ordinary and undeniable emotion of anger we experience in such circumstances suggests that there is something more at work than the standard model of our relationship to others indicates.

In epistemology for many years, roughly from the seventeenth century to the twentieth, there was a standard model of knowledge which seemed well founded, but which presented us with what appeared to be an insoluble problem. According to this model, which we owed to Descartes's attempt to discover a sure foundation for knowledge, the mind knows directly only its own thoughts and concepts. The problem, then, was how we could cross the barrier that surrounded our own mind and acquire knowledge of the external world. The solution of the problem comes only when the Cartesian statement of it is left behind and it is realized that from the very beginning we are involved in the "external" world (cf. for example Husserl's *Lebenswelt*), and that the contents of our own mind are not cognitively privileged. The mind is something which is in touch with the "external" world by its very nature.

Similarly there has been a standard model of the moral self, which appears to be well founded; but this model presents us with what appears to be an insoluble problem. According to the model, we are inextricably bound up in our own egos, we love ourselves and what is good for ourselves.

This is viewed as part of ordinary experience and as not needing special justification. But the problem then is: how is it possible for us to cross the barrier that separates us morally from others and be concerned about their welfare? How is altruism possible?

The anger of David at the treatment meted out to the poor man, and our own ordinary, similar response to the mistreatment of others even when it does not affect ourselves, suggests that the standard model is misconceived, and that we are by nature and from the beginning no more morally than epistemologically isolated from the world around us.

What belief was the cause of David's anger? Was it a belief relating to himself, that in some obscure fashion his own fate was, after all, bound up in the fate of the poor man – for example, that one day if he should become impoverished the same thing could happen to him? Since the scientific revolution of the seventeenth century it has been widely assumed among philosophers that nothing is good or bad in itself, as an end, but only as a means to an end, since the appropriateness of a means to an end can in principle be demonstrated or refuted, but not the goodness or badness of anything in itself. If Smith is robbed, we can say that is bad for Smith, but we cannot say it is bad in itself; for there is a way of discovering that it is bad for Smith, since he suffers a loss, but no way of discovering whether it is bad in itself. So we can say that being robbed of his sheep was bad for the poor man (though of course good for the rich man), and if it angered David, that can only be because it was in some way also bad for David – a consideration at bottom purely selfish. But there is nothing in the story to support such an interpretation, and it is not likely to appear a plausible explanation to those who have had a similar experience. David's anger is not self-regarding. Yet it is immediately comprehensible to us all.

Is it perhaps a case of sympathy? When we see another person suffering pain, we may feel with him because we know what it is like. For Adam Smith, an acute observer of human nature, feelings such as these were the foundation of the ethical life. Is this what leads David to feel angry, that he can imagine the anger that the poor man feels, and shares in it out of a sense of their common humanity? But no reference is made in the story to the anger of the poor man. Far less does David's anger appear motivated by utilitarian considerations: he does not take time to calculate whether more people would be better off if the robbery were allowed or punished, and then decide to get angry accordingly. Nor is David angered at the fault of logic which leads the rich man to appropriate the lamb as his property by an action that undermines property.

David is angry because something detestable has been done. The question as to who is affected by the action is secondary. The action is detestable in itself, objectively. It is an object of horror. David's anger suggests that an action can be bad in itself, and detested for its own sake, and not because of its effects on oneself, and in fact not for its effects at all. If he did not get angry, or at least if he did not have the attitude of will that naturally leads to anger (for one may be tired or sick or fail to experience appropriate emotions for external reasons without being at fault, so long as the will is right), that is a sign that he did not properly grasp what had been done morally, and had become callous. It is a question of the heart. The heart has its reasons, as Pascal said. It is not a mere random force. To be callous is to be hard of heart, to have a mind and a will that is unresponsive to what is morally good or evil. In moral knowledge or judgment it becomes plain that there is no mind without a heart. It is only when his heart was stirred that David was able to perceive the real nature of his own action.

To say that the action of the rich man was detestable is just to say that his will was detestable. David's anger is anger at his will. If the story had been that the lamb was taken by mistake, we can assume David would not have gotten angry, because he would have had no reason to do so.

Bishop Joseph Butler was one who saw that we are from the beginning members of the moral world and do not have to argue ourselves into it from a prior or more natural position of self-love. Although concern for our fellow men is very different from concern for ourselves, it has roots in our human nature just as deep, and the passions and affections which lead us to the one can also lead us to the other.[226]

By what mental act do we arrive at the judgment that an action is morally good or evil? For the most part it is, as Aristotle saw, not an act of deduction, but a perception. One sees that something is good and right. But perceptions can also be mistaken, and a mistaken perception can be corrected by deduction.

If we view justice and injustice as objective qualities of the will, it also provides us with a more plausible explanation of the opinion of Socrates that injustice corrupts the soul. For this proves not to be an argument from self-centered concern, as it is often portrayed, which would in any case be out of character for Socrates, but a statement of an intrinsic evil. To argue that injustice should be avoided because it corrupts the soul is not to argue that it should be avoided because it has bad consequences for oneself personally. It is only to say that it is evil and evil-making, that injustice is something wrong and detestable in itself. This is not an appeal to one's selfish concern for his own well-being as an individual, but to his detached and impartial concern for what is right as a universal principle. It is not an argument from the unpleasant effects of injustice, as if they were something distinct from injustice, but a display or exhibiting of the nature of injustice.

Will and punishment

David evinces two other emotions in the story. The rich man deserves to die, he exclaims. And when he discovers that he himself is the rich man, he is overcome with remorse. What exactly are these emotions, and what beliefs have given rise to them?

The rich man "deserves to die." It has become common in public discussion to refer to this sentiment as a desire for revenge, with the implication that it is a self-centered, primitive, and irrational emotion, which ought to be replaced, through an enlightened education, by the nobler desire for the offender's rehabilitation. Often an unspoken assumption behind this view is the belief that the offender was not really responsible for his offence, which ought to be seen as the product of his social environment and perhaps his biological inheritance. This view has dominated opinion in certain circles now for several decades, and has shown itself in not a few "liberal" responses to the current Islamic terrorism.

David can scarcely be accused of desiring revenge, however, since (as the case was presented to him) he was not personally affected adversely by the rich man's action. The concept of punishment is different from the concept of revenge. It is that the original objective equality of dignity between the criminal and his victim, to which Locke and Kant refer, has been destroyed and needs to be reinstated, and that it can only be reinstated by the infliction of pain. Not to desire the reinstatement of their equal dignity is to become complicit in the crime. This is the concept of desert. The rich man "deserves to die because he has done this thing and because he had no pity." The desire that a criminal should be punished is an impartial and impersonal desire, which has no relation to any personal benefit to be obtained by the victim.

Just as justice does not originate out of considerations of utility, so neither does punishment. The true purpose of judicial punishment is not and cannot be to rehabilitate the criminal, but to make him suffer: as he ought, but no more than he deserves. Admittedly, this is a very difficult view for an educated and sensitive person, who has an ardent desire to reduce the amount of suffering in the world. But the universe is a complicated place, and though our ideals may well ultimately harmonize with one another, this does not necessarily take place easily. What currently passes for the "progressive" view of punishment stands in stark contrast to the opinion of Socrates. For him, punishment heals the soul of the criminal, and the criminal who goes unpunished can never be truly happy, because he remains in contradiction to the objective order of right. Hegel puts the point even more vividly, arguing that the criminal has a *right* to punishment, that any other treatment is also a retreat from him and from his worth as a moral being, a way of disregarding his freedom and his ability to take responsibility for his life and actions.

That way of putting the point reminds us that justice and desert are connected. It is unjust to treat someone in a way that he does not deserve; but if he deserves his punishment, then the punishment is just. And this connection between justice and desert carries over to the discussion of social justice. One of the main objections to be made against the concept of social justice as equality is that it inevitably severs the link between justice and desert, redistributing advantage and property without regard for who has done what to deserve that treatment.

Will and remorse

"David said to Nathan, 'I have sinned against the Lord.'" He acknowledges he has done evil. He does not make excuses. He accepts his responsibility and confesses his guilt. This acknowledgment is an integral element of the process of justice, which is not complete without it. A court sentencing a convicted criminal rightly looks for some sign of remorse from him, and if it perceives none, is rightly inclined to impose a more severe penalty.

David does not say he has sinned against Uriah, which modern sentiment would expect him to say, but that he has sinned "against the Lord." Of course he has sinned against Uriah. But the moral significance of his action is not limited to the personal relationship between the two individuals; it is a contravention of the objective moral order which is embodied in the will of God. The "will of God" is not a mere personal preference of a powerful being but the objective order of right.

Remorse is a form of suffering, a painful emotion of self-criticism, and there are different kinds and degrees of it. There is a form that is defensive and self-centered, and a natural reaction of human nature, as when we are chagrined to discover we have made a fool of ourselves in public. But there is also a virtue of remorse, consisting in sorrow at the fact that we have caused harm to others. This is a rational emotion in someone who has committed an injustice. It arises from applying to an action we have performed the objective and impartial standard of the universal rule of reason, and finding – allowing ourselves to find – that it does not measure up, and that in consequence we are guilty.

True remorse is therefore difficult for human nature, and far from automatic, but rather the result of a process of cultivation. Since we naturally wish to have a good opinion of ourselves, as human beings it is easy for us to deceive ourselves about our true dispositions and intentions when they are unpleasant. True remorse arises only when we insist on being honest with ourselves. For Freud, remorse is a victory of the "super-ego," the force in our psyche that represents the voice of society rather than our natural instincts, and so is a step on the way to neurosis. But just because virtuous remorse is not a natural instinct, it is a sign of a good will, the one thing that can "be conceived in the world, or even out of it, which can be called good without qualification," as Kant remarks. Remorse is in a certain way the beginning of the ethical life.

The fundamental belief underlying true remorse is belief in one's own freedom of will, and therefore in one's responsibility for one's actions. But it is one thing to be responsible, which follows from the fact of freedom, and another to accept one's responsibility. At the present time the ideas of freedom and responsibility are often attenuated, in accordance with the idea of "social justice." "Responsibility" then can be taken to mean only that one's action caused a regrettable effect, without implying that the action was genuinely free. But true remorse means acknowledging that one could have acted differently.

Freedom

Free will

We have stated that persons possess dignity and deserve respect because they have freedom of the will. In the course of the last hundred years, as psychologists and others have attempted to probe into the depths of the human psyche, we have become more aware of the forces that can impinge on our motivation. In some quarters this has led to a large degree of skepticism regarding freedom of the will. And this skepticism has fed into the current socialistic conception of social justice. The advocate of the egalitarian conception of social justice sees the actions of the disadvantaged, and even of all human beings, as predominantly, if not entirely, the product of forces over which the individual has no control, namely the external influence of societal conditions and the internal influence of biological and psychological factors. By contrast, the traditional conception of justice presupposes that the actions of sane, conscious adults are not predetermined but are the products of their free choice. This is in some ways the most fundamental difference between social justice and ordinary justice. For it is a consequence of this that the two theories have very different views of individual responsibility.

Free will is generally taken to mean that a person could have done something different from what he is actually doing, that he had the power to make a real choice. In general there are three opinions among philosophers regarding the relationship between freedom of the will and determinism. One is that determinism and free will are not compatible, and determinism is true. A second is that determinism and free will are not compatible, and free will is real. The third is that determinism and free will are compatible, and both are, or may be, true. Various explanations are advanced for this.

The chief reason for believing in free will is the universal testimony of sane, adult human beings that they are conscious of making choices, and are directly aware they could have chosen to do something different from what they are actually doing. As Dr Johnson said, kicking the stone, "Sir, we know our will is free, and there's an end on't."[227] However, freedom cannot be demonstrated by the methods of empirical science, because it is not an empirical concept. The same is true, strictly speaking, of determinism. However, the modern science of physics, since its advent in the seventeenth century, when explanation by reference to purposes or teleologies was abandoned, has depended on the deterministic assumption of universal causation, that all movement and change in the physical world is necessarily the product of causes. Initially this was understood in the sense of strict necessity: a cause was something that necessarily produced its effect, and an effect was something necessarily produced by a cause or causes. A scientific explanation was a causal explanation. With the development of quantum physics in the twentieth century a somewhat different picture of physical reality emerged. On the level of particle physics, what results from a cause is a probability. In one direction the probability may be extremely high, vanishingly close to 1, and in another direction it may be extremely low, vanishingly close to zero, but neither the one nor the other is ever absolute. Neither the 1 nor the zero are ever reached. Even on the macro level of ordinary, everyday life, this remains theoretically true, but the probability comes so close to certainty that it is impossible to detect the difference. On the macro level it is still possible, and necessary, to have explanations involving universally quantified laws.

Although it seems, then, that a certain amount of indeterminacy is built into the physical world, yet this indeterminacy is far removed from what we mean by free will. It is still possible, in regard to the will of human beings, to be a determinist.

Einstein was one who shared this view, and tells us why he found it attractive:

> In human freedom in the philosophical sense I am definitely a disbeliever. Everybody acts not only under external compulsion but also in accordance with inner necessity. Schopenhauer's saying, that "a man can do as he will, but not will as he will," has been an inspiration to me since my youth up, and a continual consolation and unfailing well-spring of patience in the face of the hardships of life, my own and others'. *This feeling mercifully mitigates the sense of responsibility* which so easily becomes paralysing, and it prevents us from taking ourselves and other people too seriously . . . [228] (My emphasis)

He unabashedly points out what he considers the great advantage of determinism, that it diminishes one's sense of responsibility. It is telling that he does not suggest any other argument for it. Conceivably this is also the chief motive that leads its supporters to embrace it. It was not an accident that Einstein went on to write one of the most lucid defenses of socialism ever published. It was also consistent with this that he refused to accept the indeterminism of quantum mechanics.

The determinism of "social justice"

The determinism based on the science of physics is not, however, the kind of determinism that mainly distinguishes "social" justice. It remains rather in the background, as a "resource" available when necessary. The kind of determinism associated most distinctively with "social" justice is one based on the condition of the disadvantaged in society. The disadvantaged must not be considered responsible for their condition or their actions, for that would be to "blame the victim." The cause of the social pathologies so often associated with the disadvantaged should be sought, not in any deficiencies of their character, but in their social and psychological conditions, which are considered effectively to remove any possibility of free choice.

An ardent supporter of this viewpoint over several decades has been the philosopher Brian Barry, until his death not long ago professor at Columbia University. In a recent book, *Why Social Justice Matters*, which gives in some respects an up-to-date account of the theory of social justice, although, surprisingly, without attempting to provide any philosophical arguments to justify it, he addresses the question of free will. For those not familiar with what passes for reasoning in the school of social justice, his approach can shed light on this arcane topic. It is worth following him through some of the details of his argument, since they illustrate common conceptions and misconceptions, without which the egalitarian view of social justice would have far fewer adherents than it has. It might be objected that I am making things easy for myself in targeting Barry, since his views are extreme to the point of caricature, but I will not take advantage of that for the moment beyond quoting him.

Free will, Barry suggests, is not at all an obvious truth, but a belief that derives mainly from the attempt of religions to explain the existence of evil – an attempt of which, as of the religions themselves, he has a low opinion. Religions (unnamed, but presumably Christianity) relieve God of the responsibility of creating evil by transferring it to human free will, he argues.

> . . . if God is good and omnipotent, how come there is so much suffering in the world? And we are all familiar with the answer: because God endowed us with free will, so we, rather than God, are responsible for everything bad about the world. To the response that this was a pretty rotten trick to play on people, the standard reply is that free will was endowed (sic) on human beings as a punishment . . . The implication is, then, that the power to employ our free will to commit sins (and thus qualify for eternal torment) is God's savage revenge for "man's first disobedience."[229]

Leaving aside the question of the historical accuracy of his surprising view that some religion has considered free will a punishment for sin, Barry sees the politics of free will as an extension of this savage desire for revenge. After Darwin and the decline of Christianity, he asserts, it took the secular form of meritocracy. "How can we justify the enormous inequalities that are common in capitalist countries?" Those who accept free will answer that "The rich owe their wealth to hard work, enterprise and frugality, while the poor have a bad moral character, which leads to laziness, fecklessness and the kind of behavior that is liable to land them in prison."[230]

Barry holds that there is no such thing as natural inequality. On the contrary, "we can bury any notion that the division between the successful and the unsuccessful – with the concomitant divisions in wealth and privilege – reflects 'natural inequalities.'" There is only natural equality, he maintains.[231]

But belief in free will has "had its ups and downs." "The Great Depression in America made manifest nonsense of the notion that the unemployed could all get jobs if they tried harder."[232] We shall see shortly what leads Barry to attribute this exaggerated notion to those who believe in free will.

He goes on to point to what he considers obvious limitations on free choice, not only for the disadvantaged but also for the advantaged.

> One obvious but crucial point is that there are quite stringent conditions for a choice to count as a voluntary one for whose consequences the person taking it can legitimately be held responsible . . . Even at the age of 16, a child's decision to leave school at the minimum age possible cannot make it responsible for the outcome if its earnings are needed to keep the family in basic necessities. It would be absurd to say that this child's truncated career prospects are just in comparison with those open to a child who benefits from parental support and encouragement while attending a school in which proceeding on to a university is a norm among the students. Neither child could be said to have much choice: certainly, one cannot be held responsible for leaving, while for the other staying on is simply following the line of least resistance.[233]

There are several interesting things about this paragraph. One concerns the object of responsibility. In the traditional view, as we shall see, the main question concerns one's responsibility for one's actions. This is where freedom lies. But for Barry, the question is about responsibility for the *outcomes* of one's actions. There is an important difference. The reason is that for him, this is where freedom lies – or, more accurately, does not lie – not in the interior, subjective sphere, but in the exterior sphere of society and social relationships. To this too we shall return shortly. Second, since neither child, in Barry's view, had a wide range of choices readily available, he draws the conclusion that the choices were not voluntary, and the children were not responsible for them.

For the proponents of "social" justice, lack of information is a crucial limitation on freedom and responsibility. And the amount of information needed is not minimal.

> Inadequacy of information also reduces responsibility for the outcomes of choices among adults. To choose between options sensibly, you need to understand the nature of the options. There will normally be a range of possible outcomes arising from each choice, and you need to have at least some estimate of their relative likelihoods. Each of those contingencies will then open up a further range options, and so on.[234]

This is only one example, though an important one, of the innumerable limitations on choice that in the end not only reduce but eliminate freedom. Fundamentally, no one has free will because everybody's choices are limited. We must ask "the basic question: can people ever properly be held responsible for choices made from a certain choice set?" For it must be assumed "that people have certain mental and physical capacities at any given time and that no 'effort of will' can overcome the limits imposed by these capacities." ". . . people cannot, by an effort of will, completely transform their personalities."[235]

These statements are significant, because, taken with the earlier ones, they manifest a conception of free will and responsibility fundamentally at odds with what these terms have traditionally been understood to mean. The freedom of the will, as Barry understands it, consists in the objective scope or range of a person's available choices, and is restricted by any limitations on them. Since everybody's choices are limited, not only by their external circumstances but also by their individual personalities, which, as he says, have certain mental and physical capacities whose limitations cannot be overcome by any effort of the will, and therefore the choices available to anybody exist only within a certain "choice set," nobody truly possesses free will, and nobody is truly responsible for their actions or their consequences. The only person who would truly possess free will would be one whose choices were not subject to any limitations or restrictions. In Christian theology this would scarcely apply even to God.

We see, then, why Barry would say that believing in free will would mean believing that the unemployed during the Depression could all get jobs if they tried harder. The term "freedom" or "free will" for him means an objective situation in society where there are no limitations on choice.

We see also why for him the kind of responsibility that counts is not subjective responsibility for one's actions, but objective responsibility for the societal outcomes of one's actions. This requires a new concept of responsibility – which he is going to attempt to provide.

We should not be surprised, then, that Barry dismisses with little consideration what he regards as the two main arguments in favor of free will. The first argument is the one we have mentioned above, based on our interior experience of making choices between alternative courses of action, the argument Dr Johnson supported with his kick. Barry rejects this with the remark that "everything we 'know' from our own experience is entirely compatible with determinism."[236] He does not attempt to support this contention with any further argument, but since determinism for him evidently means having a limited range of choices, which is always the case when dealing with human beings, even with Dr Johnson, we can sufficiently imagine what his argument would be.

The second argument for free will he takes up is that the consequences for society of a general acceptance of determinism would be catastrophic because all responsibility would be abandoned. Barry, however, believes there is a sense in which "responsibility" can still be maintained even by those who do not believe in free will, namely that the action in question "flowed from the actor's will in the right kind of way." When we say an action was done by a person's "own free will," we do not mean that the person actually has free will. ". . . we mean only to rule out certain alternative explanations such as coercion or mental abnormality."[237]

What, then, about *mens rea*? Barry maintains that it does not have any deep philosophical implications but is a purely legal concept set up as a requirement for legal responsibility. It asks only "if the action flowed from the actor's will in the right kind of way." It "is unaffected by any questions about determinism in general."[238]

What, then, is this "right kind of way" in which an action should flow from a person's will in order for him to be responsible for it and for its outcomes even though he does not do it freely since his choices are limited? How does it differ from the traditional idea of interior, subjective freedom and responsibility? At this crucial point, on which everything hangs, his argument unfortunately dries up. He has told us some things it excludes, such as coercion and mental abnormality, and he now adds to those automatism. But he does not attempt to give a positive account of it.

At this point I am going to attempt a conjecture. Barry's conception of "responsibility," if I am not mistaken, seems analogous to the kind we attribute to an animal. Finding food overturned at a campsite, we might say, "A bear was responsible for that." We do not attribute free will to the bear, but a particular kind of causality. The obvious question, of course, is whether such a thin concept of "responsibility" can be sufficient for the needs of a society composed of human beings. Since it is a responsibility without free will in the traditional interior or subjective sense, it has no room for guilt, and therefore none for innocence; no scope for blame, but also none for praise; no allowance for punishment, but also none for reward. It is a purely external conception, which would enable us to identify an individual as a link in a causal chain, but without that interior dimension which, as we have seen, is the mark of human presence.

However, there is a reason why Barry does not do more to give us an account of individual responsibility. It is because he does not believe in it. He concedes that this modified conception of individual responsibility is a makeshift approach devised for those who, whether they accept or reject determinism, "do regard personal responsibility as a potential justification of inequality." He makes it plain that his deeper sympathy is with those who reject the concept of responsibility altogether, because at bottom it is incompatible with "social" justice. ". . . if we once took seriously the implications of determinism, we would realize that the assignment of responsibility is a charade." ". . . anyone who rejects personal responsibility altogether will be led to the conclusion that has panicked so many people into promoting 'free will' – i.e. that there is no basis in justice for differential outcomes."[239] And of course conversely, anyone who accepts that there is no basis in justice for differential outcomes will be led to the conclusion that the assignment of responsibility is a charade.

That this is his true belief becomes plainer still in a later chapter where he argues that responsibility for social problems lies not with the individual, but with society. We will come back to the question of responsibility in the next section. Here we are concerned with the question of freedom. Our aim in discussing Brian Barry has been to convey how and why and in what sense this leading representative of the school of "social" justice rejects it. Perhaps the reader may feel that Barry's view is an exaggeration and that a less extreme conception could be plausible. But the merit of his position is that it brings out with devastating clarity the true implications of the current conception of "social justice."

The possibility of freedom

Our conception of free will is very different from Brian Barry's. We consider that the will possesses in itself an internal, subjective power of rational choice which is independent of the external range of choices available. Several lines of reasoning support this view.

One, in response to Barry, is that human beings have the ability to expand their range of choices. A "choice-set" is not something fixed forever. People often refuse to be bound by these limitations. They can reject them collectively or in groups, but also as individuals. What mainly prevents them from doing so is coercion, whether by government or crime. Where an individual is not subject to hostile coercion, the expansion of his range of choices is usually mainly a question of his ingenuity. The defender of social justice may reply that ingenuity is a product of society. But it can manifest itself even in the worst slum. The studies of the Peruvian slums by Hernando de Soto and the efforts of the Bangladeshi micro-loan entrepreneur Muhammad Yunus have demonstrated the ability of the poor to create new structures for themselves when the heavy hand of coercion is lifted from their shoulders. In a different way, many constraining circumstances have been overcome by the expedient of travel. Relocation to other places is one of the commonest ways people have used to expand their range of choices. The immigrants who flooded into the New World from Europe in the nineteenth century did what human beings have always done: they found a way out of the "choice-set" they had been given.

The meaning and existence of free will have been the subject of intense debate among philosophers in recent decades. This is perhaps not the place to present and defend our full theory of freedom of the will, but we will attempt to outline it in terms of current debate.

It is important as a preliminary step to formulate the problem rightly. It is not a conflict between a demonstrated certitude, namely universal causation, and a mere undemonstrable theory, free will, as if we had an indubitable experience of the one, guaranteed by the whole apparatus of the physical sciences, and a mere imagination of the other, locked in the secret recesses of a totally private mind. Universal causation, even and precisely in the sense of quantum theory, is a theory. While it is no doubt an exceptionally strong and well-founded theory, on which we feel entitled to rely unquestioningly in the ordinary actions of life, it cannot have the untouchable status of a dogma, since genuine science does not have dogmas. It will persist as long as it is the best explanation of the phenomena it describes, and no longer. (Strictly speaking quantum theory does not explain, but only makes predictions; which however is largely the purpose of explanations in science, and its predictions have proven to be remarkably correct.)

Our freedom of choice, on the other hand, is something we experience, and we all experience, every one of the billions of us adults, every day. In this regard I consider Kant was mistaken in maintaining that the freedom of the will lies entirely beyond experience. If by "experience" we mean only what can be perceived by the five senses and what can be duplicated by others reporting the deliverances of their senses, no doubt we do not "experience" our own freedom of choice. But by that measure, we also have no experience of memory or imagination. Yet it seems entirely reasonable to say that we have the experience of remembering and imagining.

We know many things that we cannot prove. In my view, for which I hope to make a more developed argument on another occasion, the immediate knowledge of our own actions belongs to a different category from our knowledge of the world we observe. There is a special kind of knowledge directly associated with and involved in our own actions: we know what we are doing in and by the fact that we are doing it. How do I know I am swimming? I don't have to look in a mirror or ask an observer. I know it just because I am swimming. By a parallel kind of argument I know I am exercising an ability, such as memory or choice, because I am exercising it. And just as I can be aware of constraints on my choice, as in the heat of sexual passion, I can also be aware of the absence of constraints.

Some such view would adequately explain why adult human beings universally believe and correctly believe that they possess freedom of the will and are consequently personally responsible for their actions. The Kantian thesis that we can do no more than *assume* it because it is a necessary practical requirement for morality attributes to us both too little and too much for such an explanation: too little, because everybody in the ordinary course of life who is not a skeptical philosopher considers that we *know* with certitude that we have this ability of free choice and consequently are personally responsible for our actions, and only the awareness of such certain knowledge could justify thoughtful people in inflicting severe penalties on those who do wrong; but also too much, because it involves sophisticated reasoning, which it is a stretch to attribute to all adults, that the concept of morality has prerequisites of this nature. Add to this that the generality of mankind are fully capable of judging when others are temporarily deprived of their ordinary freedom of the will by such things as drugs or alcohol or a stroke.

Free will and emergence

In recent years certain advances in the science of physics have hinted at an exceedingly strange new possibility. These advances are referred to as the phenomenon of "emergence." The prevailing assumption in modern science has always been reductionist, that higher-level or more organized phenomena can be explained by lower-level or less-organized phenomena, that everything in psychology will prove to be explainable eventually by biology, biology by chemistry, and chemistry in turn by physics. This assumption requires that the more organized should be predictable, at least in principle, from the less organized. But recently striking examples have been found to the contrary, where the higher level produces phenomena that are genuinely new and cannot be predicted or explained by the lower level, but rather the reverse: it is the higher level that successfully predicts and explains the lower level. These phenomena that "arise" out of the lower level but are not "caused" by it or predictable from it are referred to as emergent. The Newtonian laws, for example, are simpler, and the laws of quantum mechanics are more complicated, but Newton's laws can be predicted by quantum mechanics as a limiting case. Within physics, emergence refers especially to phenomena that occur at macroscopic scales but not at microscopic ones, even though macroscopic realities are usually viewed as built up out of microscopic ones.

One remarkable example of this is sound quantization. Sound, as everyone knows, consists in a wave motion through the molecules of a medium, such as air or glass, as when we hear the noise of traffic through a window. The molecules of the medium vibrate, each passing its vibrations on to the next. It turns out, however, that under certain circumstances sound no longer consists of a wave, but of particles. The physicist Robert B. Laughlin, winner of a Nobel Prize in Physics, describes it in this way:

> Suppose, for example, a sound transducer is attached to a solid and turned on, thus beaming sound into the solid, and then reduced in intensity to make the amount of sound small. A sound receiver on the other side of the solid detects not a faint tone but sharp pulses of energy arriving at random times. This quantized transmission of pulses evolves into the more familiar transmission of tone when the intensity is increased – an everyday example of the emergence of Newtonian reality out of quantum mechanics . . . the conclusion becomes inescapable that particules of sound exist, even though they do not exist when the solid is disassembled into atoms. The particles emerge, just as the solid itself does. Sound quantization is a particularly instructive example of particle emergence because it can be worked out exactly, in all its detail, starting from the underlying laws of quantum mechanics obeyed by atoms . . . The analysis also reveals that the particles of sound acquire more and more integrity as the corresponding tone is lowered in pitch, and become exact in the limit of low tone. Very high-pitched sound quanta propagating through a solid can decay probabilistically into two or more quanta of sound with a lower pitch, this decay being aptly analogous to that of a radioactive nucleus or an elementary particle such as a pion. . . . The quantum properties of sound are identical to those of light. This fact is important, for it is not at all obvious, given that sound is a collective motion of elastic matter while light ostensibly is not.[240]

The discovery of emergence constitutes a profound revolution in our way of seeing both the world and science, a revolution at least as important as the discovery of quantum mechanics. It implies that no particular level of reality is epistemologically privileged. The micro level is not more fundamental than the macro, nor the macro than the micro, but both are of equal importance for understanding the universe. Many of the collective phenomena are not necessarily caused by the single phenomena out of which they appear to be built, but each must be understood in the light of the other. As P. W. Anderson said in the title of his groundbreaking paper on the subject, "More is Different."[241]

Emergence theory is admittedly in its infancy and is still highly controversial. The basic concepts involved in it are not entirely clear, nor even the line of demarcation between what emerges and what does not. But, without making any premature assertions, it does perhaps give us a glimpse of how something that has appeared for centuries to be a logical impossibility could prove to be a reality: that free will should be compatible with determinism, determinism, at least in its quantum form, being a micro or low-level phenomenon and free will being a macro or higher-level one.

If mind, and with it free will, arises out of matter, but matter is not privileged, matter in turn must in some sense, it would seem, arise out of mind or be intelligible only in relation to mind. This surely says something about both of them. Exactly what it says in detail remains for the moment a mystery. But at the least it appears we will have to revise our concept of matter, which, whatever it is, seems to be a far more mysterious thing than the purely inert and passive, "material" thing it has so long been taken to be.

If this approach should be correct, the interesting philosophical question regarding free will is no longer so much whether it exists, but precisely how it is possible. To have free will, for example, a being must be alive. Even lower forms of life exhibit, it can be argued, a kind of spontaneity which may well be the forerunner of will and freedom in a higher form. Although many people seem to assume, with Richard Dawkins, that life is entirely mechanical and can be created by inventing a self-replicating machine, a very different account of it is needed to produce spontaneity, and *a fortiori* freedom. In point of fact we are scarcely at the beginning of understanding what life is in itself and what is needed to create it.

Freedom and the person

The power of free choice, so intrinsic to our conception of ourselves and others, is a quality of the will. It shows itself especially in moral action, the ability to will and act against our own interests for the sake of others. For this is freedom from the domination of causation. Animals and very young human beings are under the dominion of their feelings, they are constrained in their actions by their natural instincts and their emotions and do not have the power of acting against their inclinations. Animals remain forever in this condition of unfreedom; but human beings grow out of it. The significance of adolescence is that it is the time when they gradually, over a sometimes tumultuous period of several years, escape from the bonds of predetermination and develop the unique power to ignore and choose against their instincts and feelings.

This power, which enables us to choose against ourself, against the causal dictates of our natural instincts and feelings, is something unique in the universe. It has a claim to be considered a higher form of being than anything found anywhere else. To describe it properly there seems to be no other language than that of "lower" and "higher," even though this language is sometimes objected to as unscientific. We are not just human animals. We are persons, and personality emerges from our biological condition in something like the way that higher orders of explanation in physics emerge from – and take over –the micro-organization on which they are usually thought to depend. Everything else in the universe appears to be subject either to the iron law of causation or to quantum probability. What we mean by free choice, what we experience when we make a choice, is neither the one nor the other, but something entirely different from both. A free choice is a new thing. It is something we originate. It can rightly be viewed as the pinnacle of created life. It is the foundation of morality and therefore inherently something worthy of respect, which is not true of any product of a mechanical causation or of a quantum process.

The fact that an act of the will is free does not, of course, mean that it is necessarily easy. On the contrary, as we all know only too well, it may require an immense effort of the will. The struggle so many people find they must engage in to accomplish such a prosaic task as losing a few pounds of weight is a testimony to the far more intense effort that must sometimes be made to reach higher and more self-sacrificing goals. But the fact that an action is difficult, even extremely difficult, should not be confused with impossibility.

The freedom of the adult human will given by our inherited biological nature does not exhaust the internal freedom of the will: there is also a different kind of freedom that comes to it through its own action, by the habitual choice of moral virtue. Although the biologically given will has the inherent power to reject the causative influence of inclination, if it does not use this power, it can lose it to a large degree, though never totally. The person who regularly chooses only to follow his inclinations finds it harder and harder to resist them. By sufficiently resisting his inclinations and choosing virtue, the individual in a sense creates his own freedom. Perhaps we can call this kind of freedom ethical, in distinction from the biological.

I do not mean to say that only virtuous actions are free in this natural or biological sense of freedom. The actions of every conscious, sane adult are free in that sense, including the evil ones. But I mean to point out that in addition to that biological freedom, as I am calling it because it is inherited along with our biological nature, there is another kind of freedom of will which I am calling "ethical" and which has often also been called "spiritual" freedom. This is the freedom that comes from the habit of choosing what is right. I am arguing that our experience of this latter freedom is a strong testimony to the existence of the former freedom.

It is true we sometimes feel we are "compelled by circumstances" and "have no choice" but to do a certain action. And it is also true that we sometimes welcome this restriction, as relieving us of the burden of responsibility. Many convicted criminals insist they could not help doing what they did. So it is in conformity with "social justice" to assume that the disadvantaged, when they rob, are compelled to rob. Yet others who suffer from the same difficult circumstances somehow manage not to rob. In the absence of external force, the feeling that one is compelled by circumstances is usually simply the feeling that the reasons for doing the action vastly outweigh the reasons against it. It does not negate our realization that if we were foolish enough, say, to be determined to act otherwise, we could do so. Whatever my external circumstances, in the last analysis it is "up to me," to use Aristotle's phrase, what attitude I take to them.

The common law has long recognized "mitigating circumstances," such as "the heat of passion" or "diminished responsibility," circumstances that reduce the degree of responsibility attributed to the defendant, especially in criminal trials, and may well result in a reduced sentence. But they are not considered to eliminate responsibility entirely. That can be accomplished by a defense of insanity, following the M'Naghten Rule, which asks whether the person could distinguish right from wrong. But it is not usually asserted that the disadvantaged are incapable of distinguishing right from wrong.

Freedom and spirit/materialism and secularism

The concept of the person is connected with another that has fallen into disuse, but which, rightly understood, helps us to articulate what is peculiar in the human condition: the concept of spirit. Although not much talked about in modern philosophy this is still common in our ordinary language. It is associated with liveliness, courage, dynamism, morale, resolve, and determination. It suggests the power of an individual mind and will to resist, and to act freely and responsibly as an individual. It is the ability to defy domination by external forces, whether of other people or of circumstances, and to resist even one's own inclinations. Thus the ethical act, in which one goes against one's own desires and interests, and perhaps against the expectations and demands of others, because it is right, is well described as an act of spirit.

The power that is meant in speaking of spirit cannot be properly understood as the necessary and predetermined effect of a cause, but is spontaneous. It is a power of self-movement, to use Plato's term. Thus it is a power that bears witness to life. It is a universal view that a being that possesses spirit is one that is patently alive. An inanimate being, or a dead one, is characterized by the fact that its movements originate outside of itself. In the perspective of "social" justice, however, this description applies to all human beings.

The conception of freedom of the will that goes with ordinary justice is a spiritual one. For the freedom exercised in any difficult ethical act is a spiritual freedom, a freedom from ourselves, from the prison of our desires. As we have just remarked, it is something unique in the universe and absolutely precious. It confers dignity on the human person. Freedom in this sense is an interior, spiritual quality that has the power to reject the limitations in which it finds itself. This ability exists by nature in all human beings, though to be actual it must, in the course of life, be acted on, and developed by practice, since even the spirit can grow dull and inert.

By contrast, the conception of freedom of the will that goes with the socialistic conception of social justice is merely a matter of opportunities and constraints. On this view the rich man has more "freedom" than the poor man, since more options lie open before him. Freedom is simply an external state of affairs, and if we are all to be equally free, therefore, we must all enjoy complete equality of options. On the view that I am advocating, however, which identifies freedom with that metaphysical core of the human being in which personality and accountability are rooted, we are all equally free, regardless of social inequalities, and equal respect involves recognizing this, and holding each person accountable for his will and all that expresses it.

This is why Hegel remarks that "spirit is the foundation of justice." It is this because the human will is free, and freedom – interior freedom, the freedom of the will – is the hallmark of spirit. Where there is spirit, there is interior freedom, and where there is interior freedom, there is spirit.

Justice, as he says, meaning true or ordinary justice, is "the realm of actualized freedom, the world of spirit brought forth out of itself."

The affirmation of interior freedom is the affirmation of spirit; and the denial of interior freedom is the denial of spirit. But the denial of spirit, even an unconscious and merely implicit denial, leads one into a dead materialism. The gospel of "social" justice, with its accompanying determinism, is necessarily associated with a materialistic view of life. It sees the fundamental reality of human life as economic. Even though Marx and Engels disclaimed any intention of making large philosophical statements, it was no accident that their followers described their viewpoint as "historical materialism" and "dialectical materialism." The true regime of justice stands over against all forms of materialism. An individual who lives a life in obedience to true justice is one who values what is of the spirit. A society that is concerned about true justice and implements it in practice despite its often heavy costs is a society that embodies and manifests spirit.

The ultimate self-mover, of course, according to Plato, is God. Spirit is not confined to the empirical world, but is open to possibilities that may lie beyond the realm of sense. By contrast, the gospel of "social" justice, being inherently materialistic, is also inherently secular. From its beginning, the movement for redistribution did not regard belief in God as merely neutral, but as "opium." It is one of the many ironies associated with "social" justice that the Roman Catholic church in the person of Pope Pius XI, in his encyclical *Quadragesimo anno,* rightly condemned socialism as secular, but then went on to approve and applaud the socialist concept of "social" justice, failing to see that social justice itself is inherently secular. At the present time, many Christians in the United States ask themselves why Europe, which for much of the nineteenth century was unquestioningly Christian, should now have become so intensely secular. Some have attributed this to Europe's "rationality," but this rationality is not overwhelmingly evident in other areas of existence. The more likely explanation for Europe's conversion to secularism is its conversion to "social" justice, which by a curious coincidence took place at the same time. Similarly, there can be little doubt that the general lack of sympathy with, and even outright hostility to, theism and religion among the intellectual and academic classes of the Western world at the present time can be explained in large part by their adoption of the gospel of economic equality.

One special way in which spirit manifests its presence is by the willingness to accept responsibility. In the next section we shall investigate this controversial notion.

Responsibility

Our ordinary conception of ethical judgment is not only that it applies primarily to the will and rests on the belief that the will is free, but also that it involves responsibility and accountability for one's actions. Because a person's actions are expressions and embodiments of his will, he bears responsibility for them, and – making a distinction between that and accountability – he is also accountable or answerable for them to others. Responsibility and accountability are inherent and necessary qualities of any action that can claim to be ethical. The actions of a child, a madman, or a sleepwalker are universally deemed to lie outside the realm of ethical judgment because it is recognized that they are not the expressions of a genuine will, and therefore the person is not responsible or accountable for them. But the actions of a sane, conscious adult are the expressions of a will and he is accountable for them to others.

The term "responsibility" made its appearance with its equivalents in the languages of Europe only toward the end of the eighteenth century. Its original use in philosophy was in connection with the idea of representative government, which ought to be responsible to the people. The word is derived, of course, from the Latin for "answer," "*respondere.*" To be responsible to someone for something is in general to be answerable or accountable to him for it, although these words in English now have slightly different ranges of meaning. The root of "*respondere*" is "*spondere,*" to promise, guarantee, give one's word, a term associated by the Romans especially with the undertakings given at the time of marriage.

In ordinary usage today the term is not restricted to the human world, but as applied to the non-human world it usually implies simple causality, as in statements like "the storm was responsible for the destruction of the trees." As applied to human beings, while it can retain this sense of simple causality, it can also combine with that the concept of duty, in a variety of ways: an individual is said to be responsible for an event not only when he causes it, but also when the causing of it is within his discretion ("each employee is responsible for providing his own transport"), or when he has a duty to cause it ("the manager is responsible for security"), or when he had a duty to prevent it and did not do so ("the captain was responsible for the sinking of the ship"). In other words, it suggests the particular kinds of causality appropriate to human or rational beings capable of moral action, as distinct from other kinds of being. We refer to this as "moral responsibility." Although "responsibility" is a relatively recent word, its meaning in these cases is ancient and well-known. What links them is the reference to causation. We shall call this therefore the ordinary concept of responsibility.

This ordinary concept of responsibility has a central importance for the discussion of justice because it provides the main basis for assigning guilt or innocence, praise or blame, and reward or punishment, that is assigning or releasing from duties.

Imputability and responsibility, which both emphasize the bond of causation between the individual person and his action, can be considered first attempts at stating the moral-societal link between them which is reflected in the concept of accountability. Because actions are imputable to persons and persons are responsible for their actions, persons are accountable for the effects of their actions on others.

Imputability

To say that an action is to be imputed to a person is to assert that it has originated with him. The imputation of an action to an individual means that he owns it, it belongs to him, it depends on him, it is his production. This is what Aristotle means when he says that our actions are "up to us," ('εφ' 'ημιν), they are within our power to do or not to do, we create them from within ourselves. ". . . a human being originates and fathers his own actions as he fathers his children."[242]

To be imputable to a person, an action must be an act of his will, it must be voluntary in the sense of not being physically forced, and of not being the product of ignorance. And provided it fulfills those conditions it *is* an act of his will and imputable to him, even if it is performed under duress. For an action performed under duress or threat is still originated by him and would not be performed if he did not intend to perform it. Yet there are greater and lesser degrees of imputability.

It is generally considered that the degree of imputability of an action to a person is proportionate to the obstacles that he has to overcome to perform it. The greater the obstacles placed in the way of the action by physical nature, and the less the moral obstacles to it, the more a good deed will be accounted meritorious. For example, if I rescue from great need at considerable sacrifice to myself a man who is completely unknown to me. On the other hand: the smaller the obstacles placed in the way by physical nature, and the larger the obstacle created by moral principle, the more a transgression will be imputed. As, for example, if I can easily help myself to the money in the till, but have a strong obligation in gratitude to the owner not to do so because of special favors he has done me. Therefore the mental state of the agent, whether he did the deed as the result of strong emotion or only after calm deliberation, makes a difference to the imputability of the deed.[243]

Imputability applies equally to our good actions and our bad ones. We cannot argue that our good actions belong to us but not our bad ones. Both of them are up to us, they are equally our creation. And since, as everyone knows, good actions give rise to good habits or virtues, and bad actions to bad habits or vices, and our character consists of our virtues and vices, therefore our character depends on us and belongs to us as our own work. Our moral fiber, whatever it is, for good or ill, is of our own making and is not the work of anyone else. Consequently, we and no one else are responsible for the kind of person we are.

The same holds true in regard to our circumstances in society. We cannot blame our bad character on "society" unless we are equally willing to praise society and not ourselves for our good character. But even if we should be so willing, our evil actions are still imputable to us and not to society because we always have the ability to reject what society proposes to us, even when that has drastic consequences for us. Although "society" can suggest many things to us, in the last analysis the decision rests with us whether to go along with society's suggestions or not.

No doubt there are situations where a person's responsibility for his actions is diminished, and this is well recognized by the law. While the law typically punishes those who injure others because it views them as responsible for their actions, it makes exceptions for cases where the action is forced, or is caused by ignorance that the individual is not responsible for. Yet ignorance is not always an excuse, since it is possible for us consciously to decide to remain ignorant of something. And the law imposes penalties in other cases for ignorance that seems to be caused, not by a deliberate decision to be ignorant, but by the agent's inattention: it is assumed that it is up to the individual not to be ignorant because he controls whether he pays attention or not. And a person cannot claim that his character made him inattentive, and so he was not responsible for it, for each person has created his character by the kinds of actions he has done. A man makes himself responsible for having a weak character by easily giving in to external pressure and living without much regard for principle. Similarly he makes himself responsible for having an unjust character by getting into the habit of cheating. For each type of activity tends to produce the corresponding kind of character, as everyone knows. Consequently, if someone does what he knows will make him unjust, he is unjust willingly.

Choice plays a fundamental role in the ethical life. It is especially our choices that make our virtues and our vices, and distinguish one person's character from another. A choice is not the same thing as desire or emotion or wish or belief, but a decision about what to do. Choice involves reason and thought, and is the result of deliberation about alternative courses of action. Not everything is open to deliberation. As Aristotle remarks, we deliberate only about what is "up to us," what we view as within our power, what we personally are capable of doing. An action that we deliberately choose to do is imputable to us.

But "social" injustice is by definition not the product of deliberation or choice. Inequality can be condemned as "social injustice" even though it is entirely the product of accident and not intended by anyone. The U.S. Supreme Court rejects policies that have "disparate impact" on protected categories of people even though it is clear there was no intention to discriminate. And of course a person who deliberately chooses to live in poverty or inequality is by that fact not a victim.

The fact that a person is recognized as originating an action gives it in effect a new meaning. Until that point it is a mere event. As Kant remarks, the fact that an action is imputable transforms it into the *deed* of a person. This makes it possible for the action to be governed by law.

It is generally recognized that only voluntary actions can be imputed to persons, and so can be governed by law. Involuntary actions are not considered deeds, are not imputable, and cannot be governed by law.[244] An imputation can be made with legal force which brings legal consequences. This happens when it is made by a court of law. But of course it can also be made by private opinion without having such consequences.[245]

The sharp distinction between what an individual can be responsible for, namely his own acts, and what not, namely everything else, was well brought out by Epictetus, who made it into the foundational insight of Stoicism.

Of things, some are in our power, and others are not. In our power are opinion, movement towards a thing, desire, aversion, and, in a word, whatever are our own acts. Not in our power are the body, property, reputation, offices, and, in a word, whatever are not our own acts. And the things in our power are by nature free, not subject to restraint or hindrance . . .

It is clear enough that Epictetus did not limit this responsibility for actions to the wealthy and powerful, but extended it to the "disadvantaged," since he was himself very much among their number, being a slave.[246]

Imputability is the hallmark of a person. The exploration of imputation reaches into the very core of personhood, into the place in the mysterious freedom of his will where the person decides to act or not to act.

Now we know what it means for an action to belong to an individual person and to be imputed to a person as its originator. But it is not clear what could be meant by imputing an action to "society." An organization – a community, a nation, an institution – can be provided by its organizers with someone to represent it, and through the actions of that representative person it can act. But "society" as such is not an organization and does not act.[247] A society can act, for example it can pass laws through its legislature, for in speaking of *a* society we are speaking of a particular organized body.

Responsibility

The concept of responsibility is different from that of imputability. While both are concerned with causation, imputability is concerned with the agent's ownership of the action, but responsibility is concerned with the consequences of the action. A person possesses responsibility to the extent that he has performed an action which brings a change about in the world, so that some aspect of the world can now be said to be "his." He acquires responsibility by putting his stamp on the world, so to speak.[248] An action can be imputed to me only if I am responsible for it, but not everything I am responsible for can be imputed to me. There is an important distinction between intentional and unintentional or accidental causation. If something belonging to me accidentally causes harm to someone, that is not my deed, but it is nevertheless to some degree my responsibility. I am responsible to some extent for all the consequences of my act, including the purely accidental ones, but only the consequences I intended can be imputed to me.

By doing the action the person commits himself to it, and to many of its consequences, though not to all. If it is a bad action, its bad consequences belong to him. If it is a good action, its good consequences also belong to him.[249]

Responsibility implies only the judgment that I have done something or not. But this judgment is not always a simple matter. Often it will be a matter of choice to say which particular factor or factors should be considered responsible for an event. Any actual event is part of an almost limitless web of factors. Any and every single element which appears as the cause of one such factor, and so has contributed its share to the event in question, can be regarded as responsible for the event, or at least as sharing the responsibility for it. So that in the case of a complex event, such as the French

Revolution, it is largely up to the observer to choose which of an endless number of factors he will maintain to be responsible for it. When we are asking about the responsibility of a person for an event – for example was Louis XVI responsible for the French Revolution? – the answer to this question will depend therefore on the degree to which he made a contribution to the causation. There are widely different degrees of responsibility because there are widely different degrees of causation.[250]

Full responsibility is not that of accidental causation but the responsibility of the will. While I am responsible to some degree or other for all the consequences of my action, including those that are merely accidental, I am fully responsible only for those I willed or intended. But to intend an effect I must have an idea of it beforehand: it must be in my consciousness. My responsibility in this full sense of the word is always limited by my knowledge of the situation. My will is responsible for the deed only in so far as I know what I am doing.

Not only are we not fully responsible for the effects produced accidentally and unintentionally by things that merely belong to us, but also our deliberate and intended actions have consequences that we did not intend and that may be very different indeed from what we intended, and these also, although we are responsible for them, we are not fully responsible for. Once we act, our action escapes from our control and becomes part of the realm of objective reality or the public domain.

To act is therefore to expose oneself to bad luck. The arsonist, let us say, wishes to burn down only the house of the person who he believes has injured him, but as luck would have it the fire catches on to the house next door. He is responsible for this. He cannot argue that it was not his intention. By the fact that he deliberately set fire to the first house, knowing that fires are violently dangerous and liable to get out of control, he incurs responsibility for whatever damage the fire does.

Every action is ultimately therefore a gamble. It will be judged by its actual consequences, whatever they may be. Although we are responsible in the full sense only for what we intend, we are nonetheless genuinely responsible, even though not in the full sense, for all the consequences of our action.[251]

Imputation together with responsibility gives rise to the concept of accountability. Since our actions belong to us and we are responsible for them and their consequences, we are accountable to others for them. This accountability can be asserted at law, so that we can be legally responsible and accountable or "liable" for harm that we cause.

The socialization of responsibility

We know, then, or at least we have a good idea, what it means for an individual to be responsible and accountable. It is above all a question of action and causation. Individuals are responsible for the effects their actions cause. But in the course of the twentieth century two radical changes have been introduced into the concept of responsibility by advocates of "social justice." On the one hand the claim is made that an individual can justly be considered responsible for harm, not on the ground that he caused it, but solely because he has the means to remedy it. The rich or powerful are made responsible for the fate of the poor or the less powerful even though they played no causal role in it. On the other, responsibility is attributed ultimately no longer to individuals at all but only to "society." When the poor commit a crime, this is not the fault of the poor individuals in question, but of the society in which they live. A certain concept of causation is maintained here: society is held to cause the crime of the poor. In both of these conceptions responsibility is socialized. Thus the innumerable controversial tort cases in recent decades alluded to in Chapters 1 and 2.

It is Brian Barry who explains and defends most clearly the very different conception of responsibility implied by the doctrine of social justice. He decries altogether the very idea of individual responsibility and wishes to see it replaced by the concept of "the responsible society." We have already seen some of his thoughts about this in the course of discussing free will, but they will bear examination again from this slightly different viewpoint. Part IV of his recent work on social justice is devoted entirely to the topic under the title "The Cult of Personal Responsibility," which already conveys something of his approach.

Barry considers that individual responsibility is an illusion. He attributes the origin of this illusion to monotheistic religion, which, in order to avoid placing the blame for evil and suffering in the world on God, where it would rightly belong if there were a God, places it instead on individual human beings, who are therefore to be punished for their "sins," not only in a future life but also in this one. This view was carried over into public policy.

> Thus, unmarried mothers were treated with gratuitous harshness so that they could expiate their sin. Their children, conceived in sin, were also made to suffer in about as many ways as human ingenuity could devise. Charities distinguished between the "deserving poor" and the "undeserving poor," leaving the latter to the only state-funded institution, the

workhouse, whose conditions were deliberately designed to be as repellent and degrading as possible. (132)

With the decline of religion, an alternative justification "had to be found" for systematic inequality, according to Barry, and it was found in the idea of natural inequality, that by nature people "have different capacities and personal characteristics." Barry does not accept this, however. It "can safely be laid to rest," apparently because at one stage it led to the emergence of eugenics. "And with it we can bury any notion that the division between the successful and the unsuccessful – with the concomitant differences in wealth and privilege – reflects 'natural' inequalities." People are "born equal" (135). For Barry, the differences between the successful and the unsuccessful are entirely the result of inequalities of opportunity.

In spite of what Barry considers to be this obvious fact, some persons remain perversely determined to defend inequality, and their current method of doing this is

> to accept that people are in principle equal in potential, but to attribute inequality to unequal merits. The rich owe their wealth to hard work, enterprise and frugality, while the poor have a bad moral character, which leads to laziness, fecklessness and the kind of behavior that . . . is liable to land them in prison.

But for Barry, this is "manifestly false." Differences in moral character are entirely the result of differences of opportunity.

The fundamental reason why in Barry's view there cannot be individual responsibility is that there is no such thing as free will. ". . . if we once took seriously the implications of determinism, we would realize that the assignment of responsibility is a charade" (139). We have already examined his reasoning about determinism. However, his concept of individual responsibility is not precisely one that would be accepted as representative by many who believe in individual responsibility. In his view, "the principle of personal responsibility" means that those who are "successful" are so entirely by their own achievement with no room for luck. Those who have had good luck cannot be responsible for their achievements. Similarly, he takes it to mean that those who are "unemployed could all find jobs if they tried harder" (135).

Although Barry rules out any individual responsibility in the strict and proper sense, he is willing to admit that there is a version of the idea that, while no doubt fundamentally mistaken, is "so far as it goes, an honourable one." This is the principle of *noblesse oblige*, which means that those who have benefited most from a system of individual rights have a responsibility to use their benefits for the good of the disadvantaged. This responsibility of property-owners and the wealthy should be imposed by law. By contrast, the statement sometimes made in public debate regarding welfare rights for the disadvantaged, that rights imply responsibilities, so that welfare recipients should acknowledge that in turn they have responsibilities and obligations to the society, Barry rejects with some passion, accusing it of "reeking hypocrisy."

In place of individual responsibility, Barry suggests the concept of "the responsible society." When bad things happen, instead of placing blame on individuals, we should seek the cause in "the structure of society." The institutions of society should be so structured that they "shield individuals from exposure to danger rather than creating a dangerous environment and demanding that individuals adapt to it" (157). He calls this "the public health approach." ". . . the effects of unskilful or unlucky decisions on people's health should be eliminated, and where that is impossible they should be minimized" (158). Far from expanding the range of choices available to people, this will often require the opposite: "The object of public policy should much of the time be to reduce the significance of choice rather than enhance it" (158).

Barry's account of social responsibility is undoubtedly faithful to the tradition of social justice thinking. Equally undoubtedly, it is entirely incompatible with the account of individual responsibility which characterizes our ordinary and traditional conception of justice. One cannot consistently accept both of these: they are mutually exclusive. The whole point of Barry's theory is to eliminate the traditional one.

Surprisingly, however, Barry proceeds to hold a very large number of individuals responsible for their actions: namely, his opponents. If one rejects the idea that individuals are morally responsible for their actions, one cannot very consistently then go on to condemn their moral characters. Yet that is just what Barry does, and not merely accidentally, as it were by a lapse of memory, but very deliberately. His work is filled with implicit and explicit moral denunciations referring not merely to actions but to personal character. To give all of them here would be tedious, but a few should suffice to convey the fact. The "legion of comfortably situated ladies" who take measures to ensure their charitable donations are not misspent are described as "nauseating" (133). "As religious belief declined in the last quarter of the nineteenth century, some alternative justification had to be found (namely, by Barry's opponents) for systematic inequality" (133).

In its context in the book this remark is a clear accusation of bad faith on their part. President George Bush and Prime Minister Tony Blair come in for bitter moral condemnation, Mr. Bush for having "notoriously failed to make up for his lack of intellectual capacity by applying himself diligently to his studies" at Yale, and having "unshakeable confidence in his own judgement, regardless of all rational argument," which "appears to derive from his daily sessions with God," and having "shown no signs of wondering if he has a wrong number" (136). His "climb to riches" "was . . . achieved by skulduggery rather than by honest toil." – this argued at some length over several pages in regard to what Barry regards as the suspicious purchase and sale of shares (". . . Who the hell bought such a large block of crummy stock ? Someone out there was sure looking after George W." [Quoted]) (143), and so on. Why does Barry not blame "society" and its "structures" for these deficiencies?

The answer to this question is that moral judgments are simply impossible without an attribution of individual moral causation and responsibility. Barry is forced to assign moral causation and responsibility to his opponents because he is not content merely to describe what they did but wishes to pass a moral judgment on them.

If there is no true free individual moral causation and responsibility, not only can no individual be truly innocent or guilty, no one rightly praised or blamed and no one justly rewarded or punished, but no moral judgments can be made at all.

Summary and Conclusion

We have argued in this chapter that justice and injustice are categories of thought that belong to the realm of ethics or morality. They are concepts of ethical evaluation. All such concepts possess certain features as an intrinsic part of their meaning. First and most fundamentally, they are qualities of a will. Every ethical virtue and every ethical vice resides in a will. Kindness, generosity, or compassion, for example, can be attributed meaningfully only to a being that has a will and in so far as it has a will. The same is true of justice and injustice. They can be qualities of something other than a will only if that something else is itself the product of a will. A state of affairs in society such as poverty or inequality of the kind that social justice concerns itself with is *not* the product of a will.

Second, as qualities attributed to a will, attributions of justice or injustice, like any other ethical attributions, presuppose that that will has the power of free choice. It makes no sense to attribute injustice, or any other ethical vice or virtue, to a will that is acting under the domination of some force outside itself. For that is what is meant by "ethics." An ethical judgment is a judgment on the free choices a person makes. Though freedom can be diminished by circumstances, that diminution can and must be taken into account in the ordinary ethical evaluation of the action.

Third, it is a presupposition of all attribution of ethical qualities that since the individual person is acting freely, he is responsible for his actions and accountable for them to others. An ethical judgment is a judgment of personal responsibility. Hence the concept of justice, if it is to be used as part of a moral judgment, must be connected to concepts of desert and responsibility – concepts which connect states of affairs to the human beings who can be held to account for them. This connection lies deep in the nature of moral judgment.

Our conclusion, therefore, is that the ascription of justice or injustice to a state of affairs in society which can exist without anyone having done anything wrong, or even without anyone having done anything at all, is incoherent. "Social justice" in its current socialistic or neosocialistic sense is not only not justice, but cannot even qualify as a term of ethical evaluation.

A Historical Note on Responsibility in Christianity

The concept of individual moral responsibility underwent a notable strengthening with the advent of Christianity. For Christian doctrine taught with some force that every individual would undergo after death a judgment by God in regard to each of his actions, that would seal the person's fate for all eternity, either for weal or for woe. The criterion of the judgment was the accordance of each action with the will of God. The exact content of the will of God was to receive detailed and sophisticated discussion by theologians during the centuries that followed, with eventually a large measure of agreement that, apart from the special deliverances of revelation, it was at bottom identical with the natural moral law, but we can leave this question aside for the moment. The point to notice is that Christian doctrine eliminated entirely any concept of collective responsibility, and also any concept of a divine judgment based on grounds that were not moral and therefore did not engage the responsibility of the individual at the deepest level.

In the preaching of Christ, it was not the Jewish people or any other collectivity that would be judged by God and assigned to heaven or to hell, but the individual. And the grounds on which the fate of the individual would be decided were exclusively of a moral nature. "Come, ye blessed of my Father, and enter into the kingdom prepared for you, for I was hungry and you gave me to eat."

The effect of this doctrine on the moral consciousness of the West was substantial. For both Jewish and Gentile worlds had accepted from time immemorial both the idea of collective responsibility and also the idea of a divine judgment based on factors that lay outside the realm of morality. The Hebrew Bible was largely the story of God's holding the Jewish people (and not only them) to account as a collective entity in which innocent individuals could rightly be punished along with the guilty. It is true that with Jeremiah a new policy was announced according to which only guilty individuals would henceforth be the object of divine punishment, but in point of fact the belief continued alongside this that God would reward and also punish the people as a whole, for this lay in the Covenant God had made with Abraham which created the people, and which was recited continually in the synagogue. The concept of collective responsibility remained so long as the fate of the Jewish people as a people remained a divine concern. The Roman occupation, for example, was a punishment inflicted on the people, and not only on individuals. Which did not serve to legitimize it, however, in the minds of many.

Furthermore, the Law of Moses had recognized, in addition to morality, another and very different criterion of divine judgment, namely ritual cleanliness, legislated in the rules of kasher. Ritual uncleanliness could happen to a person by accident, and consequently he could suffer the divine condemnation for something for which it was perfectly clear he was not personally responsible. Many incidents of this kind are narrated in the Hebrew Bible. Of course, this judgment was one that took place in this life, not in a life to come, but it could nonetheless be fatal. Jesus, however, rejected the concept of ritual uncleanness as "traditions of men." "It is not what goes into a man that makes him unclean, but what comes out of him."

For the pagan world of classical Greece and Rome, the categorical Christian doctrine of judgment after death was equally a new departure. The typical thoughts of classical man about the afterlife seem to have been well summed up by Plato's Socrates: either death brought extinction, or a shadowy existence as depicted in the myths, very likely accompanied by a judgment. The consciences of men were governed perforce by the will of "the gods." But like Charon and his passage over the Styx, the "will of the gods" was a shadowy and uncertain concept. The gods of the myths were far too much like human beings, affected by all the failings that human beings are heir to, and then some, to be reliable as just judges. In practice, it is true, classical man seems to have essentially ignored the failings of the gods narrated in the myths, and attributed to them divine perfection. But the gods owed their authority to their ability to punish in this life, which the educated came more and more to doubt. Cicero assured his readers that "there is no such thing as the wrath of the gods."[252]

The classical world that still accepted the wrath of the gods accepted also that that wrath could be incurred by an individual for reasons other than contravention of the moral law. The punishment suffered by Oedipus was, no doubt, in their view the result of an infringement of an objective law established for human conduct by the divine order, but it was not the result of any moral offense.

The Christian world had, then, from its very beginning in the preaching of Christ, a powerful concept of individual moral responsibility, which placed it in deep contrast to most other religious movements, and in fact still at the present day distinguishes it from the generality of religions, with the sole exception perhaps of Zoroastrianism.

It is true that the concept of a divine judgment that took place on the individual after death and that was wholly based on moral criteria had come to be accepted by the Pharisees through the influence of Persian religion during the two centuries before Christ when Judaea was subject to Persian rule (538–333 BC). But this belief remained only that of one particular sect of Israelite religion, to which other sects such as the Sadducees did not subscribe. The concept of ritual uncleanliness would survive, to reappear in Islam. The Christian elimination of ritual uncleanness and its restriction of moral responsibility to the moral actions of individuals can be considered with some justice as a historic step forward in the development of human consciousness toward rationality.

It is also true the theological tradition of the Church recognized that morally good human actions owed their origin fundamentally to God. As Augustine wrote, "*Opera nostra dona Dei sunt.*" (Even Plato had accepted this.) The Catholic tradition generally maintained that this principle must be understood, however, in a way that retained the responsibility of men both for their actions and also for their eternal fate, which depended on their actions. The Reformers, on the other hand, made of this principle their foundational insight, preserving men's responsibility for their actions, but not for their fate, which did not depend on their actions, but was pre-destined by God. Although, on the Reformers' view, salvation was predetermined by divine grace and not awarded on human merit, the fact that one was saved, as one believed, created an obligation to live accordingly, and in this obligation men's responsibility for their actions was maintained.

As we have seen, official Roman Catholicism has in general and for the most part enthusiastically adopted the doctrine of social justice. And, as we have also seen, this doctrine logically eliminates individual responsibility in favor of societal responsibility. Nevertheless, paradoxically, as we have already remarked above (p. 91) the Church has managed to continue to maintain the traditional Christian doctrine of individual responsibility alongside the doctrine of social justice. The only explanation I can see for this strange but welcome fact is that it has not perceived the contradiction. Perhaps if it should once succeed in perceiving it, it might become a little more skeptical about the validity of "social justice" in its current sense.

It might be thought that a religious conception of responsibility has no role to play in a philosophical account of it; worse, that it is precisely what is wrong with the concept of individual responsibility, that it is a product of religious beliefs that have no other foundation than faith or hope. But this particular religious conception is at its core simply the concept of an unbiased observer. I believe this will be clear from the following discussion.

Chapter 7

The Concept of Justice

In the previous chapter we argued that any conception of justice and injustice must necessarily possess certain features in virtue of the fact that they are qualities of ethical evaluation. In particular, like all other ethical qualities, they are qualities of the will. In this chapter, by contrast, we wish to explore rather those qualities of justice and injustice that are unique, distinctive, and peculiar to themselves.

Although justice and injustice are to be found in the will, they are found in it not in isolation, but in its relationship to other wills. And since, as we have also seen, the human will must be considered, and actually is, free, justice can be described as a quality of the free will in relation to other free wills.

The freedom of the will shows itself above all, as we have repeatedly observed, in the power to be moral, to act, when necessary, against one's own interests and inclinations and for another, and is, we argued, the highest form in which the phenomenon of life expresses itself, and so the highest form of being in the universe. With it there appears in the world for the first time natural dignity. Dignity is a worthiness to be respected. A being possessing the astonishing power of free will, which manifests itself especially in the power to be moral, deserves respect. By respect we mean not just any feeling of subservience, but a rational feeling originated by the recognition that something imposes an obligation on me, and together with that a steadfast will to behave in ways that are compatible with that obligation, and especially to avoid the kinds of actions that flout that dignity.

Now we wish to ask what that way is, what that respect entails or consists in. How ought a being with free will to be treated? And since respect is something that only a free will can give, as well as receive, our question is: how ought a being with free will to be treated by other beings with free wills?

Our answer is not complicated, at least in its initial formulation. It is freedom. A free will has the right to receive freedom from other free wills. The freedom of the will in itself is the interior ability above all to act against itself and its own interests, to do what is morally good and right even at detriment to oneself. But while the will's freedom manifests itself most unambiguously in moral action, it is not limited to that. All the voluntary actions of a free will are free. More than that, all the imputable actions of a free will are free. But this interior freedom can only be exercised in action if there is external freedom from coercion, or liberty. An action is just when it respects that liberty. This is our definition of justice. Justice is the quality of a free action in virtue of which it is compatible with the freedom of will of other persons. Not with the particular purposes of other wills, but with their interior freedom.

We owe this viewpoint to Kant. It is the doctrine he develops in the Introduction to his *Rechtslehre*.[253] This does not mean we necessarily endorse everything to be found in the rest of that work, much of which is devoted to conceptions taken from Roman law, though there is little that does not well repay careful investigation.

Our thesis can be arrived at by considering the way justice is ordinarily regarded. For it is a distinguishing feature of justice when compared with other concepts or principles that offenses against it can, in the common view, legitimately be punished by coercion. This is not true of any other virtue. No one believes that imprudence, or intemperance, or cowardice (taken by itself), for example, or any other of the vices or failings that human flesh is heir to can properly be punished by coercion. Why is this? It is because coercion is uniquely hostile to justice. Acts of injustice, all of them in their immense variety, are coercive, and only coercion can balance out and overcome coercion. In itself, coercion is unjust. Only injustice can be punished or abolished by what itself would otherwise be injustice. For only in coercion do we discount, override, and trample on the freedom of will of the other, negating its inherent and natural liberty. What is wrong with coercion is not that it eliminates the object or purpose of the will or prevents that from being achieved, but that it overrides the will's *freedom*.

By contrast, "social injustice" cannot legitimately be punished by coercion. For first, since social injustice is not primarily a quality of will, but of external states of affairs in society, namely inequality, there may be no one to punish. For as we have noted, inequality can arise entirely by accident without anyone intending it or being responsible for it. It is not an action, or the product of an action. Second, there is nothing about inequality or poverty that demands the use of coercion against them. Poverty, though it may limit the effectiveness of the will of the poor, as many other conditions of life do, does not negate, override, and trample on the will's interior freedom. Inequality does not invalidate the will of those who are unequal, as coercion does. On the contrary, it is arguable that both poverty and inequality are more effectively overcome and removed through the voluntary activities of actors in a market economy. And while an injury can be prevented or punished by another injury, discrimination is not an injury. For to constitute an injury, an action must directly worsen the condition of the other person, which discrimination does not do. Discrimination invariably consists in not providing a benefit. But not providing a benefit is very different from inflicting a loss. If I take your property without your permission, I am injuring you because I am negating your freedom. But if I refuse to provide you with a job, I am not injuring you, because I am not negating your freedom but merely leaving you in the condition you were in beforehand.

Discrimination can consist, not in performing any action in regard to the person discriminated against at all, but simply in providing a *benefit to others*. As we have noted above (p. 6), the Swiss pharmaceutical firm Novartis has recently been convicted by a New York court of gender discrimination and subjected to heavy fines: an important part of the evidence was that it paid its salesmen on average $75 a month more than the women. The benefit given to the men was treated as if it were an injury to the women.

As we have remarked, the conception of justice in terms of freedom is in its essentials that of Kant. It is also, with some additions, that of Hegel. For Kant, an action is just when it is such that the freedom of the will of each person can coexist together with the freedom of everyone else in accordance with a universal law. Justice is the sum of those conditions under which the will of one person can be conjoined with the will of another in accordance with a universal law of freedom. The universal law of justice, he writes, is: act externally in such a way that the free use of your will is compatible with the freedom of everyone according to a universal law. For Hegel, freedom is both "the substance of justice and its goal," that is, justice consists in freedom and it produces freedom. The organized system of justice in a society is therefore the realm of "freedom made actual."[254]

Justice as freedom can apply only to deeds, the actions of a person that can have an effect on others. By the same token, it applies only to the relationship of a will to other wills, not to people's wishes, desires, or needs, for these are not questions of freedom. An action may go against another person's wishes, desires, or needs and yet may fully leave him his freedom. The virtue that responds to people's wishes, desires, and needs is benevolence, charity, or humanity.

The concept of justice as respect for freedom is formal or procedural. It says nothing about the content of the will, such as the motivation of the action or the particular purpose it aims to achieve, only about its relationship of harmony with the ability of other wills to act freely. Hegel agrees with this, but adds that there is also a material side to justice in addition. For our part, we hold that justice requires respect for property. Property is not a material concept, however, but a further specification of the formal concept of justice.

What does it mean, to respect another person's freedom of will? The answer to this question is well known. We will set it out in a number of theses.

Thesis 1: *A person's freedom of will is infringed upon when he is subjected to force, the threat of force, or deliberate deception for the purpose of inducing him to perform or not to perform an action.*

The first part of this thesis is not likely to be disputed by many. The most obvious kind of action that transgresses on another's freedom of will is the use of physical force, and *a fortiori* the use of violence or injurious physical force, on his body against his will, since physical force on an individual's body overrides his will altogether. It can do this in a variety of ways: by directly causing harm to the person, for example by killing or injuring him; by compelling him directly to perform an action, as can happen when he is placed under arrest; and by constraining him from acting, as imprisonment does.

To be unjust an action must not only use physical force on the body of a person, but do so against his will. The use of physical force, even injurious force, on the body of a person who knowingly and willingly permits it, as in surgery, cannot be unjust. But it may be immoral on other grounds, as may be argued in the case of actions such as suicide and dueling.

The second part of the thesis has been the subject of more debate. The threat to use force against me if I should perform an action certainly infringes on my freedom of will. But it does not remove my physical ability to act. Nor does it automatically remove or even lessen my will to act. It is up to me to decide whether to give in to the threat or to perform the action. I still, therefore, bear some responsibility for my action or lack of it. The extent of the infringement depends on several factors: the extent of the force threatened, the credibility of the threat, and in the case where the threat is conditional on the threatened person performing or not performing some action, the nature of the action. Supposing that the action demanded should be extremely serious (e.g. an assassination), but the force threatened trivial and the threat incredible, it would not ordinarily be considered that the individual's freedom was significantly reduced; he would undoubtedly be judged severely if he carried out the assassination.

Whereas if the action forbidden were of small importance, but the force threatened grave and the threat credible, the normal conclusion would surely be that the individual's freedom was severely impaired. But if the force threatened was equally grave and the threat equally credible as in this latter case, yet the action demanded was extremely serious, it would normally not be considered that the individual's freedom was overridden. The greater seriousness of the action demanded counterbalances the force threatened, so that a higher degree of force is required to annul the individual's freedom.

It is generally agreed, thirdly, that an individual's freedom of will in regard to the doing of some action is reduced or eliminated by another person's lie, when the lie is told deliberately in order to induce him to perform or omit that action. This is what we mean by fraud. Fraud and force are alike in overriding another's freedom – and indeed they are paradigms of treating another as a means in violation of Kant's second formulation of the categorical imperative.

The term we will use for all these infringements on the freedom of the will is coercion. It is true that in recent philosophical literature this word has come generally to be restricted to threats to use force, rather than including the use itself of force. But popular usage retains the more comprehensive sense, as can be seen from any dictionary, and for our purposes here it is helpful to have one word for everything that we mean, in order to avoid constant repetition of "force, the threat of force and lies told in order to induce a person to perform or omit an action."

Why, however, it may be asked, make so much fuss about coercion? There are many kinds of restriction on our choices and coercion is only one of them. If I wish to fly to North Korea but cannot because I have no money for a ticket, this is a very effective restraint on my desire. How is it essentially different from the North Korean government policy that prohibits me from doing so, or even from being unable to fly because I am in jail?

The difference between coercion and other limits on freedom of choice lies not so much in restrictions or lack of restrictions in themselves as in the immense difference between initiative and activity on the one hand and passivity on the other that the different kinds of restriction involve. Under coercion my actions are nothing more than the continuation of previously existing forces. But in the absence of coercion I can initiate action and creating a new beginning. If the police arrest me, putting handcuffs on me and compelling me to go with them to the police station, my action in going with them is entirely the product of their action and contains no component of mine. But when I do the action of my own free will, I am the initiator of the action, it is my creation, it is something new in the universe, which would not have happened unless I had willed it, and it belongs to me. It is to that extent an embodiment of my personality.

As we have pointed out, the concept of justice is everywhere considered to provide a justification for the use of force to correct injustice. This can only be because it is recognized at least implicitly that every injustice already itself involves a use and misuse of force. Injustice can be punished by coercion because coercion can be punished by coercion. Justice is coercive because injustice is always coercive.

There are degrees of disrespect for a person's freedom of will that fall short of coercion. They are generally not felt to be as serious. Many of them are considered cases of faulty character or bad manners rather than strict injustice. See the discussion below on desert and ingratitude, p. 183.

Since justice entails freedom from coercion, a certain kind of coercion is necessarily if paradoxically justified, as we have observed above, namely the coercion necessary to prevent or punish unjust coercion. Kant has explained this clearly enough.

> Any opposition that counteracts the hindrance of an effect promotes that effect and is consistent with it. Now, everything that is unjust is a hindrance to freedom according to universal laws. Coercion, however, is a hindrance or opposition to freedom. Consequently, if a certain use of freedom is itself a hindrance to freedom according to universal laws (i.e. unjust), then the use of coercion to counteract it, inasmuch as it is the prevention of a hindrance to freedom, is consistent with freedom according to universal laws; in other words, this use of coercion is just. It follows by the law of contradiction that justice (*Recht*) is united with the entitlement to use coercion against anyone who violates justice (*Recht*).[255]

Yet in 1799, only two years after publishing this treatise on justice, Kant published a short essay, "On a Supposed Right to Lie because of Philanthropic Concerns," in which he maintained that telling a lie under any circumstances whatever was unjust, even if it caused no harm to any individual, but rather brought a benefit, for example by preventing a murder, because every lie "wrongs mankind," "vitiating the source of justice." But this is a case of Homer nodding. The use of a lie to prevent a hindrance to freedom, such as robbery or murder, is just as consistent with freedom as the use of force in similar circumstances would be. For this reason moralists have traditionally allowed the use of deception against the enemy in a just war.

All three of these as categories of unjust action are fairly uncontroversial: the use of force, the threat of force, and deliberate deception for the purpose of causing another to perform or omit an action. The application of our criterion of justice to them may help us to understand better *why* they are considered unjust, but it is not generally needed in order to convince us *that* they are unjust. But there are other categories of actions that in modern times have been very much in dispute as to their justice and injustice. One of these is the private ownership of property; others are acts of bias, discrimination and unequal treatment.

Property

Ownership

Pierre-Joseph Proudhon is famous for having asserted that "property is theft."[256] It is not so widely known that he arrived later in life at the view that "property is freedom."[257] What the founder of peaceful anarchism meant by property in the two cases was admittedly somewhat different: in the first that of large landowners and capitalists, whom he considered analogous to the exploitative state; in the second, that of craftsmen and peasants obtained through their own labor. Still, in this second opinion he came closer to the truth. The greatest threat to human freedom, he argues, comes from the state.[258] There must be a counterweight to the State, Proudhon argues, and it can only be private property.

> A State constituted even in the most rational, the most liberal manner, animated by the best of intentions, is none the less an enormous power, capable of crushing everything around it, unless a counter-weight is created against it. What can that counter-weight be? . . . Where can we find a power capable of balancing out this formidable power of the State? Only in property. If you collect together all the forces of property, you will have a power equal to that of the State.[259]

Proudhon placed a restriction on property, that it could be just only to the extent that it was earned by personal labor. Though a self-proclaimed revolutionary, he was in this respect insufficiently so, but adhered to the traditional conception that economic value was objective. For like Adam Smith and Karl Marx he fell victim to Locke's seductive labor theory of value, and to a particularly restrictive form of it, about which we will see more below.

In the meantime, the thesis we wish to defend can be formulated in Proudhon's words: property is freedom.

We agree with Proudhon's argument that property provides a powerful counterweight to the power of the State. But we do not consider that this can provide a moral foundation for property, for this is an argument from need, and we do not argue that the right to own property is derived from need. Need cannot create a right. What is at stake in the ownership of property and what ultimately justifies it is the freedom of the individual human will which creates it. Ownership is a part of natural liberty. Liberty means that I have the right to do as I please, so long as no injury is inflicted on another. The right to own property consists in the ability to exclude others from using it. But no one is injured by being excluded from the use of any particular object. For to injure a person is to infringe upon his freedom of will, and your ownership of an object does not infringe on my freedom of will, nor mine on yours. The freedom of my will is not negated and trampled on by the fact that you own an object, say an acre of land. As Kant remarks, my will to use an object as I please does not conflict with the law of external freedom. It is therefore possible for an individual to own an object absolutely, in the full and complete sense of the word. This includes the right to destroy it, always on condition that no one else is thereby harmed.

To own an object means that I have a relation to it of such a nature that anyone else who uses it against my will, or who hinders me from using it as I wish, does me an injury – the injury, namely, of infringing on my legitimate freedom of will.[260]

Property is the embodiment of the individual will. To own an object is, as Hegel expresses it, to "put my will into" it. I can do this to any "thing." There is no thing that cannot be owned. The concept of a "thing" stands in contrast to that of person. Persons cannot be owned, since they are ends in themselves. They are free subjects, and to own them is to abolish their freedom, to reduce them from person to thing, so that in effect they are depersonalized. They cannot be owned as persons, but only owned as something else – as chattels. Properly speaking we do not even own ourselves, for whatever we own we can destroy. But we have an obligation to respect ourselves, as we respect other persons, since we possess freedom of will as they do, and the dignity that comes from that. There are actions we may not do toward ourselves without degrading ourselves. A thing, by contrast, is what is different from a person. In Hegel's words again, a thing is something "not free, not personal, without rights." Things do not belong to themselves; unlike persons, they are not ends in themselves; they are brought into the realm of purpose and meaning by the human will. Human beings, and all rational beings, have an absolute right of appropriation over all things.

A thing is always something external to a person. Something that is an integral part of a person, such as a limb or organ, is never merely a thing.

Ownership consists in having authority over a thing. This is different from simple power. If I have an apple in my hand, I have power over it and can eat it or throw it away. But to have authority over it is to have the right or moral power to do that, in contrast to others who do not have that right.

In property, as Hegel remarks, my will becomes objective to me. This is why property can be private and exclusive. My property is the embodiment of my will. If a piece of property is of such a nature that it can be owned by a number of people in common, this is a partnership, in which each person's ownership of his share is an embodiment of his personal voluntary preference.

The right to own property Hegel appropriately calls "the right of personality." That is, it is a right that comes immediately with the possession of personhood, with the fact that one is a person, because it is the embodiment of what is most distinctive of the person, his freedom of will. All persons and only persons can own property.

Against this thesis of the absolute right to own private property, however, it is asserted that there must be ethical and legal limits on the right of exclusion, since otherwise a person could starve to death in the midst of plenty. In other words, although ordinary need may not create a right, extreme need does create one. This has the appearance of being a serious difficulty, but it is not the simple one it is often made out to be. For all its presumably good intentions and its emotional force, it is an incoherent conception. "Need" is not an objective concept but a subjective one. It is in the eye of the beholder. I may consider that you have great need of something, but you may reject that view. The demand to pass an objective judgment on a subjective reality cannot be met, or at least cannot be met rationally.

A right is something that must in principle be capable of being calculated by a court. How will the court make this calculation? If 100 people can be expected on average to die from all causes every day in a particular city, all of whose lives could be extended by at least some amount by medication or food or other remedy, and all of whom therefore have need of them, what precise quantity of medication or food or other remedy belonging to which precise people should the court take from those people and give to which of the dying in order to extend their lives by what length of time? This calculation is impossible to make in any objective fashion. Contrast this with stealing medication or food from them: the calculation of what to repay them is objective and easy.

To make need the basis of a right is to endorse a right to rescue. But the Common law has never recognized a right to rescue. The purpose of the Common law is to settle disputes, but failure to rescue cannot be the ground of a dispute. For no criminal can be identified. If you have stolen my car, your identity as the criminal is established by the historical chain of action that removed the car out of my possession. But if I have an accident and a hundred people drive by without rescuing me, which of them can be singled out as the criminal? The first? But perhaps she had a good reason not to stop. Several U.S. states have now legislated a right to rescue, but the legislation is generally ignored and not enforced. There is a good reason for this. Even in Europe, where civilian law reigns and so the imposition of a right to rescue is much easier, enforcement is rare.[261]

Hegel considers that in extraordinary circumstances the state (and only the state) may cancel private ownership. It is difficult to disagree with this entirely, since complex and tangled situations can develop in the course of history where this seems the only possible solution. Yet there is no easy theoretical criterion for when circumstances are extraordinary.

Thesis 2: *No one's freedom of will is infringed upon by the fact that another individual has exclusive ownership of an object.*

Original acquisition

If a person has just possession of an item, and transfers it to another person by just means, then the resulting distribution is just, as Robert Nozick has rightly argued. But assuming no one has possessed it before, how do we obtain just possession of the object in the first place? Locke argued that we accomplish this by our labor. We own ourselves, and so we own our labor. When we "mix" our labor with the item, we come to own it. The truth of this is seen most clearly in the case of the creation of a work of art. It is generally recognized that whoever creates a work of art owns it (provided no one else already owns the materials or is paying for his time, etc.). He has imposed a new form on the material, which links him to it in a unique way, and this link perseveres even if he becomes separated from it spatially. The object exists as his creation independently of him. The validity of this argument is not limited to works of art; but applies equally to the cultivation of the soil, the growing of food and the breeding of animals, and wherever human labor bestows a new form on a natural object.

But although Locke's argument invoking labor to explain possession is valid, it is not necessary. In order to obtain initial or original just possession of an item that has not belonged to anyone else, all that is necessary is (a) to take physical possession or occupancy of it, (b) to have the will to make it one's own, and (c) to declare or otherwise make evident that we will to exclude others from owning it.

Physical possession or occupancy is an important part of original acquisition because the right of property is an exclusive right to use objects, and one can use an object only by physically controlling or occupying it. If an object has never before had an owner, we must take physical possession of it in order to use it. Furthermore, just because my property is the embodiment of my will, my interior and invisible will alone that some object should be mine is not enough to make it so. I must occupy it or take physical possession of it so that its status as my property will be recognizable to others.[262]

In order to own an object, it is not enough, however, to control it or occupy it *de facto*. We must have the will to own it. Our will to own it is *the* central and decisive condition of ownership. An object that accidentally falls under my control but that I have no desire to own does not become my property.

Again, it is not enough to control or occupy the object, and to have the interior and secret will to own it, but I must also manifest publicly my will to own it in some way to others. There are many ways of doing this, some formal and some informal. It can be done simply by placing a mark on the object.

How far does the right of first ownership extend? How much of an object can I acquire as its owner in this way? Locke answers in terms of use. "As much as any one can make use of to any advantage of life before it spoils." The reference to spoilage seems to suggest he has in mind mainly food. But this is too restrictive. The better answer is in terms of control, that is as much as I have the physical ability to exclude others from.[263] This includes Locke's condition, since in order to use objects I must control them; but it also extends further, for example to the possession of land. Control is a more appropriate criterion because it applies to all kinds of property, not only food, and it goes with occupancy and physical possession. It also has more recognition in international law, for example in fixing the extent of territorial waters.

One takes possession of a natural object and makes it one's property for a purpose: to serve a need. Property is for use. My use of it is the external manifestation of my need. Some people conclude from this close relationship between ownership and use that a property that is not used loses its ownership. But this is a mistake. The decisive thing in my ownership of an object is my will to own it. This can intend future use, or future use conditional on need. Ownership does not require actual need or actual use.

On the other hand, if a person has complete use of an object, the right to use it in every way, including destruction of it, then he owns it. There is no difference between total right of use, and ownership.

But if the will to own and to use an object entirely evaporates, ownership lapses; the object becomes ownerless. This happens to public monuments that were significant in the past history of a society but are now abandoned and no longer honored or cared for. Many monuments and works of art which were created in ancient societies but have since lost meaning for their successor-societies have been saved by Western nations that appreciated their significance. Now, tutored by the West in the historic values of these monuments, the successors of these ancient societies wish to be recognized as their owners, and demand their restitution. But it is too late for that: by losing interest in these objects and monuments, in some cases for a thousand or two thousand years, they lost their rights of ownership over them to others willing to honor them and care for them.[264]

Since the central fact in my ownership of anything is my will to own it, I have the power to give up this will and either discard the object or give it or sell it to another. Not everything, however, which can be possessed can be discarded or sold. As we saw, persons cannot be either owned or sold, because the defining quality of the person is his dignity stemming from his freedom of will. My property is always something external to me. The question is sometimes asked as if it were a puzzle, whether a person can sell himself into slavery. But one cannot sell one's right to life: as the Declaration of Independence states, there are rights that are inalienable. Can I sell my kidney? I can give it as a gift to a member of my family who needs one, and even to a person outside the family as an exceptional act of charity. But to sell a vital organ as if it were an ordinary external commercial object is degrading. I do not have that kind of ownership rights over my kidney, any more than over myself. My kidney is not my property, any more than I can be property. It is an integral part of myself. In judging whether an action is degrading, however, we should not look only at the external action: the motive of the action plays an important role. An action done for the sole purpose of aiding another person must be judged differently from the same action done in order to make money, even where the purpose of the money is to save my own life. Should actions that are degrading be prohibited by law? That would be going too far: the coercive penalties of the law can only be justified as remedies for coercive wrong.

Thesis 3: *Property is sacred.*

What is sacred is set apart and forbidden (Durkheim[265]). It is to be treated with respect and reverence; it is taboo, inviolable. This holds for every person, and it holds also of the rights of persons over what belongs to them, because their property is the embodiment of their will. We have no right to interfere with a person's will or action, to put our will above theirs, unless it causes or threatens harm to others; for the same reason we have no right to interfere with another's property. As Plato puts it,

> You shall not, if you can help, touch that which is mine, or remove the least thing which belongs to me without my consent; and may I be of sound mind, and do to others as I would that they should do to me.[266]

The sacredness of property is not merely an ideology of the powerful, much less the inertia of a thoughtless convention. What is at stake in property is the freedom of the human will and respect for that freedom. Property is sacred because the freedom of the will of each individual human being is sacred. A person who denies that the human will is free is no doubt unlikely to see the sacredness of property, but he is also unlikely to see the sacredness of human existence. For there can be nothing sacred about a machine or purely mechanical causation. If a person is to have respect for human dignity, the first requisite is to respect the freedom of each and every human will. This includes having respect for one's own dignity and therefore one's own freedom of will. It is easy enough when we do something we ought not to do to excuse ourselves by saying we were compelled to do it. Perhaps in some sense we may be, yet not in a sense that relieves us of our responsibility.

The moral argument for property is not an argument from need, as if the fact that we need property laid a foundation for a right to it, although this argument is often made. As we have noted above, need cannot create a right. For a genuine right is a claim that can be legitimately enforced through coercion, and the sole fact that a person needs something cannot be the foundation for using coercion to fill that need, since only unjust coercion can justify the use of coercion to remedy it. The right to property comes from a genuine right, the natural right to freedom, the freedom of our will.

Legitimate liberty is sacred, and Hegel is right to say that property is the first embodiment of legitimate liberty. To attack any person's property is to attack the person, because it is to attack the freedom of his will to make the arrangements he considers necessary or desirable for his existence. Your property causes me no harm, nor mine you. On the contrary, for anyone who understands what it means to exchange something freely with someone, which is of course the most basic concept of economics and the foundation on which our economic life depends, the exclusive possession of property by individuals is an indispensable condition for material progress.

If we do not have the freedom to acquire property, it is hard to see what freedom we can have. This is true not merely of the amount of property we need to live, but of any amount of it.

Although the moral right to own property is not grounded on its economic consequences but on ethical values, the economic effects of a regime of respect for property make a strong consequentialist or prudential argument for it. An example of this is the matter of incentives, which in economics is a question of decisive importance. If anyone can take freely what you have labored on, you have no incentive to labor on anything. The first prerequisite for any society that wishes to make material progress is to have firm laws guaranteeing strict property rights.

This is not to say, however, that every conception of property is equally valid. In the theory of the feudal system, all land belonged to the king, who was considered to earn this right in battle and who could dispose of it as he wished by bestowing it on his followers. But this is an exaggeration of the rights of kings. The sole fact that one army defeats an enemy army, even in a just war, though it may transfer the rights of ownership over governmental property to the victor, does not negate and destroy or bestow on the victor the rights of the existing private owners of property, even though they are enemies. Locke recognizes this explicitly. The true role of the king is to acknowledge and defend the existing just ownership rights of individuals. Yet in England it is still the rule that all title to land must ultimately be traceable to royal grant.

Poverty

Although poverty and inequality are often mentioned in the same breath by some, they are far from being the same thing. Poverty is a quality of an individual, but inequality is a relationship between two or more individuals. The logic of these two concepts is different. Poverty no doubt limits the range of choices available to the poor person, and if freedom of the will should be mistakenly defined as an objective range of choices, then poverty is a condition of limited freedom of the will. But we have seen that the inherent or essential freedom of the will is not that, but like the will itself something wholly interior and subjective. In the absence of coercion, the sole fact of poverty does not infringe on the freedom of will of the poor person. What infringes on any person's freedom of will is coercion, which is exercised not by facts or states of affairs but by other persons.

The idea of poverty is properly not that of a condition that may be merely temporary, as of persons who happen to lose all their possessions owing to a natural disaster and are destitute, but a more or less permanent and hopeless state of affairs in which people's lives are inextricably mired. Graduate students in America may live on tiny incomes, but are not for that reason judged "poor." In pre-capitalist societies permanent poverty was ordinary and the fate of most people, but with the discovery of the power of free trade and the capitalist system of production, it came widely to be felt that this no longer needed to be the case. In American society everyone had the power to do well through hard work, and, as the mass immigration of the nineteenth and twentieth centuries testified, it came to be felt that there was no reason for anybody to be poor in America except through some deficiency of character. One was ashamed to be poor, and so far as possible pretended not to be. One tried to "keep up appearances." The word "poverty" sounded alien and overwrought, as something that belonged only to remote and primitive societies. Even during the Great Depression, when times were very hard indeed, few people spoke of their poverty, so far as I can discover. After the Second World War, "poverty" as a distinct phenomenon was still little noticed in the United States until the publication of *The Other America: Poverty in the United States* (New York: Macmillan) published by the socialist and formerly Roman Catholic writer Michael Harrington in 1962.

Just as a single book, Rachel Carson's *Silent Spring*, also published in 1962, can be said to have essentially launched the environmental movement, so Harrington's book effectively launched the poverty movement. I am not saying that poverty did not exist or was not a very serious problem, on the contrary, but that the public attitude toward it changed dramatically at that time, from something it was considered one had good reason to be ashamed of, and that was not discussed publicly, as being one's own private responsibility, to something that was the responsibility of society and should be eliminated by action of government. It was understood at the time that the "other America" was chiefly black. Then, within a few short months, the scene changed dramatically. The book made a tremendous impact on the national consciousness, as only those who were alive at the time will remember. The publicity it was given directly influenced the policies of the Kennedy and Johnson administrations, lying at the origin of Mr. Johnson's War on Poverty, of the Civil Rights Act of 1964, and the Social Security Act of 1965.[267]

Equality

We should not speak of the injustice of nature in the unequal distribution of possessions and resources, because nature is not free and is therefore neither just nor unjust.[268]

Human beings are equal in their moral dignity because they each equally possess freedom of will. That is, they are equal as persons, in the rational human nature and personhood from which possession springs. What follows from this is that they have an equal right to possess property, not a right to possess equal property. Justice does not require that everybody should possess the same amount of property, but that everybody should be equally able to possess property, that is should not be coercively prevented from gaining property.[269]

Even if a materially equal society should happen to be created, it would quickly become unequal, because the possession of material goods depends on human industriousness. Goods are not a stable possession but are consumed and must be replaced. But if a project cannot in principle be carried out, arguably it ought not to be carried out.[270] Robert Nozick has shown that any artificial pattern imposed on a society by force must destroy freedom, and freedom in its turn destroys patterns.

Inequality is by no means necessarily the product of coercion. The fact that my income is a thousandth part of someone else's, or that this state of affairs prevails between different segments of society, does not infringe upon the freedom of will of those who are less equal.

Thesis 4: *In the absence of coercion, neither poverty nor inequality infringes upon the freedom of will of the poor.*

Fairness

Fairness is a genuine virtue, and all things else being equal there is a moral obligation to be fair, but fairness is not the same as justice. Whatever is unjust is *ipso facto* unfair, but not everything that is unfair is necessarily unjust.

A claim in fairness is a genuine moral claim. An unfair action is more than a mere absence of kindness or charity: treating someone unfairly is not like refusing to make a donation to a charitable cause. There may be no moral obligation to make a charitable donation, but there is a moral obligation to be fair. Fairness has a moral foundation and is a true virtue. But while true injustice always involves coercion, unfairness does not, and therefore coercion cannot be rightly used to remedy it. A literary critic's comments on a novel by an author he does not like may be unfair, but even the most distraught author, provided he lives in a democratic society, is unlikely to demand the critic should go to jail. Consider again the well-known parable in the New Testament about the landowner who contracts with laborers to work in his vineyard (see above, p. 113). To those who came to work late in the day he pays as much as to those who commenced early. The latter thereupon expect more, which seems only fair, since they had worked longer, and when they do not receive it, but only what they contracted for, accuse the owner of unfairness. But the owner's response is that he has committed no injustice, since they receive what they bargained for: he has not employed any coercion against them, he has not robbed or defrauded them. It follows that they cannot take him to court. It is easy under some circumstances to slip from one to the other, from the concept of fairness to that of justice and vice versa, since all actions that are unjust are unfair. The person who treats another unjustly also always treats him unequally. But the proposition cannot be reversed: it is not the case that an unfair action is always unjust. The coercive power of the law, which can rightly be used to remedy injustice, cannot be rightly used to remedy unfairness.

Again, it is widely assumed that unequal treatment, that is peaceful discrimination, is unjust. We have already discussed this question in Chapter 5 above. But for the sake of completeness we will here reiterate our conclusion.

Thesis 5: *In the absence of coercion, unequal treatment does not infringe on the freedom of the will of those so treated.*

Ronald Dworkin makes a distinction between two sorts of rights people may be said to have. The first is the right to "equal treatment," which he describes as the right to an equal distribution of some opportunity or resource or burden. Every citizen, for example, he believes, has a right to an equal vote in a democracy. The second is the right to "treatment as an equal." This is the right, he states, not to receive the same distribution of some burden or benefit, but to be treated with the same respect and concern as anyone else.[271] Dworkin considers that the right to treatment as an equal is fundamental and the right to equal treatment derivative. In some circumstances the right to treatment as an equal will entail a right to equal treatment, he states, but not in all circumstances. Dworkin employs this distinction to justify reverse discrimination, such as discrimination against majority whites in order to promote minority blacks, since the whites would be treated as equals (he asserts) even though they would not receive equal treatment, while ruling out "ordinary" discrimination against blacks. In his view "a more equal society is a better society even if its citizens prefer inequality."

Dworkin believes that the Equal Protection clause of the US Constitution confers "an individual right to equality," and that that should be interpreted as a right to be treated as an equal.[272]

But injustice, as we have argued, consists in coercion, except where coercion is needed to remedy unjust coercion. The decisive consideration in regard to discrimination is whether the discrimination is peaceful or coercive. Coercive discrimination against either whites or blacks is unjust, not because it is discrimination but because it is coercive; peaceful discrimination, whether it is against blacks or whites, not being coercive, cannot be unjust. It will be sufficiently obvious to the reader by now that not treating a person as an equal is by no means the same as using coercion on him. Therefore:

Thesis 6: *In the absence of coercion, "not to be treated as an equal" does not infringe on one's freedom of will.*

It is a misreading of the U.S. Constitution to take it as conferring an individual right to economic equality or equality of power. The Fourteenth Amendment, sometimes alleged to confer such a right, asserts only that no State may deny to any person within its jurisdiction "the equal protection of the laws." The plain meaning of this is that within each State the laws must be enforced by the government of the State without favoritism.

Aristotle

In order to bring out the difference of our own theory, we will briefly review some other theories of justice and their relation to our own. In Aristotle's conception justice is always a quality of the will, rather than of objective states of affairs which are not the product of will, and to this extent his view is in agreement with our own. Beyond that, justice in general as explained by Aristotle consists in due proportion. A just distribution of profits is one proportionate to the original investment, or more generally to the ground of the distribution, a just price is one proportionate to the object's value, a just penalty one proportionate to the crime, a just criticism one proportionate to the fault. There are two basic kinds of justice: justice in distribution and corrective justice; and the latter is of two further kinds, justice in exchange and criminal justice (Nic. Eth. Bk. 5, chapter 3).

Our thesis, by contrast, is that an action is just when it respects the freedom of will of others and unjust when it does not. Aristotle's exclusive interpretation of justice as proportion and injustice as disproportion, while in a sense true (we will see more about this below), is inadequate to explain the wickedness of serious injustice. When Cornwall puts Gloucester's eyes out in *King Lear*, this is more than a case of disproportion. What makes Cornwall's action unjust is that it injures Gloucester against Gloucester's will. If Gloucester had freely consented to it, it would not have been unjust.[273]

Let us take as an example of justice in distribution the act of a man distributing to himself and his partner the proceeds of a trading voyage. The just distribution will be the one proportionate to their respective investments, says Aristotle: one partner, let us say, has contributed twice as much as the other, and therefore should receive twice as much of the proceeds. But in our view this proportion holds only because it is agreed to and is voluntary. A situation can be imagined where for some reason the agreement is to divide the proceeds in a different ratio, such as three or four to one, perhaps because of family considerations or some non-commercial gratitude or who knows what. In that case that will be the just distribution. A distribution in which the distributor "gives too much to himself and not enough to his partner" will be unjust, not because of the abstract proportion, but because it is against what was agreed to and is coercive. Aristotle's views on this question are influenced by his common but mistaken assumption that exchange values have objective existence. For he believes that for an exchange to take place, the value of the goods exchanged must be equal. This overlooks the fact that the goods are valued differently by the two sides. The buyer values the goods he buys more than he values the money he pays for them, while the seller values the money he receives for his goods more than he values the goods themselves. It is true Aristotle recognizes that the correct unit for measuring the exchange value of goods is demand, but he does not allow for the difference in demand between the two sides, which is the true explanation of the exchange (Nic. Eth., V, 5).

Aristotle and many others have accepted the concept of a "just price," which was the price equal to the value of the goods, on the supposition that that value is objective. Locke, Adam Smith, and Marx held this view, and considered that the value of anything exchanged was created by the quantity of labor that went into making it. But the truth was stated by Hobbes:

the just price of any item is whatever anyone is willing to pay for it. More recently this truth was emphasized by the members of the so-called Austrian School of economics. Economic or exchange value is not objective, but subjective. It is a matter of voluntary agreement. It is dependent therefore on time. The economic value of my house today is whatever anyone is willing to pay for it today. Tomorrow it may be very different.

As explained by other writers, beginning with Plato, justice consists in rationality, so that an injustice is always an irrational action. This needs to be properly understood: it does not mean there cannot be reasons for an unjust action. Obviously there can be reasons of a certain kind, but they are outweighed by others that are of a more fundamental nature and more powerful.

For Plato, justice is first and foremost a quality of the soul, namely a soul governed by reason. The soul, he states, consists of three parts, desire, spirit, and reason, and when the soul is rightly ordered the power of reason controls the other two (*Republic*). We have no difficulty agreeing with this. It is entirely rational to respect the freedom of will of persons and to avoid coercion. To do that it is no doubt necessary for reason to control our desires and spirit (in the Platonic sense). Plato is far from holding anything even resembling a theory of social justice.

But a serious injustice seems to be more and worse than merely irrational. To describe the gas chambers at Auschwitz as irrational, however true it may be, does not seem to capture the enormity of what was done. An action may be exceedingly irrational yet not be unjust. Every unjust action is no doubt irrational, but the proposition cannot be reversed.

Moral values cannot be explained by reducing them to nonmoral values. If moral values are to be explained as a demand of rationality, as they are explained by Plato and Aristotle, it cannot be merely rationality in general but must be a special moral kind of rationality. If moral values are to be explained as a form of coherence, as they are explained by Kant, it cannot be mere coherence in general but must be a special moral kind of coherence. It is not mere incoherence in general that would lead a person to say he would not be able to live with himself if he did a certain unjust deed: some degree of incoherence is part of human life. If moral values are to be explained as a form of utility, as they are by Mill, it cannot be mere utility in general but must be a special moral kind of utility. But then in all these cases what is distinctive and special about moral values must still be accounted for.

Criminal justice raises the question of desert.

Desert

Desert is a consequence of the freedom of the will, and of the fact that the justice of an action consists in its compatibility with freedom of the will. It is only in virtue of the fact that persons possess free will and could have acted differently from the way they did that they can deserve to be treated in a certain way. A being that does not possess free will cannot deserve anything. If, as we argue, human beings possess free will, and are therefore responsible for their actions and answerable for them to others, and if justice means respecting that freedom of will, it means also recognizing and respecting the fact that people are as we have just described them: responsible for their actions and accountable for them to others. Justice means, therefore, treating people in accordance with their actions, that is, with their deserts. Those who use their freedom to do good deserve to receive good in return, and those who use it to do harm deserve to receive harm in return. This is natural desert. According to true or genuine justice, there is such a thing as innocence, and such a thing as guilt; there can be such a thing as praise and such a thing as blame; there can be reward and there can be punishment. To treat people as they deserve is to honor their freedom of will and their dignity as rational beings. Not only just reward but also just punishment is a form of respect. This is why Plato's Socrates could say that punishment heals the soul, and why Hegel could hold that the criminal has a *right* to punishment.

A criminal deserves a punishment proportionate to his crime. A person who wishes to prevent such punishment makes himself complicit in the crime. To impose a heavier punishment than the criminal deserves is to commit a new crime.

In the view of John Rawls, however, there is no such thing as natural desert. For no one deserves his natural endowments, Rawls argues, and so no one deserves what he accomplishes with them. We do not deserve even our own moral character, because many factors besides our own actions have contributed to making it possible for us to have that character. Only within the framework of some institution, such as an agreement or a promise, can it make sense to talk of desert, he believes. If the organizers of the race have promised that the first one past the post wins the prize, and if you are the first one past the post, then you deserve to win the prize. But if no one has made such a promise, you do not deserve to win.[274] Of course, if we do not deserve our good character, it should follow, though strangely he does not discuss this, that we also do not deserve our bad one, and so we do not deserve to be penalized for the crimes we commit. Although Rawls does not draw this conclusion explicitly, many have.

Even if it is true that we do not deserve our natural talents, however, that does not prevent them from being rightly ours. I do not deserve my existence, but anyone who takes it away from me commits a crime. If someone gives me a gift, say for my birthday, it may well be that I don't deserve it, but that does not make his action in giving it, or mine in accepting it, unjust. A gift may be given precisely *because* it is undeserved. People are entitled to give gifts, and to accept them. When they accept them, they own them, and anyone who takes them away by force commits the crime of theft, which deserves punishment. But if your natural talents are rightly yours, then what you achieve by using them is also rightly yours. The thesis that there is no such thing as natural desert is little more than another way of denying that there is freedom of the will.

But Aristotle refuted that viewpoint decisively in pointing out that it depends on us, it is "up to us," what kind of character we have, because everyone knows that our character is built up over time by our behavior, for which we are responsible. That other factors also contributed is irrelevant. Nothing is ever accomplished without luck; but that does not mean that all accomplishment is mere luck. It is right to admire a person for his excellent character. Suppose that someone has had every conceivable advantage in regard to leading an ethical life, has had exemplary parents, teachers, and friends, good instruction, and no temptations arising from poverty, ill health, etc. It was still possible for him to fail calamitously, because his will is free. You might say it was unlikely, but it was not impossible, and in actual fact such things happen not infrequently. If it did not happen in this case, that is to his credit.

Contract

Contracts are binding only because they are a product of free will. When two persons make an agreement, their free wills are joined; each offers to suffer a loss to the other in order to obtain a gain from the other. Each one thereby has an obligation to provide for the other what he has agreed to provide, for if he fails to do this, while the other does it, he causes the other to suffer a loss without the gain that justified it. The obligation exists only because it has been entered into freely. A person coerced to give consent is under no moral obligation to keep the contract. In which case neither is the other. Although there may be an appearance of a contract, there is no contract.

This also applies to conditional coercion. A law which states: if you employ A, you must also employ B, whether you wish to or not, coerces the employer into hiring B if he hires A. This is an infringement on the employer's free will, and the resulting contract of employment with B is an empty formality which, whatever power may be bestowed on it by the law, is devoid of moral force.

Justice as a Virtue

We have argued that justice is a quality of the will and of actions, and can be a quality of states of affairs in society only in so far as they are the product of a will that can be responsible and accountable for them. Since justice is a quality of actions and of the will, it is also a quality of personal character: it is a virtue. What does it mean, to possess this virtue? What are the qualities of a just person?

In recent decades the school of "virtue ethics" has drawn attention to the importance of moral virtue, and not only of moral action, for the ethical life and for moral education. An important motive for leading an ethical life is the desire, not only to do the right thing in particular cases, but to be a certain kind of person: to be generous, or kind, or truthful, or just. The idea or the aim of becoming a more generous person is a powerful incentive to think about and to do the particular kinds of action that a generous person does, and similarly the aim of becoming a more just person provides a strong motive to do the kinds of actions that a just person does. Moral education means, among other things, showing the attractiveness of those kinds of personal character, and their superiority over their opposites, so that they become deeply rooted in the individual's heart.

From the viewpoint of the socialistic conception of social justice, however, concern for the personal virtue of justice is misguided, for, as we have seen, according to it one's personal character is the product of one's environment and not something the individual is truly responsible for. The social justice school believes that the harmony of society depends on objective economic equality. From the perspective of ordinary justice, however, the question of subjective personal character is of paramount importance. In our ordinary dealings with others, we consider nothing more important than the moral quality of the person we are dealing with. For the state of society itself, the truth is that peace and harmony depend in the first place on how its citizens act toward one another, and so on the moral quality of its citizens' character. This is not something that can be replaced by societal "structures," for the structures themselves depend on it. There may be laws, but whether there is the rule of law depends on whether the members of the society demand that of one another. It is for good reasons that the first question we typically ask ourselves, consciously or unconsciously, when dealing with someone for the first time is: what kind of a moral character does this person have?

What kind of person, then, is one who is just? It may seem at first sight that this kind of character is not so attractive as those of other virtues. The person who is generous inspires others to be generous; the one who is kind can stimulate others to be kind; but the person whose paramount quality is a respect for the demands of justice will possibly be thought, by contrast, censorious and severe. Hume describes it as "the cautious, jealous" virtue. Yet if we are once the victims of injustice, we may speedily discover the desirability of having those who "hunger and thirst for justice."

The description of the just man given by Plato's Socrates (see above, p. 121) provides a good starting point for an account of justice as a virtue. As we pointed out, he teaches that justice is first and foremost a quality of the soul. This is already a valuable and penetrating observation. It is of course wholly at odds with the socialistic conception of social justice, which has no room for the soul. But more than that, it points out that the virtue of justice is not merely a matter of repeating certain external actions or even of having the habit or custom of so doing. For it is possible to imagine such a custom as something superficial, merely the result of one's upbringing and without any deep roots. The virtue of justice lodged in a person's soul, that is, a commitment in the depths of his personality to leading an ethical life, is the essential cause of human happiness. For it means that his life is governed, not by arbitrary whim and caprice, but by practical moral reason. The just man is just, not on the spur of the moment, but because he has a settled reason for doing what is just, and through repeated exertion of his will against his inclinations has given that reason an actual force in his life so that it is not merely an idea in his mind but an effective motive that reaches into his heart. The person who is genuinely committed to leading a just life has a great degree of harmony with himself on the deepest level of his personality.

Justice and injustice as we understand them represent fundamentally different and contradictory views of human life and the world. The unjust person attributes to himself a unique importance in the overall scheme of things, so that his will is inherently superior to the wills of others and his freedom is more valuable than the freedom of others. He arrogates to himself rights and powers above those of others. The other is defined by the fact that he is not me. It is natural for such a person to make exceptions for himself from the general rules, which he sees as applying only to others. The just person, by contrast, places himself on the same level as others, views himself as one among others, accepts that the will of the other is as important as his own will, and the freedom of others as valuable as his own freedom. He has a disposition to see himself from the outside, to take a third-person view of his own behavior. He is in that sense detached from himself, he can stand back and view a case in which he is personally involved from the perspective of an impartial and disinterested judge, despite the fact that his own individual interests pull him perhaps in an opposite direction.

This aspect of justice is reflected in many of the typical calls to justice: "How would you feel if someone did that to you?" "How would it be if everybody did that!" "Forgive us our trespasses as we forgive those who trespass against us." "Don't jump the queue," and so on – all emphasize this aspect of justice. We could perhaps say that this is the truth in egalitarianism. The error of socialism is to try to rewrite that in terms of a simple distributive formula for the exterior of society – all that we have to do is to make people equal in respect of their privileges and advantages, and we don't have to bother about their interior virtues.

We have argued that justice is at bottom a formal concept: an action is just when it is compatible with the universal freedom of will of persons. If this is correct, a just person is, first and foremost, one who habitually respects the freedom of will of all persons, both others and himself, and therefore respects their personal dignity that flows from that freedom. Consequently, a just person is one who recognizes his own responsibility and accountability for his actions.

Above that basic level, the person who is habitually just is likely to be sensitive to the aspect of human relations that has to do with pressure on other people and their freedom of will. When we want something urgently, it is easy to fall into the way of exerting pressure on others who can give it to us, even though they may not have any special obligation to do so. It is even easy to exert pressure unwittingly. A just man is more likely to think about the effects of his actions on others, whether he may be exerting unjustified pressure. Refraining from unnecessary pressure is a traditional axiom of good manners. This is one reason among many why the just man makes a good friend. Aristotle points out that true friendship can exist only between the good. For the good help one another, he argues, while the malicious harm one another.

A person who is accustomed to behaving in just ways is equipped to resist certain kinds of temptation; for example, the temptation to help himself at the expense of others. He will not corruptly expect to receive payment where it is not due to him. He will not even be tempted to commit fraud or embezzlement. We prize different virtues in different situations. In physical danger we prize courage; in hardship, compassion and charity. Justice is a quality of character we prize particularly in the realm of commerce and the handling of money. It accords with this that the just person will resist supporting a system of redistribution of wealth. George Bernard Shaw remarked that a politician who proposes to take money from Peter and give it to Paul can usually count on the support of Paul. This was an ironic observation, since it reveals the corruption of the redistributive society Shaw himself advocated.

We have noted in an earlier chapter the prominent role that Christian religious authorities have played in developing and spreading the gospel of socialistic "social justice." It follows from our arguments that they should abandon that teaching. But that does not mean they would be left without a social message. Religious communities are in an especially strong position to make the case that the success of civil society depends inherently on the individual practice of moral virtue. And while all the moral virtues have a role to play in laying the foundations of civil society – it will make an immense difference to any society if the majority of its citizens have the personal habit of being generous, kind, thoughtful, and humane in their dealings with others – the chief role must go to the virtue of justice. Justice is the foundation of social order. This is not merely justice in the external arrangements of society, but above all in the interior character of its members. To see the force of this it is only necessary to think of the devastating effects of corruption. Societies whose members are generally honest are typically successful, including in the economic sense. Those whose members are habitually corrupt are predictably unsuccessful. To explain the immense differences in economic development between different countries, little more is required than the presence or absence of corruption. But to resist corruption can require great strength of character. Where can that spiritual power of resistance come from? The Christian church can play a central role in this. The Founding Fathers of the United States generally gave a great deal of emphasis to the proposition that a republic can be successful only to the extent its members are virtuous. The idea that a free society could prosper while its citizens habitually lived lives of dishonesty or even self-indulgence rightly seemed to them incredible.

Although justice is a moral quality rather than an intellectual one, it has implications in the cognitive realm. It is difficult for human nature to concede that we have made a mistake. For it is a natural instinct of our ego to want to place ourselves above others, and a mistake undermines this.

Yet the just man is more willing to acknowledge his mistakes than others. This is a consequence of the fact that he is more inclined, as we saw above, to see himself habitually as one among indefinitely many others, without special privileges or exceptions. The recognition that we have been in error is often a precondition of progress. A great part of the progress made by the physical sciences has come from the fact that they have developed a system that requires this question to be raised. It is not enough in physics or chemistry to put forward a theory and point to the reasons that commend it, which is what human nature would most like to do, but it is above all necessary to test the theory, that is, to confront it with the evidence or the reasons against it. This requires a frame of mind that has much in common with justice.

Habits are easier to acquire when we are young. Aristotle therefore rightly remarks that the first important thing in acquiring moral virtue is a good upbringing. But this commonsense idea is not easily compatible with the socialistic conception of social justice, which views it as "elitist" and discriminatory, and as exalting what it tends to consider the regrettable role of the family as a source of privilege. If our personal characters are the product of our social environment, family upbringing will be viewed as simply reflecting and reinforcing that. Social justice in this sense has in fact no role for personal character, since it views justice as exclusively an objective quality of society such as economic equality. The nearest thing to moral character from its point of view is zeal to impose social justice on others. But from the perspective of ordinary justice, zeal to redistribute other people's money does not entirely qualify for the accolades of high virtue.

The unjust character can take surprising forms. One is a willingness to disown one's inherited culture. Even a modest degree of enthusiasm about one's own cultural inheritance is denigrated as excessive egoism and "chauvinism." One sees the virtues of other cultures but only the faults, real or imagined, of one's own. Roger Scruton has labeled this the "culture of repudiation." A form of it is the rejection of one's own species and an excessive sentimentality over animals, under fear of committing the crime of "speciesism." Adopting the ideology of social justice enables one to offload the burden of charity onto the impersonal state, and to live without making judgments of desert and liability (except of course against conservatives).

Freedom Above All? The Role of Government

According to the account we have given of justice, it consists essentially in respect for the freedom of will of other persons. But, it may be objected, this makes freedom the supreme value, which trumps all other values.

Is this not exaggerated? Is it not the case that we recognize other goods as being sometimes of equal or even greater good than freedom? We are willing on occasion to sacrifice our freedom for the sake of other things we hold precious. The Christian command to love one's neighbor as oneself, and sometimes even more than oneself, surely points to a higher and greater duty, the power of which can be recognized as belonging to the human condition even by those who are not Christians. If this is so, must it not be accepted that society has the right to care for its poor and needy by collective public measures, such as redistributive taxation and health care programs, even though they infringe on the freedom of will of the individual? Accepting the thesis that justice consists in respect for freedom, can it not be that compassion sometimes trumps both freedom and justice?

This kind of question confuses what is right for the state with what is right for the individual. An individual may very well in an important sense place other values above freedom and justice in his decisions for his own life. He may legitimately decide to sacrifice his freedom or his life for the sake of love, or show compassion rather than demand justice in the case of someone who has injured him.

But the decisions of a state fall into a fundamentally different category. Government acts always and only by the use or threat of force. This is its defining characteristic. The only justification of its existence is that this is necessary to protect its citizens. That means *all* its citizens. If it deliberately harms some in order to benefit others, it acts directly against its own *raison d'être*, and commits gross injustice. It is a gross *social* injustice in the original sense of that term. The actions of government must be intended to benefit either its society as such and as a whole, or its individual citizens broadly equally. People pay taxes, and government can legitimately require them to pay taxes, only for their own benefit. This is an integral condition of the legitimacy of taxation. To compel people to pay taxes for the benefit of others whom the government wishes to privilege, whether they be rich or poor, is an abuse of power.

A similar mistake is made by those who equate the state with a family, as Hegel and many others have done. Within the family it is natural to sacrifice one's own interests for the sake of the other members. It is true the state is very like a family in certain respects. It is an object of love, pride, and loyalty for very many of its members. But the state is not a family. The family arises out of the intimate and voluntary relationships of love and procreation, while the state arises out of, and is maintained in existence by, the use of force. The family exists for the purpose of mutual support and care in the circumstances of life generally, while the state exists for the vital but limited purpose of defense against aggression, foreign and domestic. Even the least act of government is coercive. Its power must therefore necessarily be restricted to cases where the use of coercion is justified. But coercion on its own citizens can be justified only when it is for their own benefit.

The argument is often made that policies of redistribution are necessary for the good of society as a whole because otherwise without them the society will break apart. But it is easy to exaggerate this likelihood, which is typically not based on evidence but is a judgment entirely *a priori*.[275]

The forcible redistribution of income or property from some individuals to others is iniquitous. This principle is foundational to a just society. Robin Hood's popularity with the broad public notwithstanding, few people actually believe one is entitled to rob the rich in order to give to the poor. In my experience this is often true even among the very poor. To substitute charity for justice is to turn moral values, and with them civil society, upside down. In the absence of justice, social order evaporates. This is not true of the absence of charity, even though charity is, of course, a very great virtue. *Fiat iustitia, ruat coelum!* is right. Let justice be done even if the heavens fall.

Consent

Where there is consent there is no injustice. If redistribution is consented to, it cannot be opposed on the ground of justice. But the consent must be individual: it is not enough for it to be collective. Collective consent can justify governmental policies, such as defense, that are intended to provide equal benefits for all. But collective consent cannot justify taking from some for the purpose of giving to others. For, as we have just pointed out, government exists to benefit all the members of society, not to benefit some and to harm others. This is the true meaning of the requirement of the U.S. Constitution that the protection of the laws should be equal.

Most modern societies, however, have taken a collective path down the road of injustice. It may be useful, then, to consider the question whether some paths, although unjust, are not closer to justice than others. One form of this question might be: under what circumstances is there most likely to be individual consent to the use of tax monies to help the poor? Experience seems to show this is when the charity is local. Both England and colonial America once provided for the care of the poor through the parish.[276] These local programs have now all been swept away by the tide of larger government. But on the local level it is more likely that people will know their neighbors personally or have convenient sources to find out about them, and so their help will be more efficacious, and it is also more likely they will feel a personal concern about their fate and be willing to give consent to public assistance for them, so that liberty is better respected. If it is a question of helping the people of our own village or street, most of us are more likely to be engaged. If a system of collective assistance to the poor is to be devised, there are good reasons to think it should be on this level rather than that of the state or nation.

This includes such concerns as health care and education. Economists are generally agreed that if these are to be the province of government, despite the very good reasons against making them such, it is preferable to provide for them by direct payments to the individuals using them, so that they can buy these services on the market, rather than by setting up grandiose and inflexible systems of public health care or public education. It is better both economically and morally to have a system of private schools, where the fees of the poor are subsidized by government, than to have a system of public schools (in the U.S. sense of the term). It is better to have a system of private hospitals, which poor patients pay for with money they have received from the government, than a system of public hospitals. This will make less of a demand on the public's charity because it is more economical, and will increase the likelihood the public will give their consent.

If, despite these considerations, it should be decided to administer public assistance on the state or national level, the public should so far as possible be consulted directly by a referendum which gives them the opportunity to vote on a case-by-case basis. Should Great Britain send aid to Haiti in the wake of an earthquake? Let the government name a sum of money and ask the public expressly to approve the taxes that must raise it.

No human system of government can be perfect; there will always be some degree of injustice. But it can make a great deal of difference how we conceive of the ideal. If the argument of this book is correct, the society that strives in its laws to maximize respect for people's freedom of will will be not only the most just but also the most humane. We can add, with a high degree of confidence, it will also be materially the most successful.

Chapter 8

Some Conclusions

The True Concept of Social Justice

True social justice is not a distinct species of justice different from ordinary justice, but is ordinary justice as it pertains to society rather than to individuals. Thus it is a formal or procedural concept and not a material one. It does not give expression to any particular goal for society to achieve. Like ordinary justice, social justice is at bottom a virtue of individuals: a quality of will, namely, respect for the freedom of will of individuals.

Injustice becomes social when it affects the society in some way as a whole, or at least in large part. The prevalence of certain customs can have this effect, such as corruption. If corruption is widespread in a society – which invariably happens only when it is tolerated at the top – there can come a point where it becomes plausible to view not only particular individuals but the society itself as corrupt.

A more trenchant form of social injustice than that of custom is the injustice of laws, and institutions supported by laws. A law or institution is unjust if it exerts coercion on individuals beyond what is necessary for the prevention or punishment of unjust coercion. Any genuinely unjust law will cast its shadow across the entire society. An egregious example of social injustice in the past history of the West as well as of other societies was slavery, an unjust institution supported by unjust law.[277] More recently, the brutal, mass-homicidal policies of the Communist, Fascist, and National Socialist regimes have been equally a moral horror.

The most obdurate form of social injustice occurs when it is present not only in laws, and the institutions they support, but in the laws for the making of laws, or the constitution, and in constitutional law, or the body of law interpreting the constitution.

The purpose of all constitutional government is to place limits on the power of government in order to protect the just liberty of citizens. In the absence of a constitution, the power of government is in principle unlimited. Yet the project of constitutional government has so far failed.[278] No constitution has been able to protect itself against subversion by those who wish to extend the powers of government beyond the limits of justice. The constitution of the just society, to survive, requires the consistent support of the nation's political will. The foundation of this, it seems, can only lie in a general education to the true conception of justice and liberty.

The idea of a "living constitution," now being put forward in some quarters, defeats the purpose for which constitutions are created, for it means that, in the case of the U.S. constitution, for example, the laborious procedure the constitution itself lays down for changing its text can be bypassed by the simple expedient of changing its meaning. If this doctrine is once accepted, the power of government becomes again unlimited. A constitution that can be easily changed or bypassed will not fulfill its purpose. The first move of the Communist, Fascist, and National Socialist regimes was to bypass their constitutions and set up alternative structures of government enshrining their own political party as the source of power so that they could carry out whatever policies they wished.

The most basic requirement of social justice is that the constitutional provisions of every society should respect the freedom of every person's will in accordance with ordinary justice. This requires constitutional respect for commercial liberty or freedom of contract. It is widely recognized that a just liberty includes liberty of thought and opinion, liberty of religion, liberty of the press, liberty of association, liberty to carry arms, and so on, roughly those liberties guaranteed in the first ten amendments to the U.S. Constitution, known in the United States as the Bill of Rights. Missing there, though at least equally important, is the right and liberty to earn a living. Freedom of contract means that a person should be free to make or not to make whatever agreements he may wish in order to earn a living, within the limits of ordinary justice.

Another basic requirement of justice is the constitutional protection of property. All ownership of property that has been justly acquired should be protected by the constitution. This has consequences, for example, for taxation. The purpose of taxation is to provide the government with the revenue it needs to carry out its constitutional tasks. It is not the purpose of taxation to redistribute wealth. The redistribution of property by government, whether from the rich to the poor, as so often intended, or from the poor to the rich, which is in many cases what actually happens, is simply legalized theft.[279]

A further conclusion is that while coercive discrimination is inherently unjust in all cases where coercion is unjust, non-coercive or peaceful discrimination, as we have explained this concept, is not unjust. Rather, peaceful discrimination on whatever grounds is a natural right.

The Just Society

The just society will be one where, first, the constitution is designed to protect the freedom of will of every citizen by restricting the kinds of laws that can be made to those that serve that end. Following on that, it will be one where all the laws are directed to that goal. Finally it will be a society where every person respects the freedom of will of all other persons. This would come close to what Kant envisaged by his "Kingdom of Ends," and also to what Christians understand by the "Kingdom of God." As Kant remarked, it is only an ideal.

Some Advantages of This Theory of Justice

1. It explains well the ordinary intuitions people have about what is right and wrong. It shows why the common crimes committed by individuals and recognized as evil by all civilized peoples, such as murder, robbery, rape, and fraud, are blameworthy. All these involve a trespass by one person's will on another's freedom, overriding it, discounting it, so that only one's own freedom is valued, although the entitlement I have to my freedom has no stronger foundation than the entitlement others have to theirs.
2. By placing the freedom of the will not only of the agent but also of the recipient of the action at the heart of justice, this theory creates a new and powerful conception of the human person as an inviolable being. Freedom of the will is seen to be the defining feature of human existence. An injury inflicts not merely physical or mental damage but trespasses on a sacred space.
3. Our theory also explains the peculiar, unconditional power of the judgment that an action is just or unjust, and why there is universal agreement that unjust actions may be punished coercively.
4. The theory explains why we should regard all rational beings as having an equal fundamental moral dignity and therefore why we should respect others and ourselves.

5. It explains why the viewpoint of an impartial judge has a special authority.

6. The theory suggests a powerful conception of social justice to take the place of the current socialistic one. The just society is a free society, in which the basic or constitutional law is designed to protect property and freedom of contract, and ideally in which everyone respects the freedom of will of everyone else.

7. This concept of justice applies also to laws in general, providing a powerful criterion for the traditional distinction between laws that are just and those that are unjust. A just law is one that prohibits actions in themselves unjust, and a law which prohibits actions in themselves just is unjust. This is a truly liberal conception, which establishes a firm foundation for the concept of limited or constitutional government, and with it the moral foundation of the free society.

8. The theory that justice is a formal or procedural principle of this kind explains far better than any consequentialist theory the absolute and unconditional character so widely attributed to justice.

9. The theory explains better than utilitarian theories do the anger we can feel at injustice done to others.

10. The theory explains why people have a motive to be just, and how human happiness might depend upon just behavior and the acquisition of a just character.

Appendix: A Note on Hegel, *Sittlichkeit,* and His Criticism of Kant

The account we have given of justice draws, among others, on insights of both Kant and Hegel. In this note we propose to discuss certain aspects of their relationship, which are also of significance for our own theory.

It is well known that Hegel criticizes Kant's theory of morality severely. This criticism has been influential, especially in Europe, where learned opinion tends to view Hegel as having effectively relativized or historicized the idea of justice. Here we will briefly summarize some further aspects of Hegel's account of justice, then explore his criticism of Kant against the backdrop of his overall philosophy. The question for us is: does someone who wishes to follow Kant in his basic doctrine – which is also essentially that of Hegel – have good reason also to follow Hegel in his critique of that?

For both men the societal background of their theories is important because their aims were defined with reference to it. Kant's work was consciously part of the Enlightenment and his aim was conditioned by that fact. The society in which he lived was still structured largely according to the rules of feudalism, which he wished in principle to overturn. For example, the law gave him the right to prohibit his servant, Martin Lampe, from marrying (which Lampe nonetheless succeeded in doing, though against Kant's wishes, by holding the ceremony secretly).[280] He welcomed the French Revolution even though many of its actions went contrary to his published philosophical standpoint. Hegel, by contrast, was writing after these changes had taken place, or at least, in his earlier years, after they had begun to do so. After the chaos of the Revolution and the Napoleonic wars he wished to reconcile his audience to the basic institutions of their society. He aimed to do this especially by pointing out the rationality embodied in them. Consequently, the fundamental concrete institutions of society play a larger and more positive role in Hegel's philosophy than in Kant's.[281]

Kant wanted to highlight the importance of the will in ethics, and therefore he wanted to distinguish it carefully from feelings and inclinations. His ethical theory contrasts them. Hegel, however, although he had essentially the same view of the will, wished to enlist the feelings and inclinations of his audience in the cause of ethical behavior and reconciliation with society, and views the basic institutions of society as the place where those feelings and inclinations, and so the habitual character of individuals, are formed, and should be formed positively.

Both Kant and Hegel discuss justice chiefly in terms of *Recht*. This is a difficult word to translate precisely into English, since it connotes an implied focus on the external system of justice rather than on the abstract concept or the interior virtue of justice in individuals which the English term can also suggest. But that there should be an external system of justice is itself a demand of abstract justice, and what cannot in principle be implemented in an external system cannot in reality be part of justice. As Hegel remarks, what we cannot do we ought not to do.

Kant describes *Recht* as a relationship between wills, and more specifically as a quality of the will that is compatible with universal freedom of will. Hegel begins from a similar view: *Recht* consists in the freedom of the will; but with his own twist: specifically it is "the self-development of the Idea of the absolutely free will."

Böhme

To understand this and the significance of Hegel's overall philosophy for the Kantian project, as well as to grasp his specific criticism of Kant's conception of justice, it will help to investigate Hegel's fundamental theory. For this our point of departure is best taken from its religious background, which is to be found especially in the writings of the Lutheran mystic Jakob Böhme (1575–1624), which Hegel became acquainted with at an early age through his father, a Lutheran pastor. Böhme's theology is distinguished by the positive cosmic role he assigned to the fall of Satan and of Adam and Eve, and to sin and evil in general. He taught that sin, rebellion against God, was a necessary stage in the development of the universe. At the beginning, God is an undifferentiated unity, a state of pure innocence. Through the creation of the angels and man, God begins a process of separation from himself, leading to desire, conflict, evil, and differentiation. This is eventually overcome through the redemption brought by Christ's love and suffering, which ushers in a new state of cosmic harmony more perfect than the original state of innocence. Through the process of separation of his creation from himself through sin and its eventual reunion through redemption, God attains a new level of self-awareness.[282] Böhme taught that this was true of all original unities, which in order to arrive at a state of maturity or completion must first pass through the process of what Hegel was later to call "the seriousness, labor, patience and painfulness of the negative." This was not very orthodox Christian belief, which agreed with Plato that God was perfect and not subject to change, but it made a profound impression on the young Hegel.[283]

The Dialectic

Out of Böhme's teaching Hegel developed his theory of the "dialectic." He presents this in different but related forms in several different contexts, among them: (1) as a theory of philosophy and knowledge, (2) as a theory of self-development, (3) as a theory of ethics, and (4) as a theory of institutions. Let us look briefly at each of these.

1. In the opening paragraph of the *Philosophie des Rechts* he explains that philosophy is to aim at explicating the rationality of whatever object it studies, which he calls its idea (*Idee*). This is to be found in the concept (*Begriff*) of it, not simply as a bare or abstract concept, however, but as actualized or realized in the real world. Not, however, the actualization given to it by the accidental vicissitudes of history, but the actualization which "it gives to itself," and which therefore represents its own true nature. For

> The shapes which the concept assumes in the course of its actualization are indispensable for the knowledge of the concept itself. They are the second essential moment of the Idea, in distinction from the first, i.e. from its form, from its mode of being as concept alone. (#1)

The task of philosophy "is to develop the Idea – the Idea being the rational factor in any object of study – out of the concept, or, what is the same thing, to look on at the proper immanent development of the thing itself."

In the *Wissenschaft der Logik* Hegel explains this more fully. He begins by asserting the identity of thought with the object of thought.

> . . . the older metaphysic [which Hegel is here defending] laid down as fundamental that that which by thinking is known of and in things, that alone is what is really true in them; that what is really true is not things in their immediacy, but only things when they have been taken up into the

form of thought, as conceptions. Thus this older metaphysic stands for the view that thinking and the determinations (*Bestimmungen* or specific forms) of thinking are not something foreign to the objects of thought, but are rather of the very essence of those objects; in other words that things and the thinking of them are in harmony in and for themselves – indeed language itself expresses an affinity between them – that thought in its immanent determinations, and the true nature of things, are one and the same content. (Introduction, p. 55)

On this basis Hegel goes on to construct a threefold conception of every concept: a concept is not a single, static thing which could be summarized in a single sentence but rather a dynamic process, which is propelled by reason's inherent power of negation through three phases (*Momente*) that progressively reveal the concept's rationality. To repeat, these phases do not constitute a temporal sequence but simultaneous logical aspects of it. The first phase is represented by the concept as it presents itself in the immediacy of particular experience. Hegel calls it in this phase "abstract" and purely "formal." But this abstract phase suggests or "passes over into" its negation, which is no longer immediate but is said to represent the concept both in its singularity and, by that very fact, in its universality. This negation then suggests a further negation which subsumes both the earlier ones in a higher or more comprehensive and complete conception.

The one and only thing for securing scientific progress (and for quite simple insight into which, it is essential to strive) – is knowledge of the logical precept that negation is just as much affirmation as negation, or that what is self-contradictory resolves itself not into nullity, into abstract nothingness, but essentially only into the negation of its particular content, that such negation is not an all-embracing negation, but is the negation of a definite somewhat which abolishes itself, and thus is a definite negation; and that thus the result contains in essence that from which it results – which is indeed a tautology, for otherwise it would be something immediate and not a result. Since what results, the negation, is a definite negation, it has a content. It is a new concept, but a higher, richer concept than that which preceded; for it has been enriched by the negation or opposite of that preceding concept, and thus contains it, but contains also more than it, and is the unity of itself and its opposite. On these lines the system of concepts has broadly to be constructed, and to go on to completion in a resistless course, free from all foreign elements, admitting nothing from outside. (Introduction)

Hegel does not exactly overwhelm the reader with concrete examples of what he is talking about. But let us see if we can make this any more transparent. As an example, let us take the concept of "experience." The term conveys a certain idea. But as soon as we reflect on this idea, it raises the concept of everything that is not experience: what precedes experience, or may be a precondition of it as an *a priori*, or associated with it or follows from it but is not contained in the idea of experience itself. Now we find that the initial idea of experience is enriched by our realization of these things that are not experience: the concept acquires definite boundaries which help to define it. When we put the two together, experience and non-experience, we have a more complete or satisfying conception of what it means to experience something. This suggests the concept of a particular experience, which is both concrete, an experience that some actual person may have, and also at the same time universal, since it will apply to all actual experiences.

2. The Dialectic as a Theory of Self-Development. In several of his writings[284] Hegel uses his dialectic to analyze the development of personality. The individual exists at first (again, the "at first" is from the viewpoint of logic) only as a conscious person, "in itself" (*an sich*), lacking self-consciousness. It becomes self-conscious, "in itself and for itself" (*an und für sich*), through the encounter with another person, in the process of mutual recognition and acknowledgment. In encountering the other, each one "has lost itself, since it finds itself as an other being." But at the same time it has subsumed or sublated (*aufgehoben*) the other, because it does not regard the other as a being in its own right, but only "sees its own self in the other." The other is an implicit threat, which must be overcome. There follows a struggle for superiority, in which each risks its life, for "It is solely by risking life that freedom is obtained."

But if one dies in the struggle, the mutual recognition is cancelled out. This is a kind of negation, but "not the negation characteristic of consciousness, which cancels in such a way that it preserves and maintains what is subsumed, and thereby survives its being subsumed." If both survive, two forms of consciousness emerge, one independent, "pure self-consciousness," the other dependent, "a consciousness which is not purely for itself, but for another." The one that prefers honor to life becomes independent; the one that prefers life to honor becomes dependent. The one is master, the other slave or serf (*Knecht*). The master now has what he wanted: he "exists for himself." But this independence is at bottom illusory, because it is true only so long as he has his servant. Ironically, his conception of himself is dependent on his servant's acknowledgment of him. "Just where the master has effectively achieved lordship, he really finds that something has come about quite different from an independent consciousness." Now the logic of the situation leads to a reversal of roles. The servant works on objective tasks and through his labor rises to consciousness of self. The master, not engaged in objectifying labor, but in the fulfillment of frivolous desires, loses his consciousness of self and descends into futility. The servant is in a position to become the master. Marx was to turn this image to his own advantage as a description of the situation of the working class.

3. The Dialectic in Ethics. This is the self-development of the free will, which takes place in the three stages or phases, which are to be understood, again, not as a historical sequence, but as logical and therefore simultaneous aspects of the concept of the will. In the first or immediate phase where it is encountered, the free will is only implicit: it does not yet reflect consciously on itself. The will, he says, is "in itself" but not yet "for itself."[285] It is embodied in external realities: property, contract, and the punishment of crime. In this phase or aspect of the concept, Hegel describes the individual as a person, but not yet as a subject; and the concept of justice involved in this first phase is merely formal or abstract. The good "ought to be but is not."

In the second phase, the will passes over into conscious reflection on itself and awareness of itself. It is now no longer merely "in itself" but also "for itself": it is no longer merely implicit but explicit. It begins, in other words, to think about the subjective conditions which make an action just or unjust: purpose, intention, and conscience. The individual is no longer merely a person, but becomes a subject. Hegel calls this phase the sphere of "morality." In relation to the first phase it can be seen as a contradiction or negation – a definite or partial one, however, not a complete one: it rejects certain things while keeping others. The subjective good ought to be but is not.

In the third phase of the concept of the will, its freedom becomes objectively embodied in certain fundamental institutions: the family, civil society, and the state. Hegel terms this phase "*Sittlichkeit.*" This term is often translated as "ethical life"; Muller however suggests "normative institutions."

> . . . ethical life is the concept of freedom developed into the existing world . . .
>
> The right of individuals to be subjectively destined to freedom is fulfilled when they belong to an actual ethical [social] order, because their conviction of their freedom finds its truth in such an objective order, and it is in an ethical order that they are actually in possession of their own essence or their own inner universality. (#153)

4. The Dialectic as a Theory of Institutions. In the *Philosophie des Rechts* Hegel employs the dialectic to analyze several institutions in a characteristic way. As an example of this we may take his treatment of the family, which occurs in Part III of the treatise, on "Ethical Life" (*Sittlichkeit*, as opposed to Part II, *Moralität*). The family is the "immediate substantiality of mind." That is, it is an embodiment of reason. The individual exists in the family not as an independent person but essentially as a member. The concept of the family as Hegel presents it is realized in three phases or aspects: marriage, the family property or capital, and the education of the children and the consequent dissolution of the family. The immediate form of the family is given by marriage. Although this is founded on sexual union, which is part of nature, self-consciousness changes it "into a union on the level of mind, into self-conscious love." Whatever the particular subjective feelings of the two persons may be, the objective source of the marriage lies in their free consent to make themselves one person. However, although it begins in a contract, marriage is not a contractual relationship, but a contract to transcend the standpoint of contract, which is the standpoint in which persons are regarded as self-subsistent units. It is the family itself which is self-subsistent.

As a self-subsistent person, the family "has its real existence in property." In the family, the "seflishness" of individual property is "transformed into something ethical, into labour and care for a common possession." It becomes the capital which the family needs for its self-subsistence. This is the second phase in the development of the concept of the family, the "embodiment of its substantial personality."

While the unity of marriage is initially only "a unity of inwardness or disposition," it acquires outward and objective existence in the children. In due course these grow up and are educated into freedom of personality, so that they are recognized as independent persons who can found families of their own. This constitutes the "ethical dissolution of the family." Its natural dissolution is brought about by the death of the parents. With this third phase we have the completed concept of the family.

Hegel's Criticism of Kant's Ethics

According to Hegel, as we have just seen, the entire realm of rights and duties exists in three levels or phases. On the first or immediate level, conceptually speaking, rights and duties are conceived of "abstractly," that is, without reflection or questioning by the individual conscience. This is the standpoint of the will which is merely "in itself." On the second level, they advance into the sphere of "morality," where they become the object of reflection and examination by the individual conscience. This is the standpoint of the will which is no longer merely in itself but "for itself." On the third level, the will advances further, beyond the morality of conscience, into the realm of society, where rights and duties are embodied in customary institutions, "the objective ethical order" and "self-conscious action." This is the realm of "necessary relations," institutions which necessarily flow from the rationality of *Recht*: the family, civil society, and the state.

Hegel criticizes Kant chiefly on the ground that his philosophy does not make room for this dimension of *Recht*. His analysis, says Hegel, remains on the level of "morality," the individual conscience and its universal principles, without entering into the realm of the "objective ethical order" of society and its institutions, where the rationality of right goes, as he asserts, beyond the purely negative requirements of the categorical imperative.

> Kant generally prefers to use the word "morality" and, since the principles of action in his philosophy are always limited to this conception, they make the standpoint of ethical life (*Sittlichkeit* as he understands it) completely impossible, in fact they explicitly nullify and spurn it. (#33)

More specifically, the ground of Hegel's criticism of Kant's theory is that "what is fundamental, substantive and primary" according to Kant is "the will of a single person in his own private self-will, not the absolute or rational will, and mind as a particular individual, not mind as it is in truth." Hegel accuses this view, which he attributes in the first instance to Rousseau, of being "devoid of any speculative thinking" and says it is "repudiated by the philosophic concept." He adds that "the phenomena which it has produced both in men's heads and in the world are of a frightfulness parallel only to the superficiality of the thoughts on which they are based." This would seem to be a reference to the French Revolution, though according to his biographers Hegel supported that event.

The harshness of this indictment is a trifle mysterious, considering that Hegel does not actually disagree with Kant's account so far as it goes. His complaint is just that it does not go far enough. The reason for this charge is the for Hegel apparently scandalous fact that Kant does not follow Hegel's peculiar conception of philosophical method.

Hegel's *Sittlichkeit* represents a canonization of the distinctive customs and institutions of particular peoples. He describes these customs and institutions as "freedom actualized." In the *Phaenomenologie des Geistes* he writes that "wisdom and virtue consist in living in conformity with the customs of one's people" (Inwood, 91). He could echo Glanvill's remark that "custom is a form of reason." But if this is true, it is so only in virtue of the fact, and to the extent, that those customs and institutions respect the dignity of persons and are compatible with the freedom of their will. Hegel's curious defense of slavery betrays him here. He grants that from the perspective of absolute freedom slavery is wrong. Yet on the other hand he blames it also on the slave, for if a man is a slave, his own will is responsible for his slavery, Hegel writes. But more than that, slavery occurs, he states, in the transition of society from the state of nature to a genuinely ethical condition: it occurs in a world where wrong is still right; and at that stage "wrong has validity" and so is "necessarily in place" (Phil. Right, Addition 36, to par. 57). Hegel's *Sittlichkeit*, it seems, can justify anything. To my mind this is a powerful vindication of Kant.

The Welfare State and *Sittlichkeit*

In the *Philosophie des Rechts* Hegel, in some apparent contradiction to his previous analysis (that civil society is the negation of the family), assimilates civil society to the family. The legal order of society (*Recht*) must reflect not only the universal demands of abstract justice but also the unique requirements of the family, civil society, and the state (paragraph 239 ff). Because of the requirements of *Sittlichkeit*, Hegel's state is far from being a minimal one as a Robert Nozick or even perhaps an Adam Smith would conceive of it. Long before Bismarck, Hegel's state is one essentially burdened with welfare obligations. This is not primarily a question of redistribution, though it involves that, but of the nature of civil society as a community. It is not a socialist but a conservative conception, though the effect is in many ways similar.

Civil society, he states, has the character of a "universal family." He views this as having direct consequences for education, which cannot be allowed to be a private responsibility of parents: the state has the right and duty to supervise the education of children, a right "paramount over the arbitrary and contingent preferences of parents . . . " "Society must provide public educational facilities so far as is practicable." Similarly, the state must be seen as having primary responsibility for the poor: society has the right and duty of acting as a trustee for the extravagant, and of caring for the poor both physically and mentally, a responsibility which cannot be left to private charity. Britain provides him with a "horrible example" of the abdication of social responsibilities by the state.

In the example of England we may study these phenomena on a large scale and also in particular the results of poor-rates, immense foundations, unlimited private beneficence, and above all the abolition of the Guild Corporations. In Britain, particularly in Scotland, the most direct measure against poverty and especially against the loss of shame and self-respect – the subjective bases of society – as well as against laziness and extravagance, etc., the begetters of the rabble, has turned out to be to leave the poor to their fate and instruct them to beg in the streets. (245)

It is a puzzle for the historian to account for such views being held after the work of Adam Smith had become known. For the British approach to these questions was well supported by the new studies in economics. Smith specifically addresses the question of education, for example. However, it will help put Hegel's ruminations on matters economic in some perspective to know what Georg Lukacs reports[286], that Hegel derived his understanding of this subject chiefly from reading Sir James Steuart's *Inquiry into the Principles of Political Economy* (1767), and that this had a profound effect on Hegel's theory of society. Steuart has the distinction of being the mercantilist, or economic nationalist, whose theory Adam Smith exploded in the *Wealth of Nations*. Perhaps understandably, Steuart, though a Scot and a prominent figure in the Scottish Enlightenment, spent half his life in continental Europe and was a great favorite among economic writers in Germany, a country which to this day seems to have had difficulty grasping Smith's doctrine, as much because of conservative concerns as socialist ones. Lukacs believes Hegel also read Adam Smith, but confesses he has no evidence to support this belief. From a modern point of view, therefore, it is scarcely an exaggeration to say that Hegel was economically illiterate, and his theory of society suffers accordingly.

Civil society is not a family. Even on his own terms, Hegel's view is hard to justify because his analysis of civil society begins with the thesis that it is the negation of the family. Much less is the state a family. It is true that the state (or at least the nation, if we may make that distinction) constitutes a community, and one that, as we have mentioned above, can command the loyalty and devotion of its members even to extreme sacrifice. And it is true that economists typically do not pay as much attention as perhaps they might to that fact. But it is also true that the basic principles of economics remain valid, and have profound implications for any theory of society. A society which does not recognize them destines itself to ruin. The basic principles of economics, such as the law of supply and demand, are part of natural law, as much as the laws of physics and chemistry are. And they are just as compatible with the rule of justice.

Acknowledgements

The Earhart Foundation generously provided the initial funding for this project. Leonard Swidler, at no small cost to himself, gave financial support which saw it to completion.

Roger Scruton has earned my undying gratitude for the many hours of labor he spent over several years reading, criticizing, encouraging, and making suggestions for this book and the philosophical education of its author. It is owing to him more than to anyone else that it is finally appearing in print.

Anthony O'Hear and Robert Grant read the entire manuscript and generously gave me detailed comments, from which both the work and I personally have benefitted greatly, especially regarding the objections that can be raised against it.

I owe a special debt of gratitude to Martin Ricketts and Linda Waterman for their practical help and support; and to the sadly late Norman Barry for lively discussions about positivism and natural law.

Lastly I wish to express my appreciation to the audiences who sat and listened and sometimes agreed but also sometimes asked difficult questions in lectures in which I developed these ideas: to the faculty at Buckingham University; in the philosophy department at La Salle University, owing to the open-mindedness of its late chairman, Michael Kerlin; at Rowan University, thanks to the initiative of Denyse Lemaire; at the American Institute for Economic Research, through the kindness of Charles Murray and Walker Todd, and the Panhandle Tiger Bay Club in Florida, due to the gratifying personal interest of Mike Hill in the subject of justice. Finally, I thank warmly my students and friends at the Wynnewood Institute, especially Uli Kortsch, Vivian McLaughlin, Bill Bonner, and Bob Guzzardi, who have watched these ideas gestate from small beginnings and over the years have lent the strong support of their encouragement.

Notes

Chapter 1

1   Bertrand de Jouvenel, *The Ethics of Redistribution*, Indianapolis, IN: Liberty Press, 1990, p. 72.
2   *New York Times*, December 6, 2007.
3   For example, "Wiz wit" is the customary order in south Philadelphia for a sandwich with Cheese-whiz and onions.
4   Cf. The Wikipedia Website "Geno's Steaks."
5   Inc. website *www.inc.com* May 20, 2010. Report by Courtney Rubin.
6   Report in the *Washington Times*, April 13, 2008.
7   Office of Public Sector Information, United Kingdom.
8   *Second Treatise of Government*, Chapter 3, Paragraph 18, page 15.
9   Ibid., Paragraph 19.
10 *Firearm News*, a publication of Victims Against Crime, P O Box 2522, Clareinch 7740, South Africa. 2004, Vol. 2.
11 Ibid. This source gives numerous other such cases.

Chapter 2

12 Iuris praecepta sunt haec: honeste vivere, alterum non laedere, suum cuique tribuere. *Digesta*, 1.1.10, *Institutiones*, 1, 3.
13 Cf. Pufendorf: "By 'human action' I do not mean any motion which has its origin in man's faculties but only such as is begun and directed by the faculties which the great and good Creator has given to mankind above and beyond the animals. I mean motion initiated in the light of understanding and at the command of will." Samuel Pufendorf, *On the Duty of Man and Citizen According to Natural Law*. Translated by Michael Silverthorne. Edited by James Tully. Cambridge: Cambridge University Press, 1991, Bk 1, chapter 1, p. 17.
14 *Ethica, or Scito Teipsum*. Translated by Vincent Paul Spade in: *Peter Abelard, Ethical Writings*. Indianapolis, IN: Hackett Publishing Company, 1995.
15 Sermon 180, c. 2; Migne, *Latin Patrology* Vol. 38, col. 974.
16 *Sovereignty*, London: Cambridge University Press, 1957, p. 140.
17 *Law, Legislation and Liberty*, Vol. 2, *The Mirage of Social Justice*, Chicago, IL: University of Chicago Press, 1976, p. 63f.
18 See, for example, H. L. Cole and L Ohanain: "The Great Depression in the United States From a Neoclassical Perspective." Federal Reserve Bank of Minneapolis Quarterly Review, 1999.

19 See, for example Milton Friedman and Anna J. Schwartz, *A Monetary History of the United States, 1867–1960*, Princeton, NJ: Princeton University Press, 1971.

20 Isaiah Berlin, *Two Concepts of Liberty*, Oxford: Oxford University Press, 1958.

21 "(f) As used in this subchapter, the phrase 'unlawful employment practice' shall not be deemed to include any action or measure taken by an employer, labor organization, joint labormanagement committee, or employment agency with respect to an individual who is a member of the Communist Party of the United States or of any other organization required to register as a Communistaction or Communistfront organization by final order of the Subversive Activities Control Board pursuant to the Subversive Activities Control Act of 1950 [50 U.S.C.781 et seq.]."

22 This note provides some further detail regarding the passage of this important legislation. In a speech delivered on June 11, 1963, President John F. Kennedy asked for legislation "giving all Americans the right to be served in facilities which are open to the public – hotels, restaurants, theaters, retail stores, and similar establishments." On June 19 he sent a bill to Congress containing provisions from the failed Civil Rights Act of 1875 to ban such discrimination in public accommodations. But it omitted a number of provisions advocated by leaders of the civil rights movement, including the prohibition of discrimination in private employment. Kennedy's bill was sent to the House of Representatives and referred to the House Judiciary Committee, chaired by Emmanuel Celler, a Democrat from New York. This committee added the ban on discrimination in employment and various other provisions, for example concerning discrimination at lunch counters.

The bill was approved by the Judiciary Committee in November 1963 and sent to the Rules Committee, whose chairman, Howard Smith, indicated his intention to delay it indefinitely. On November 22, however, President Kennedy was assassinated and Vice President Lyndon Johnson became president with the avowed intention of passing it. When Congress's winter recess commenced the opposition to the bill was still too strong to pass it. During the recess, however, the president's advocacy had its effect, and after Congress reconvened, the bill passed the House on February 10, 1964. But it still faced powerful opposition in the Senate, including a 14-hour filibuster by Sen Robert Byrd. All together the debate occupied the Senate for 57 working days. But eventually, on June 19, largely owing to complex parliamentary maneuvers by Democratic leaders, it was passed, and signed into law on July 2, 1964.

23 Eugene E. Kinsey, www.kinseylaw.com. See the treatment of liability in Burke, Thomas Patrick, *No Harm: Ethical Principles for a Free Market*. New York: Paragon House, 1994, p. 140.

24 *The New York Times* recently carried a full-page ad with the headline: "Africa's misery: America's shame." Nothing was said about Africa's shame. This Western attitude has been successfully exported to the Muslim world; when Muslim terrorists occupied the Grand Mosque in Mecca in 1979, the Muslim mob in Islamabad, Pakistan, protested by attacking and burning the *American* embassy.

25 *A Theory of Justice*, Cambridge, MA: Belknap Press of Harvard University Press, 1971, # 17, p. 104.

26 See below p. 103.

[27] *Frontiers of Justice*, Cambridge, MA: Belknap Press of Harvard University Press, 2006, 69ff.

[28] *The Mirage of Social Justice*, p. 97.

[29] Ibid., 66, 67.

[30] Stephen Joel Trachtenberg, George Washington University.

[31] "No guilt without a guilty mind." "Reum non facit nisi mens rea." Leges Henrici, 5, # 28. The reference for St. Augustine is given, p. 19, note 15.

Chapter 3

[32] Unless we except John Stuart Mill's brief references to it, discussed later in these pages.

[33] Edward Gibbon speaks of "social justice," but in a sense indistinguishable from ordinary justice in reference to the punishment of crime. "Every crime which is punished by social justice, was practised as the rights of war; the Huns were distinguished by cruelty and sacrilege; and Belisarius alone appeared in the streets and churches of Naples to moderate the calamities which he predicted" (*Decline and Fall*, chapter 41). According to Hayek this was an occasional usage of the eighteenth century (*The Mirage of Social Justice.*, chapter 9, Note 2).

[34] It is true that some commentators consider the term "justice" was used in the sense of "social justice" already by Pope Clement XIII (Carlo della Torre Rezzonico, 1693–1769) in his encyclical letter, *A quo die*, of 1758, where he remarks that "Among the fruits of justice, mercy to the poor should certainly be considered the most important. That justice which comes from faith belongs to Jesus Christ" [38]. " . . . (the poor) require our generosity as their principal right" [41]. Certainly the letter stresses the importance of mercy and generosity toward the poor. However, the pope refers to these qualities not as justice, but as "fruits" of justice. The New Testament uses the term "justice" (Greek: *dikaiosune*) for the right relationship of the soul to God, which the context here would support. The statement that the poor have a "right" to generosity is a *hapax legomenon* which can be understood in the sense that they have a claim to it, it is something we ought to do because of Christ's teaching. "Social justice" would have to wait till the Risorgimento.

[35] Charles F. Delzell, Online encyclopedia cats.ohiou.edu/~chastain. Walter Maturi, D'Azeglio, *Dizionario biografico degli Italiani*, Rome, 1962.

[36] "*Osservazione sugli studi del Collegio Romano*"; "*Abbozzo del Projetto di Ordinazione intorno agli Studii Superiori.*"

[37] Cf. Essay Four, Of the Origin of Government, in *Hume, Political Essays*, ed. Knut Haakonssen, Cambridge: Cambridge University Press, 1994, 20–3.

[38] "When finally one of the parties has taken a decided superiority, when it shows all the characters of a peaceable organization, when its internal enemies quiet themselves out of fear, lassitude, or conviction, and finally when the consent of foreign nations fully gives to the victorious power all the characters of legitimacy, only then is all opposition rebellion." Maistre, "Lettres," *Oeuvres* C (7:68–69:74).

[39] *Saggio teoretico di dritto naturale appoggiata sul fatto*. 2nd edition, Vol. 1. Prato, Tipografia Giachetti, Figlio. 1883. Capo XI, Sommario. Par. 592, p. 281.

40 Ibid. par. 593.

41 *Saggio*, par. 354 (Diss. II, Capo III).

42 *Saggio*, par. 355.

43 "But in this case justice will never be rigorously satisfied, it being impossible for the son to render back to the father the existence he has received from him." Footnote to par. 356, p. 152.

44 Par. 356.

45 "If an individual receives so much from another to whose goods he had no previous right, he must give as much in return if he wishes to settle accounts according to justice. Justice between equals consists therefore in a quantitative balancing or level-ling; nor can justice be lessened on one side by increasing on the other, since the right of the person who gave extends precisely to the thing he gave, neither more nor less. Therefore this right is satisfied by an equivalent. But suppose instead that two or more individuals all seeking a common good (many sailors, for example, seeking to discover an unknown land, or many associates running a public educational estab-lishment) compete with one another to obtain a preeminence or an office: should you give to one the same that you give to the other? [*Torrete per regola di giustizia l'altrettanto?*] But no, that is a ridiculous thing even to say, impossible to execute. But is it equality? Equality consists here in equalizing the office to the person's capacity, the recompense to the merit, punishments to demerit, and the real order to the ideal proportions of means to end. And each person should be content to make the same contribution as every other to the common purpose." Par. 357, p. 153.

46 A phrase reminiscent of Robespierre's "despotism of liberty" (Speech of February 5, 1794) and Marcuse's "repressive tolerance" (essay of 1965, in Robert Paul Wolff, Barrington Moore, Jr., and Herbert Marcuse, *A Critique of Pure Tolerance*, Boston, MA: Beacon Press, 1969, pp. 95–137.

47 *Essai sur les principes philosophiques de l'économie politique.* Paris: Lethellieux, 1943. Les deux économies, p. 32. This work is a translation by Robert Jacquin of three articles by Taparelli published in *Civilta Cattolica*: Le due economie (1856), Anal-isi critica dei primi concetti de Economia (1857), and Indirizzo di future trattazioni economiche (1862).

48 Ibid.

49 Ibid., p. 33.

50 Ibid., p. 40.

51 Ibid.

52 Ibid., p. 46.

53 Ibid., p. 66.

54 Ibid., p. 66.

55 Ibid. Orientation d'études ultérieures d'économie, p. 94.

56 Ibid., p. 93.

57 Ibid., p. 93.

58 Ibid., p. 46.

59 Ibid., p. 50.

60 Ibid., p. 100. See also pp. 62 and 96.

61 See below, p. 83.

62 Franklin D. Roosevelt Presidential Library and Museum. Recording of radio address, October 2. Detroit, MI – "The Philosophy of Social Justice through Social Action" (Radio address) (9 min). Tape RLxB-85–1 65–9:1(7–8).

[63] In March of 1797, when he was born, the town was occupied by Napoleon's army, but restored to Austria in October.

[64] See *Rosmini e l'illuminismo: Atti del XXI Corso della "Cattedra Rosmini,"* ed. P. Pellegrino, Stresa: Sodalitas-Spes, 1988.

[65] Alberto Mingardi, "A Sphere Around the Person: Antonio Rosmini on Property," *Journal of Markets and Morality*, Vol. 7, No. 1, spring 2004.

[66] Ibid.

[67] On the agreements and disagreements of Rosmini with Liberatore and Taparelli, see Alejandro Chafuen, "I precursori italiani del personalismo economico: una riflessione sugli scritti di Luigi Taparelli d'Azeglio, Antonio Rosmini e Matteo Liberatore," in *Il coraggio della libertà: Saggi in onore di Sergio Ricossa*, ed. Enrico Colombatto and Alberto Mingardi, Soveria Mannelli: Rubbettino, 2002.

[68] *Filosofia del diritto*, 1841. Trans. *The Philosophy of Right*, ed. Denis Cleary and Terence Watson, Durham: Rosmini House, 1995.Vol. 1, par. 94.

[69] *Filosofia del diritto*, Vol. 1, 237. Denis Cleary, "Antonio Rosmini," *Stanford Encyclopedia of Philosophy. Spring 2002 Edition*, Edward N. Zalta , ed..

[70] "Two Concepts of Liberty," in *Four Essays on Liberty*, Oxford: Oxford University Press, 1969, p. 121–2.

[71] *Filosofia del diritto*, Vol. 1, par. 88. Mingardi, "A Sphere Around the Person: Antonio Rosmini on Property," . Note: Mingardi's article could be accessed only online and without pagination; the pagination given in these notes is conjectural.

[72] Cleary, op. cit., p. 10.

[73] *Filosofia del diritto*, Vol. 6, pars. 1640–1644. Mingardi, op. cit.

[74] *Saggi di scienza politica. Scritti Inediti*, ed. G. B. Nicola (1822, reprint Turin, 1933), p. 88.

[75] *Del rispettar la proprieta'*. Fragment in G. B. Nicola, ed. *Antonio Rosmini, Opere inedite di politica*. Milan, 1923. Cf. Mingardi, p. 77, note 94.

[76] *Filosofia del diritto*, Vol. 1, par. 338. Mingardi, p. 74.

[77] Ibid. Vol. 2, par. 347. Mingardi, p. 75.

[78] *Teodicea*, par. 921. Mingardi, p. 79.

[79] *Filosofia del diritto*. Vol. 2, par. 340. Mingardi, p. 76.

[80] Ibid. Vol. 2, par. 1631. Mingardi, p. 77.

[81] Ibid. Vol. 1, par. 359. Mingardi, p. 77.

[82] Ibid. Vol. 2, par. 908, n. Mingardi, p. 77.

[83] Ibid. Vol. 2, par. 504.n. Mingardi, p. 77.

[84] Ibid. Vol. 6, par. 1650. Mingardi, p. 73.

[85] Ibid., p. 7.

[86] *Costituzione*, Cap. II., p. 6.

[87] Ibid.

[88] Ibid., p. 6.

[89] *Costituzione* 1993, p. 109.

[90] Ibid., p. 47.

[91] Ibid.

[92] Ibid. 1997, p. 113.

[93] *Costituzione*, Cap. I., p. 3.

[94] *Filosofia del Diritto*, Vol. 3, par. 263.

95 Ibid., p. 125.
96 Ibid., p. 48.
97 Ibid., p. 49.
98 Ibid., p. 49.
99 *The Victorian Church*, Part I, 1929 to 1959, London: Adams & Charles Black, 1966–70.
100 J. P. T. Bury, art. "France," *Encyclopedia Britannica*, 1961.
101 *Tracts on Christian Socialism*, V.
102 Politics for the People, (1848–49), p. 35.
103 Ibid., p. 55.
104 Ibid., p. 37.
105 "Action" being taken here as a technical term here standing for a range of related phenomena, including such things as inaction and negligence, for which an individual can be held directly accountable.

Chapter 4

106 See Steven Lukes, *Marxism and Morality*, Oxford: Oxford University Press, 1987, chapter 4. "The moment anyone started to talk to Marx about morality, he would roar with laughter." Quoted from Vorländer, 1904. (Back cover.)
107 *Utilitarianism*, London: Parker, Son, and Bourn, 1863, chapter 5.
108 Ibid.
109 *On Nature*, 1874.
110 *On Liberty*, 1859, chapter 1.
111 *Utilitarianism*, chapter 5.
112 *Autobiography*, London: Longmans, Green, Reader, and Dyer, 1873, chapter VII. The position we will defend later in these pages is that there is no general presumption in favor of equality, including equality of treatment, as a matter of justice, though there are, no doubt, particular situations within which there is such a presumption as a matter of fairness, which is a very different matter. An additional contribution by Mill to the idea of social justice was the proposition that it is possible to cause a person harm by failing to help him. *On Liberty*, chapter 1. More about this below.
113 Chapter VII.
114 *Chapters on Socialism*, ed. Stefan Collini, *J.S. Mill, On Liberty and other writings*, Cambridge: Cambridge University Press, 1989, p. 275.
115 See esp. chapter V, "Justice and Equality."
116 Preamble to the party constitution.
117 See Russell Hittinger's article, "The Coherence of the Four Basic Principles of Catholic Social Doctrine: An Interpretation," a paper delivered to the Pontifical Academy of the Social Sciences, May 2, 2008. Hittinger believes a main concern in the papacy's development of social justice doctrine was a desire to protect the institutions of the church (24).
118 An encyclical letter in Catholic terminology is an open letter addressed to the entire body of bishops, to the church at large, or occasionally to the whole human race. The document issued by the Second Vatican Council conjointly with the

then pope, Paul VI, *Gaudium et spes*, was described not as an encyclical letter but a "pastoral constitution."

[119] See Aquinas, *Summa Theologiae*, II-II, Q. 77.

[120] Par. 55. p. 34. (St. Paul Editions, Daughters of St. Paul, Jamaica Plains, Boston, MA, 02130.) ". . . . . alteri, quod suum est, detrahere, ac per speciem absurdae cuiusdam aequabilitatis in fortunas alienas involare, iustitia vetat . . . . ." Latin text par. 30.

[121] A draft of the encyclical was composed by Matteo Liberatore, S.J., student and friend of Taparelli. Historians credit two other prominent Catholic figures with special influence on Leo's ideas: Cardinal Manning of Westminster and Wilhelm Emmanuel von Ketteler, bishop of Mainz, both of whom took a lively interest in the fate of the working classes. It is an interesting point that Ketteler publicly supported Ferdinand Lassalle's version of socialism, which gave rise to Germany's Socialist Democratic Party. However, Ketteler died in 1877, long before the encyclical was written, and Leo emphatically rejects socialism. Manning died in 1892, the year after the encyclical was published.

[122] Par. 65.

[123] Par. 11.

[124] Par. 6.

[125] Par. 7.

[126] Par. 10.

[127] Par. 13.

[128] Par. 8. References are to the translation published by the Daughters of St. Paul, 50 St. Paul's Ave, Jamaica Plain, Boston, MA, 1942. The paragraphing differs from that of some other editions.

[129] Par. 26.

[130] Par. 27.

[131] Par. 9.

[132] This term used in the Latin text (*proletarii*) owes its fame to Marx. The official English text renders it as "working classes," the meaning Marx gave it. Originally it referred to those who were wealthy only in their children.

[133] Iubet igitur aequitas, curam de proletario publice geri, ut ex eo, quod in communem affert utilitatem, percipiat ipse aliquid, ut tectus, ut vestitus, ut salvus vitam tolerare minus aegre possit. Unde consequitur, favendum rebus omnibus esse quae conditioni opificum quoquo modo videantur profuturae. Quae cura tantum abest ut noceat cuiquam, ut potius profutura sit universis, quia non esse omnibus modis eos miseros, a quibus tam necessaria bona proficiscuntur, prorsus interest reipublicae. Latin text par. 27.

[134] For example Michael J. Shuck, *That They May Be One: The Social Teaching of the Papal Encyclicals*, Washington, D.C.: Georgetown University Press, 1991, p. 85.

[135] Par. 6.

[136] "The length of rest intervals ought to be decided on the basis of the varying nature of the work, of the circumstances of time and place, and of the physical condition of the workers themselves. Since the labor of those who quarry stone from the earth, or who mine iron, copper, and other underground materials, is much more severe and harmful to health, the working period for such men ought to be correspondingly shortened. The seasons of the year also must be taken into account; for often a given kind of work is easy to endure in

one season but cannot be endured at all in another, or not without the greatest difficulty."

[137] Par. 60.

[138] Par. 61.

[139] Par. 62. "If labor should be considered only under the aspect that it is personal, there is no doubt that it would be entirely in the worker's power to set the amount of the agreed wage at too low a figure. For in as much as he performs work by his own free will, he can also by his own free will be satisfied with either a paltry wage for his work or even with none at all. But this matter must be judged far differently, if with the factor of personality we combine the factor of necessity, from which indeed the former is separable in thought but not in reality. In fact, to preserve one's life is a duty common to all individuals, and to neglect this duty is a crime. Hence arises the right of securing things to sustain life, and only a wage earned by his labor gives a poor man the means to acquire these things."

[140] Par. 63.

[141] Vera Zamagni, *Economic History of Italy, 1860–1990*. Oxford: Oxford, 1998.

[142] Par. 4.

[143] Par. 5.

[144] For a fuller account of this concept, which is a term of art for us, see above p. 10f.

[145] See above, p. 43.

[146] Burton, E., and Marique, P. (1910). Guilds. In *The Catholic Encyclopedia*. New York: Robert Appleton Company. Retrieved March 20, 2009, from New Advent: http://www.newadvent.org/cathen/07066c.htm.

[147] In this encyclical Pius uses the word "justice" 44 times, and "social justice" eight times.

It is "the law of social justice" that the riches produced by economic activity ought to be distributed among individual persons and classes to the common advantage of all.

The distribution of created goods, which "suffers from the huge disparity between the few exceedingly rich and the unnumbered propertyless, must be brought into conformity with the norms of the common good, that is, social justice."

Social justice demands that changes be introduced as soon as possible whereby a family wage will be assured to every adult workingman.

It is contrary to social justice when, for the sake of personal gain and without regard for the common good, wages and salaries are excessively lowered or raised; and this same social justice demands that wages and salaries be managed in such a way as to offer to the greatest possible number the opportunity of getting work and obtaining suitable means of livelihood.

"The right ordering of economic life cannot be left to a free competition of forces. For from this source, as from a poisoned spring, have originated and spread all the errors of individualist economic teaching."

The public institutions of the nations ought to make all human society conform to the needs of the common good; that is, to the norm of social justice.

If the right principles are observed, not merely the production and acquisition of goods, but also the use of wealth, now often so wrongful, will be brought back again to the standards of equity and just distribution.

[148] Par. 40.
[149] Par. 73.
[150] Par. 74.
[151] Par. 140.
[152] Par. 136.
[153] Par. 161.
[154] Par. 18.
[155] Par. 71.
[156] Par. 11.
[157] Par. 11.
[158] Par. 12.
[159] Par. 13.
[160] Par. 14.
[161] Par. 18.
[162] Par. 19.
[163] Par. 20.
[164] Par. 21.
[165] Par. 22.
[166] Par. 23.
[167] Par. 25.
[168] Par. 26.
[169] Par. 27.
[170] Par. 86 .
[171] Par. 44.
[172] Par. 30.
[173] *Mater et magistra* mentions that Pius XI in *Quadragesimo anno* taught that the views of communists and socialists were radically opposed to Christian belief. Par. 34. There are several passages that could be taken as indirect or implied condemnations of the communist regimes, but mainly because of their atheism.
[174] Par. 86.
[175] Par. 89.
[176] Par. 111.
[177] Par. 112.
[178] Par. 127.
[179] Harry Hearder, *Italy, A Short History*, Cambridge University Press, 1990, 2001, p. 259.
[180] Ibid.
[181] Par. 29.
[182] Par. 60.
[183] Par. 66.
[184] Ibid.
[185] Par. 75.
[186] Par. 5.
[187] Par. 23.
[188] Par. 59.
[189] Par. 61.
[190] Par. 70.
[191] Par. 35.
[192] Par. 36.

[193] Par. 37.

[194] Par. 2.

[195] Par. 39.

Chapter 5

[196] Nozick, Robert (1969). "Coercion," in *Philosophy, Science, and Method: Essays in Honor of Ernest Nagel*, Ed. Sidney Morgenbesser, Patrick Suppes, and Morton White, New York: St. Martin's Press, pp. 440–72.

[197] *The Federalist*, No. 51, February 6, 1788.

[198] Wesley Hohfeld distinguishes rights (or claims) from liberties (or privileges), powers, and immunities. In this account, the earlier "civil rights" are not rights but liberties; but the civil rights recognized in 1964 are "rights."

[199] The name "Jim Crow" came from a song-and-dance caricature of blacks.

[200] "Smith didn't give a damn about women's rights . . . he was trying to knock off votes either then or down the line because there was always a hard core of men who didn't favor women's rights." Dierenfield, Bruce J., *Keeper of the Rules: Congressman Howard W. Smith of Virginia*, Charlottesville, VA: University of Virginia Press, 1987, p. 194.

[201] It has since been claimed by supporters of the legislation that Smith's motives were mixed, and that while he opposed racial integration, he preferred that if there was to be integration, women should be protected against discrimination.

[202] Horowitz, Daniel. "Rethinking Betty Friedan and The Feminine Mystique: Labor Union Radicalism and Feminism in Cold War America," *American Quarterly*, Vol. 48, No 1, March 1996, pp. 1–42.

[203] *Second Treatise of Government*, chapter 2.

[204] "La propriété étant un droit inviolable et sacré, nul ne peut en être privé, si ce n'est lorsque la nécessité publique, légalement constatée, l'exige évidemment, et sous la condition d'une juste et préalable indemnité." Published on the website of the French Ministry of Justice, December 17, 2001.

[205] Eleanor Roosevelt, the chairman; René Cassin, a prominent French defender of sexual equality who went on to receive the Nobel Peace prize in 1968 for his work on the Declaration; the Confucian scholar Peng-chun Chang, a product of Columbia University who encouraged the commission members to embrace contradictions in the oriental style, which they proceeded to do; and Charles Malik of Lebanon, an Eastern Orthodox Christian theologian and politician.

[206] *The Universal Declaration of Human Rights: Origins, Drafting and Intent.* Philadelphia: University of Pennsylvania Press, 1999.

[207] Mary Ann Glendon, "The Forgotten Crucible: The Latin American Influence on the Universal Human Rights Idea." *Harvard Human Rights Journal*, Vol. 16, Spring 2003.

[208] Ibid.

[209] Waltz, Susan, "Universalizing Human Rights: The Role of Small States in the Construction of the Universal Declaration of Human Rights." *Human Rights Quarterly* 23 (2001), at p. 60.

[210] Glendon, "The Forgotten Crucible."

[211] Waltz, "Universalizing Human Rights."

[212] Glendon, "The Forgotten Crucible."

[213] Glendon, "The Forgotten Crucible."

[214] *Human Rights and the United Nations: A Great Adventure*, New York: Transnational Publishers, 1984.

[215] *On the Edge of Greatness: The Diaries of John Humphrey*, ed. A. J. Hobbins, Montreal: McGill Universities Libraries,1994. Perez Cisneros should "burn in hell" because his work had the unintended consequence of delaying final approval of the Declaration, which played into the hands of the Soviets who were opposed to it. From our point of view this is a somewhat ironic remark.

[216] She continued, "Neither nature, experience, nor probability informs these lists of 'entitlements,' which are subject to no constraints except those of the mind and appetite of their authors." Jeane Kirkpatrick, "Establishing a Viable Human Rights Policy." 1981. Prepared for Kenyon College's Human Rights Conference, April 4, 1981.

Chapter 6

[217] Morelly's *Code de la Nature*, advocating the abolition of private property, was published in 1755; Robert Wallace's *Various Prospects of Mankind, Nature and Providence* in 1761, and Mably's *Entretiens de Phocion* in 1763. In his *Discourse on the Sciences and Arts*, 1750, Rousseau had written of the "fatal inequality introduced among men by the difference of talents and the cheapening of virtue."

[218] Plato's Socrates argues that all action is aimed at good, we might say by definition. Therefore necessarily those who do evil do so because they have a mistaken belief about what is good. But this fails to take into account that "good" is an aequivocal term as between egoistic good and ethical good, which can contradict one another.

[219] *Nicomachean Ethics*, Book III. Rackham, p. 117.

[220] An action can be voluntary in one respect but involuntary in another. The sharpshooter who fires at the hostage-taker but hits the hostage performs a voluntary action of firing at the one but the involuntary one of hitting the other. Only the voluntary action is rightly subject to ethical judgment.

[221] *Republic*, Bk. 4.

[222] Cf. A. E. Taylor, *The Mind of Plato*, Ann Arbor, University of Michigan Press, 1960, chapter 3.

[223] This has been doubted by Jonathan Dancy in a series of works, also by Ross on *prima facie* duties.

[224] Kant, in the *Critique of Judgement*, distinguishes between technically and morally practical judgments, assigning the former to the domain of theoretical philosophy and only the latter to the realm of practical philosophy. Introduction I, par. 173. Pluhar translation, Hackett Publishing Company, 1987, p. 12.

[225] *De Republica*, Bk. 3.

[226] *Fifteen Sermons Preached at the Rolls Chapel*, 2nd ed. London, James and John Knapton, 1726 (1729); Sermon 1: Upon Human Nature.

[227] Boswell, *Life of Johnson*, 10.10.1769. Boswell quoting Johnson: "All theory is against the freedom of the will; all experience for it." 15.4.1778.

228 *The World As I See It*, Secaucus, NJ: Citadel Press, 1956 (1984). p. 2.

229 *Why Social Justice Matters*, Malden, MA: Polity Press, 2005, pp. 131–2.

230 Ibid. 135.

231 Ibid.

232 Ibid.

233 Ibid. 136–7.

234 Ibid. 137.

235 Ibid.

236 Ibid. 138.

237 Ibid.

238 Ibid. 139.

239 Ibid.

240 Robert Laughlin, *A Different Universe: Reinventing Physics from the Bottom Down.* New York: Basic Books, 2006.

241 P. W. Anderson, *Science*, New Series, Vol. 177, No. 4047 (August 4, 1972), pp. 393–6.

242 *Nicomachean Ethics*, Bk. 3, chapter 5. 1113b, 19 (Irwin).

243 Ibid.

244 Metaphysical Elements of Justice, (the Metaphysics of Morals, Part I), translated by John Ladd, 2nd ed., Indianapolis, IN : Hackett Publishing Co., 1999.

245 Kant, ibid.

246 *Manual.*

247 See Hayek, *Law, Legislation and Liberty*, Vol. 1, *Rules and Order*. Chapter 1.

248 Cf. Hegel, *Philosophy of Right.*

249 Kant, ibid.

250 Cf. Hart and Honoré, *Causation in the Law.* 2nd ed. Oxford: Oxford University Press, 1985.

251 Hegel quotes a German proverb: "A flung stone is the devil's." As I write, a similar case has been tried before the U.S. Supreme Court. One Christopher Dean, wearing a mask and waving a gun, walked into a bank and behind the teller's counter where he grabbed some cash, when his gun accidentally fired. He was caught, convicted, and sentenced to 18 years which included a mandatory additional sentence of 10 years for committing a crime in which a firearm "is discharged." He argued that the extra time should not apply to accidental discharges, but Chief Justice Roberts wrote in his majority opinion that "accidents happen." True, the chief justice said, "it is unusual to impose criminal punishment for the consequences of purely accidental conduct." But criminals, he said, must bear the consequences of the unintended consequences of their unlawful acts (*New York Times*, April 30, 2009, p. A20).

252 *De Officiis*, 3, xxix.

Chapter 7

253 The full title of the work is *Die metaphysische Anfangsgründe der Rechtslehre*. Different translators have given it very diverse English titles, such as *Philosophy of Law*

(Hastie) and *Doctrine of Right* (Gregor). To avoid confusion I refer to it simply as the *Rechtslehre* throughout these pages.

[254] Both Kant and Hegel discuss justice chiefly as *Recht*, that is, not merely as abstract justice but justice which requires to be embodied in law. This does not affect our argument, however.

[255] Metaphysical Elements of Justice, (the Metaphysics of Morals, Part I), translated by John Ladd, 2nd ed., Indianapolis, IN : Hackett Publishing Co., 1999.

[256] What is Property? Or, an Inquiry into the Principle of Right and Government (original title: Q*u'est-ce que la propriété? Recherche sur le principe du droit et du gouvernement*), 1840.

[257] *Théorie de la propriété* (Theory of Property), Paris, Librairie Internationale, 1863–64.

[258] P.-J. Proudhon, *General Idea of the Revolution in the Nineteenth Century*, translated by John Beverly Robinson, London: Freedom Press, 1923, pp. 293–4.

[259] Ibid.

[260] Kant, I, I, 1. Ladd, p. 42; I,I, 5, Ladd p. 45.

[261] *People v. Beardsley* 150 Mich. 206, 113 N.W. 1128 (1907).

[262] Cf. Hegel, #51.

[263] Cf. Kant, #10.

[264] Cf. Hegel, *Philosophy of Right*, par. 64, Addition 41.

[265] Emile Durkheim, *The Elementary Forms of the Religious Life*, New York: Free Press, 1965. Trans. from French by Joseph Ward Swain. p. 52ff.

[266] *Laws*, Book XI, 913.

[267] This at least is my personal memory of the events. I yield to any historian who can show otherwise.

[268] Hegel, *Philosophy of Right*, PR #49.

[269] Ibid., Addition 29, to par. 49.

[270] Ibid.

[271] *Taking Rights Seriously*. Cambridge, MA: Harvard University Press, 1978. Chapter 9, Reverse Discrimination, p. 227.

[272] Ibid. p. 239.

[273] Technically, no doubt, Gloucester was a rebel.

[274] John Rawls, *A Theory of Justice*, Cambridge, MA: Harvard University, Belknap Press, 102ff, 310–15.

[275] Locke's argument in the Second Treatise, # 139, chapter 11, is relevant here. Cf. "And to let us see, that even absolute power, where it is necessary, is not arbitrary by being absolute, but is still limited by that reason, and confined to those ends, which required it in some cases to be absolute, we need look no farther than the common practice of martial discipline: for the preservation of the army, and in it of the whole commonwealth, requires an absolute obedience to the command of every superior officer, and it is justly death to disobey or dispute the most dangerous or unreasonable of them: but yet we see, that neither the serjeant, that could command a soldier to march up to the mouth of a cannon, or stand in a breach, where he is almost sure to perish, can command that soldier to give him one penny of his money . . . "

[276] Cf. Thomas Jefferson, *Notes on the State of Virginia*, Query XII.

Chapter 8

[277] Certainly this is true of modern slavery, whatever may be one's ultimate judgment regarding slavery in the ancient world, which some have considered more open to debate.

[278] See Hayek, *Law, Legislation and Liberty*, p. 1.

[279] Cf. Rosmini.

Appendix

[280] Manfred Kuehn, *Kant, a Biography*. Cambridge: Cambridge University Press, 2001, 223.

[281] Jerry Z. Muller, *The Mind and the Market: Capitalism in Western Thought*, New York: Anchor Books, 2003, chapter 6.

[282] Cf., for example, *The Way to Christ*, ed. Peter Erb, Mahwah, NJ: Paulist Press, 1977.

[283] The Fathers of the Church had spoken of the sin of Adam as a felix culpa, a "fault" which was "happy" or fortunate in that it led God to send his Son to earth. But this phrase was intended as a figure of speech. St. Augustine taught that God allows evil because he can bring good out of it, but this is still far from endorsing evil as necessary, as Böhme does.

[284] *The System of Ethical Life* (1802/3), *The Phenomenology of Mind* (1807), the *Encyclopedia* (1817, 1831).

[285] This is a play on the common German phrase "an und für sich" which means something like "in principle," "per se," or "other things being equal."

[286] *The Young Hegel: Studies in the Relations Between Dialectics and Economics*, 1938. Cambridge, MA: MIT Press, 1976.

Bibliography

(Some particular topics treated in the body of the text have their own bibliographies below.)

Abelard, Peter. *Ethica or Scito teipsum*. Trans. Vincent Paul Spade in: *Peter Abelard, Ethical Writings*. Indianapolis, IN: Hackett Publishing Company, 1995.

Allison, Henry E. *Kant's Theory of Freedom*. Cambridge: Cambridge University Press, 1990.

Aquinas, Thomas. *Summa Theologiae*. 5 vols. Madrid: Biblioteca de Autores Cristianos, 1955.

Aristotle. *Nicomachean Ethics*. Trans. Terence Irwin. Indianapolis, IN: Hackett Publishing Company, 1985.

Augustine, St. Sermon 180, c. 2: Migne, *Latin Patrology* Vol. 38, col. 974.

Barnes, Jonathan, ed. *The Cambridge Companion to Aristotle*. Cambridge: Cambridge University Press, 1995.

Barry, Brian. *Why Social Justice Matters*. Malden, MA: Polity Press, 2005.

Barry, Norman. *Introduction to Modern Political Theory*. 4th ed. New York: St. Martin's Press, 2000 (1981).

Beck, Lewis White. *A Commentary on Kant's Critique of Practical Reason*. Chicago, IL: University of Chicago Press, 1960.

Berlin, Isaiah. *Two Concepts of Liberty*. *Oxford:* Oxford University Press, 1958.

Bloomfield, Paul. *Moral Reality*. Oxford: Oxford University Press, 2001.

Böhme, Jakob. *The Way to Christ*, ed. Peter Erb. Mahwah, NJ: Paulist Press, 1977.

Broadie, Sarah. *Ethics with Aristotle*. New York: Oxford University Press, 1991.

Burke, Edmund. "Thoughts and Details on Scarcity." In Isaac Kramnick, ed. *The Portable Edmund Burke*. New York: Penguin, 1999.

Burke, Thomas Patrick. *No Harm: Ethical Principles for a Free Market*. New York: Paragon House, 1994.

Butler, Joseph. *Fifteen Sermons Preached at the Rolls Chapel*. 2nd ed. London: James and John Knapton, 1729 (1726).

Chadwick, Owen. *The Victorian Church*, Part I, 1929 to 1959. London: Adams & Charles Black, 1966–70.

Chappell, Vere, ed. *The Cambridge Companion to Locke*. Cambridge: Cambridge University Press, 1994.

Cole, H. L. and L. Ohanain. "The Great Depression in the United States from a Neoclassical Perspective." *Federal Reserve Bank of Minneapolis Quarterly Review*, 1999.

Crisp, Roger, Michael Slote, ed. *Virtue Ethics, Oxford Readings in Philosophy*. *Oxford:* Oxford University Press, 1997.

Dancy, Jonathan. *Ethics without Principles*. Oxford: Clarendon Press, 2004.

Dierenfield, Bruce J. *Keeper of the Rules: Congressman Howard W. Smith of Virginia.* Charlottesville, VA: University of Virginia Press, 1987.

Durkheim, Emile. *The Elementary Forms of the Religious Life.* New York: Free Press, 1965. Translated from French by Joseph Ward Swain.

Dworkin, Ronald. *Law's Empire.* Cambridge, MA: Belknap Press of Harvard University Press, 1986.

—. *Sovereign Virtue.* Cambridge, MA: Harvard University Press, 2000.

—. *Taking Rights Seriously.* Cambridge, MA: Harvard University Press, 1977.

Einstein, Albert. *The World As I See It.* Secaucus, NJ: Citadel Press, 1956 (1984).

Finnis, John. *Natural Law and Natural Rights.* Oxford: Clarendon Press, 1980.

Frederick G. Kempin, Jr. *Historical Introduction to Anglo-American Law.* 3rd ed. St. Paul, MN: West Publishing Co., 1990.

Friedman, Milton, and Anna Schwartz. *A Monetary History of the United States, 1867–1960.* Princeton, NJ: Princeton University Press, 1971.

Gauthier, David. *Morals by Agreement.* Oxford: Clarendon Press, 1986.

Gewirth, Alan. *Reason and Morality.* Chicago, IL: University of Chicago Press, 1978.

Glendon, Mary Ann. "The Forgotten Crucible: The Latin American Influence on the Universal Human Rights Idea." *Harvard Human Rights Journal,* Vol. 16, Spring 2003.

Guardini, Romano. *Freedom, Grace and Destiny.* London: Harvill Press, 1961. (Translation of *Freiheit, Gnade, Schicksal.* Munich: Kosel-Verlag, 1948).

Gurevich, Aaron. *The Origins of European Individualism.* Oxford: Blackwell, 1995.

Guyer, Paul, ed. *Kant's Groundwork of the Metaphysics of Morals: Critical Essays.* Lanham, MD: Rowman & Littlefield, 1998.

—. *Kant's System of Nature and Freedom.* Oxford: Clarendon Press, 2005.

Hart, H. L. A. *Law, Liberty and Morality.* Stanford, CA: Stanford University Press, 1963.

—. *Punishment and Responsibility: Essays in the Philosophy of Law.* Oxford: Clarendon Press, 1968.

Hart, H. L. A. and Tony Honoré. *Causation in the Law.* 2nd ed. *Oxford:* Oxford University Press, 1985.

Hayek, Friedrich A. *Law, Legislation and Liberty.* 3 vols. Vol. 1, Rules and Order. Vol. 2, The Mirage of Social Justice. Vol. 3, The Political Order of a Free People. Chicago, IL: The University of Chicago Press, 1973.

—. *The Road to Serfdom.* Chicago, IL: University of Chicago Press, 1994.

Hearder, Harry. *Italy, a Short History.* 2nd ed. Cambridge: Cambridge University Press, 2001 (1990).

Hegel, G. W. F. *Grundlinien Der Philosophie des Rechts.* Hamburg: Felix Meiner Verlag, 1955. Reprint, 1967.

—. *Hegel's Science of Logic.* Trans. W. H. Johnston and L. G. Struthers, ed. H. D. Lewis. 2 vols. London: George Allen and Unwin, 1929.

—. *Phänomenologie des Geistes, Philosophische Bibliothek.* Hamburg: Felix Meiner Verlag, 1988.

Herbert, Auberon. *The Right and Wrong of Compulsion by the State,* ed. Eric Mack. Indianapolis, IN: Liberty Classics, 1978.

Hobbes, Thomas. *Leviathan,* ed. Edwin Curley. Indianapolis, IN/Cambridge: Hackett, 1994.

Hobhouse, L. T. *The Elements of Social Justice*. London: George Allen & Unwin, 1922.

Höffe, Otfried, ed. *Immanuel Kant: Metaphysische Anfangsgründe der Rechtslehre*. Berlin: Akademie Verlag, 1999.

Horowitz, Daniel. "Rethinking Betty Friedan and The Feminine Mystique: Labor Union Radicalism and Feminism in Cold War America." *American Quarterly*, Vol. 48, No. 1, March 1996.

Hume, David. *An Enquiry Concerning the Principles of Morals*, ed. Tom L. Beauchamp. Oxford: Oxford University Press, 1998 (1751).

—. *Hume: Political Essays*, ed. Knud Haakonssen. Cambridge: Cambridge University Press, 1994.

Humphrey, John. *Human Rights and the United Nations: A Great Adventure*. New York: Transnational Publishers, 1984.

—. *On the Edge of Greatness: The Diaries of John Humphrey*, ed. A. J. Hobbins. Montreal: McGill Universities Libraries, 1994.

Inwood, Michael. *A Hegel Dictionary*. Oxford: Blackwell Publishers, 1992.

Jaeger, Werner. *Aristotle, Fundamentals of the History of His Development*. 2nd ed. Oxford: Oxford University Press, 1962 (1934).

John, Locke. *Second Treatise of Government, Indianapolis*, 1980 (1690). Both Notes are on p. 15.

Jouvenel, Bertrand de. *The Ethics of Redistribution*. Cambridge: Cambridge University Press, 1952. Reprint, Indianapolis, IN: Liberty Press, 1990.

—. *Sovereignty*. London: Cambridge University Press, 1957.

Justinian. *Corpus iuris civilis*, ed. Mommsen and Krueger. Berlin: 1928.

Kane, Robert, ed. *The Oxford Handbook of Free Will*. Oxford: Oxford University Press, 2002.

Kant, Immanuel. *Critique of Pure Reason*. Trans. Norman Kemp Smith. London: Macmillan & Co. Ltd., 1964.

—. *Groundwork of the Metaphysics of Morals*. Trans. Mary Gregor. Cambridge: Cambridge University Press, 1997.

—. *Kritik Der Reinen Vernunft*. 2 vols. Frankfurt: Suhrkamp Verlag, 1974.

—. *Lectures on Ethics*. Trans. Peter Heath, ed. J. B. Schneewind Peter Heath. Cambridge: Cambridge University Press, 1997.

—. *Metaphysical Elements of Justice (the Metaphysics of Morals, Part I)*. Trans. John Ladd. 2nd ed. Indianapolis, IN: Hackett Publishing Co., 1999.

—. *The Metaphysics of Morals. Cambridge Texts in the History of Philosophy*. Trans. Mary Gregor. Cambridge: Cambridge University Press, 1996.

—. ed. *Metaphysische Anfangsgründe der Rechtslehre*. 2nd ed. Hamburg: Felix Meiner Verlag, 1998.

—. *Metaphysische Anfangsgründe der Tugendlehre*. Hamburg: Felix Meiner Verlag, 1990.

—. *Religion within the Limits of Reason Alone*. Trans. Theodore M. Green and Hoyt H. Hudson. New York: Harper Torchbooks, 1960 (1934).

Korsgard, Christine M. *Creating the Kingdom of Ends*. Cambridge: Cambridge University Press, 1996.

Kraut, Richard. *Aristotle on the Human Good*. Princeton, NJ: Princeton University Press, 1989.

Kripke, Saul A. *Naming and Necessity*. Cambridge, MA: Harvard University Press, 1972.

Kuehn, Manfred. *Kant, a Biography*. Cambridge: Cambridge University Press, 2001.

Laughlin, Robert B. *A Different Universe: Reinventing Physics from the Bottom Down*. New York: Basic Books, 2005.

Locke, John. *Two Treatises of Government*, ed. Peter Laslett. Cambridge: Cambridge University Press, 1960.

Lukacs, Georg. *The Young Hegel: Studies in the Relations between Dialectics and Economics*, 1938. Cambridge, MA: MIT Press, 1976.

MacIntyre, Alasdair. *After Virtue*. Notre Dame, IN: Notre Dame Press, 1981.

Maistre, Joseph de. "Lettres" in *Oeuvres*.

Marcuse, Herbert. *A Critique of Pure Tolerance*. Boston, MA: Beacon Press, 1969.

Mill, John Stuart. *On Liberty*, ed. Alburey Castell, *Crofts Classics*. Arlington Heights, IL: Harlan Davidson, Inc., 1947.

Morsink, Johannes. *The Universal Declaration of Human Rights: Origins, Drafting and Intent*. Philadelphia, PA: University of Pennsylvania Press, 1999.

Muller, Jerry Z. *The Mind and the Market: Capitalism in Western Thought*. New York: Anchor Books, 2003.

Nagel, Thomas. *The Possibility of Altruism*. Princeton, NJ: Princeton University Press, 1970.

Nozick, Robert. *Anarchy, State and Utopia*. New York: Basic Books, 1974.

Nussbaum, Martha C. *Frontiers of Justice*. Cambridge, MA: Belknap Press of Harvard University Press, 2006.

Plato. *The Republic*. Trans. Paul Shorey. 2 vols. Vol. 1, *The Loeb Classical Library*. London: William Heinemann Ltd., 1953.

Proudhon, P.-J. *General Idea of the Revolution in the Nineteenth Century*. Trans. John Beverly Robinson. London: Freedom Press, 1923.

—. *Théorie de la propriété* (Theory of Property). Paris: Librairie Internationale, 1863–64.

Pufendorf, Samuel. *On the Duty of Man and Citizen According to Natural Law*. Trans. Michael Silverthorne, ed. James Tully. Cambridge: Cambridge University Press, 1991 (Latin original, 1673).

Qutb, Sayyid. *Social Justice in Islam*. Trans. John B. Hardie. Oneonta, NY: Islamic Publications International, 1953.

Raven, J. E. and G. S. Kirk. *The Presocratic Philosophers*. Cambridge: Cambridge University Press, 1969.

Rawls, John. *John Rawls, Collected Papers*, ed. Samuel Freeman. Cambridge, MA: Cambridge University Press, 2001.

—. *Lectures on the History of Moral Philosophy*, ed. Barbara Herman. Cambridge, MA: Harvard University Press, 2000.

—. *A Theory of Justice*. Cambridge, MA: Belknap Press of Harvard University Press, 1971.

Raz, Joseph. *Engaging Reason: On the Theory of Value and Action*. Oxford: Oxford University Press, 1999.

—. *The Morality of Freedom*. Oxford: Clarendon Press, 1986.

—. *Practical Reason and Norms*. Oxford: Oxford University Press, 1999 (1975), Hutchinson & Co. (Publishers) Ltd.

Ripstein, Arthur. *Force and Freedom: Kant's Legal and Political Philosophy*. Cambridge, MA: Harvard University Press, 2009.

Ryle, Gilbert. *The Concept of Mind*. Harmondsworth, Middlesex: Penguin Books, 1949.

Sandel, Michael J. *Liberalism and the Limits of Justice*. 2nd ed. Cambridge: Cambridge University Press, 1982.

Scheffler, Samuel. *Boundaries and Allegiances*. Oxford: Oxford University Press, 2001.

Scheler, Max, ed. *Der Formalismus in der Ethik Und die Materielle Wertethik*. Bonn: Bouvier Verlag, 2000.

Schmitz, David. *Elements of Justice*. Cambridge: Cambridge University Press, 2006.

Scruton, Roger. *Kant, A Very Short Introduction*. Oxford: Oxford University Press, 1982.

—. *The Meaning of Conservatism*. South Bend, IN: St. Augustine's Press, 2002.

—. *Modern Philosophy, an Introduction and Survey*. New York: Penguin, 1994.

—. *The Palgrave Macmillan Dictionary of Political Thought*. 3rd ed. Houndmills, Basingstoke: Palgrave Macmillan, 2007.

—. *Philosophy: Principles and Problems*. London: Continuum, 1996.

—. *A Short History of Modern Philosophy*. 2nd ed. London: Routledge, 1981.

Shafer-Landau, Russ. *Moral Realism: A Defence*. Oxford: Oxford University Press, 2003.

Simmons, A. John. *The Lockean Theory of Rights*. Princeton, NJ: Princeton University Press, 1992.

Smith, Michael. *The Moral Problem*. Oxford: Blackwell Publishing, 1994.

Taylor, A. E. *The Mind of Plato*. Ann Arbor, MI: University of Michigan Press, 1960 (1922), Constable and Company Ltd.

—. *Plato, the Man and His Work*. 4th ed. Cleveland and New York: Meridian Books, 1956 (1926).

Thomas, D. A. Lloyd. *Locke on Government*. London: Routledge, 1995.

Ulpian (Domitius Ulpianus). *The Commentaries of Gaius and Rules of Ulpian*. Trans. J. T. Abdy, Bryan Walker. Whitefish, MT: Kessinger Publishing, LLC, 2007.

Waldron, Jeremy. *The Right to Private Property*. Oxford: Clarendon Press, 1988.

Waltz, Susan. "Universalizing Human Rights: The Role of Small States in the Construction of the Universal Declaration of Human Rights." *Human Rights Quarterly, Vol. 23*, 2001.

Walzer, Michael. *Spheres of Justice: A Defense of Pluralism and Equality*. New York: Basic Books, 1983.

Williams, Bernard. *Ethics and the Limits of Philosophy*. Cambridge, MA: Harvard University Press, 1985.

Williams, Matthew Clayton and Andrew. *Social Justice*. Oxford: Blackwell Publishing, 2004.

Wolff, Robert Paul. *The Autonomy of Reason: A Commentary on Kant's Groundwork of the Metaphysic of Morals*. Gloucester, MA: Peter Smith, 1986.

Wood, Allen W. *Kant's Ethical Thought*. Cambridge: Cambridge University Press, 1999.

Woolhouse, Roger. *Locke: A Biography*. Cambridge: Cambridge University Press, 2007.

Zamagni, Vera. *Economic History of Italy, 1860–1990*. Oxford: Oxford University Press, 1998.

Bibliographies on Particular Topics

Taparelli

Writings of Taparelli

Essai sur les principes philosophiques de l'economie politique. Paris, Lethellieux, 1943. Ed. Robert Jacquin. A collection of Taparelli's writings on political economy.

"La legge fondamentale d'organizzazione nella società." In: Gabriele De Rosa, *I Gesuiti in Sicilia e la rivoluzione del '48*, con documenti sulla condotta della Compagnia di Gesù e scritti inediti di Luigi Taparelli d'Azeglio, Edizioni di Storia e Letteratura, Roma, 1963, pp. 166–88.

La libertà tirannia. Saggi sul liberalesimo risorgimentale, Edizioni di Restaurazione Spirituale, Piacenza 1960, raccolta di articoli pubblicati su La Civiltà Cattolica nel 1861, a cura di Carlo Emanuele Manfredi e Giovanni Cantoni. A collection of Taparelli's writings on liberalism.

Pirri, P., ed. *Carteggi del Padre Taparelli della Compagnia di Gesù* (Bibliotheca di storia italiana recente (1800–70) XIV), Turin, 1932. Taparelli's correspondence.

Saggio teoretico di dritto naturale appoggiato sul fatto. Rome, *Civiltà Cattolica*, 2 vols. 1883/2, 1949/4 (1840–43).

About Taparelli

Armando, B. *Il concetto proprietà nel Padre Taparelli.* Pinerolo, 1960.

Behr, Thomas C. *Luigi Taparelli and the Nineteenth-Century Neo-Scholastic 'Revolution' in Natural Law and Catholic Social Sciences* (Ph.D. dissertation, SUNY Buffalo, 2000).

—. "Luigi Taparelli d'Azeglio, S. J. (1793–1862) and the Development of Scholastic Natural-Law Thought as a Science of Society and Politics." *Journal of Markets & Morality*, Vol. 6, No. 1, Spring 2003, pp. 99–115.

Brucculeri, A. "Un precursore italiano della società delle nazioni." *Civiltà Cattolica* 77/1 (1926), pp. 395–405. 77/2 (1926), pp. 28–37, pp. 121–31.

Carlo, E. di, *Diritto e morale secondo Taparelli.* Palermo, 1921.

Catholic Encyclopedia, art. "Aloysius Taparelli." New York: Robert Appleton Company, 1912.

Dezza, P. *I neotomisti italiani del XIX secolo.* 2 vols. Milan, 1942–44.

Dianin, Giampaolo. *Luigi Taparelli D'Azeglio (1793–1862).* Il significato della sua opera, al tempo del rinnovamento neoscolastico, per l'evoluzione della teologia morale.

Frattini, E. "Taparelli e il tradizionalismo della restaurazione." *Miscellanea Taparelli.* Rom 1964, pp. 171–90.

Jacquin, Robert. *Le Père Taparelli, sa vie, son action, son œuvre.* Paris, 1943.

Keim, Elisabeth. *Das Eigentum in der Naturrechtslehre Luigi Taparelli d'Azeglios.* St. Ottilien, 1998.

Legitimo, Gianfranco. *Sociologi cattolici italiani. De Maistre - Taparelli - Toniolo.* Volpe, Roma, 1963, pp. 30–51.

Lener, S. "Il 'Diritto naturale appogiato sul fatto' del Padre T. e l'antiguismo contemporaneo." *Civiltà Cattolica* 114/4 (1963), pp. 346–59, pp. 594–607.

Messineo S.J., A. "Il P. Luigi Taparelli d'Azeglio e il Risorgimento italiano." *Civiltà Cattolica*, anno 99, Vol. 3, quaderno 2356, 21/8/1948, pp. 373–86; e quaderno 2357, 4/9/1948, pp. 492–502.

—. "Il Padre Taparelli e il risorgimento italiano." *Civiltà Cattolica* 99/3 (1948), pp. 373–86, pp. 492–502.

—. "Il Padre Taparelli e la Civiltà Cattolica." *Civiltà Cattolica* 113/3 (1962), pp. 544–55.

Miscellanea Taparelli (*Analecta Gregoriana, 133*), Rome, 1964.

Perego, A. *Forma statale e politica finanziara nel pensiero di Taparelli.* Milan, 1956.

—. "L'imposta progressiva nel pensiero del Padre Taparelli." *Civiltà Cattolica* 98/4 (1947), pp. 136–44.

Pirri, P. "Il Padre Taparelli e il rinnovamento della scolastica al Collegio Romano." *Civiltà Cattolica* 78/1 (1927), pp. 107–21, pp. 399–409.

—. "Intorno alle origini del rinnovamento tomista in Italia." *Civiltà Cattolica* 79/4 (1928), pp. 215–29, pp. 396–411.

—. "Le idee del Taparelli sui governi rappresentativi." *Civiltà Cattolica* 78/2 (1927), pp. 206–19, pp. 397–412.

—. "La rinascita del tomismo a Napoli." *Civiltà Cattolica* 80/1 (1929), pp. 229–44, pp. 422–33. 80/2 (1929), pp. 31–42.

Rosa, Gabriele de. *I Gesuiti in Sicilia e la rivoluzione del '48*, con documenti sulla condotta della Compagnia di Gesù e scritti inediti di Luigi Taparelli d'Azeglio, Edizioni di Storia e Letteratura, Rome, 1963.

Rosa, Luigi di. *Luigi Taparelli. L'altro d'Azeglio.* Cisalpino, Milano, 1993.

Schmidinger, H. M. "Thomistische Zentren in Rom, Neapel, Perugia usw." *Christliche Philosophie im katholischen Denken des 19. und 20. Jahrhunderts*, hrsg. von E. Coreth u.a., Bd. 2, Graz, 1988, pp. 109–30.

Sorgenfrei, H. *Die geistesgeschichtlichen Hintergründe der Sozialenzyklika "Rerum Novarum" Papst Leos XIII. vom 15. Mai 1891.* Heidelberg-Löwen, 1970, pp. 116–21.

Thomann, M. "Der rationalistische Einfluß auf die katholische Soziallehre." In A. F. Utz (Hrsg.), *Die katholische Soziallehre und die Wirtschaftsordnung.* Trier, 1991, pp. 163–202.

Zitarosa, G. *Il diritto naturale da padre Taparelli ad oggi.* Naples, 1965.

Antonio Rosmini

Writings of Rosmini

Aristotele esposto ed esaminato. Turin, 1857.

Del rispettar la proprieta'. Fragment published in G. B. Nicola, ed. *Opere inedite di politica.* Milan, 1923. Note: Denis Cleary and Rosmini House, Durham, UK, have published English translations of many of Rosmini's voluminous writings.

Delle cinque piaghe della Santa Chiesa, 1848.

Filosofia del diritto, 1841. Trans: *The Philosophy of Right*, ed. Denis Cleary and Terence Watson. Durham: Rosmini House, 1995.

Il rinnovamento della filosofia in Italia, proposto dal c. T. Mamiani della Rovere ed esaminato. Milan, 1836.

La costituzione secondo la giustizia sociale con un'appendice sull'unita' d'Italia. Milan and Florence, 1848; second edition in *Scritti politici.* Stresa, 1997. Trans. Alberto Mingardi: *The Constitution under Social Justice.* Lanham, MD: Lexington Books, 2007. Note: The first edition was published in Milan and Florence, but between May and June Rosmini rewrote it extensively. The second version, however, could not be published because it had been put on the Index of Forbidden Books. It saw the light of day only in 1997 in a critical edition by Fr. Umberto Muratore. It is this edition, however, that Alberto Mingardi used for his translation. I had already made my own translation of the first edition, but use Mingardi's translation of some additional passages contained only in the second edition.

Nuovo saggio sull'origine delle idee. Milan, 1836. Trans: *The Origin of Ideas.* London, 1883.

Panegirico alla santa e gloriosa memoria di Pio VII pontefice massimo. Modena: Eredi Soliani, Tipografica Reali, 1831.

Saggi di scienza politica, 1822.

Teodicea sociale, 1845.

About Rosmini

Bergamaschi, Cirillo. *Bibliografia Rosminiana.* 8 vols. Milan-Stresa, 1967–96 (covers Rosminian bibliography in all languages from 1814–1995).

—. *Grande dizionario antologico del pensiero di Antonio Rosmini.* (4 vols of explanations of words and phrases from Rosmini's works in Rosmini's own words.) Rome: Città Nuova Editrice. 2001. CD version available.

Chafuen, Alejandro, Alejandro Chafuen "I precursori italiani del personalismo economico: una riflessione sugli scritti di Luigi Taparelli d'Azeglio, Antonio Rosmini e Matteo Liberatore." In Enrico Colombatto and Alberto Mingardi, eds. *Il coraggio della libertà: Saggi in onore di Sergio Ricossa.* Soveria Mannelli: Rubbettino, 2002.

Cleary, Denis. *Antonio Rosmini: Introduction to his Life and Teaching.* Durham: Rosmini House, 1992 (2nd edition forthcoming).

Davidson, Thomas. *The Philosophical System of Antonio Rosmini Serbati.* London: 1882.

Mingardi, Alberto. "A Sphere Around the Person: Antonio Rosmini on Property." *Journal of Markets and Morality,* Vol. 7, No. 1, Spring 2004.

Pellegrino, P., ed. *Rosmini e l'illuminismo: Atti del XXI Corse della "Cattedra Rosmini."* Stresa: Sodalitas-Spes, 1988.

Pozzo, Riccardo. *The Philosophical Works of Antonio Rosmini in Translation* in American Catholic Philosophical Quarterly, LXXIII (1999), No. 4.

Christian socialism

Early joint publications

The Christian Socialist (1850–51).

Politics for the People (1848–49).
Tracts on Christian Socialism (a series of pamphlets).

Individual authors

Clifford, John D. D. *Socialism and the Teaching of Christ. With a Bibliography of Christian Socialism and Particulars of Existing Christian Socialist Societies.* London: Fabian Tracts, No. 78, 1897.

Dearmer, Percy. *Christian Socialism Practical Christianity.* London: Clarion Pamphlets, No. 19, 1897.

Girdlestone, E. D. *Christian Socialism versus Present-day Unsocialism.* Limavady: Circle Co-Operative Printing Co., 1887.

Headlam, Stewart Duckworth. *Christian Socialism. A lecture.* London: Fabian Tracts, No. 42, 1892.

Kaufmann, Mauritz. *Christian Socialism.* London: Kegan Paul & Co., 1888.

Ludlow, John Malcolm Forbes. *Christian Socialism and Its Opponents: A Lecture.* 1851.

Magee, William Connor (successively Bishop of Peterborough and Archbishop of York) *Christian Socialism; or, Many Members, one Body: A Charity Sermon.* London: Bath, 1852.

Maurice, Frederick Denison. *Christian Socialism* (a dialogue), Christian Social Union. Reprint 1898.

—. *Dialogue between Somebody, a Person of Respectability and Nobody, the Writer.* No publication information.

Ramsay, Thomas. *Is Christian Socialism a Church Matter?* London, 1851.

Socialist Quaker Society. *Socialism: An Essentially Christian Movement.* 1901 Reprinted from the "Friends' Quarterly Examiner," published by West, Newman & Co., London.

Sprague, Philo Woodruff; Westcott, Brooke Foss. *Christian Socialism.* New York: E. P. Dutton & Co., 1891.

Tuckwell, William. *Christian Socialism, and Other Lectures.* London: Simpkin & Marshall, 1891.

John Stuart Mill and socialism

Capaldi, Nicholas. *John Stuart Mill: A Biography.* Cambridge, UK, New York: Cambridge University Press, 2004.

Douglas, Charles Mackinnon. *John Stuart Mill; A Study of His Philosophy.* Edinburgh, London: W. Blackwood and Sons, 1895.

Jones, H. S. *Victorian Political Thought, British History in Perspective.* Houndmills: Macmillan, 2000.

Mill, John Stuart. *Auguste Comte and Positivism.* London: N. Trübner & Co., 1865.

—. *Autobiography.* London: Longmans, Green, Reader, and Dyer, 1873.

—. Chapters on Socialism, in Stefan Collini, ed. J. S. Mill, *On Liberty and Other Writings.* Cambridge: Cambridge University Press, 1989.

—. *Considerations on Representative Government.* London: Parker, Son, and Bourn, West Strand, 1861.

—. *The Contest in America.* 2nd ed. Boston, MA: Little, Brown and Company, 1862.

—. *An Examination of Sir William Hamilton's Philosophy and of the Principal Philosophical Questions Discussed in His Writings.* London: Longman, Green, Longman, Roberts & Green, 1865.

—. *Nature, the Utility of Religion, and Theism.* 2nd ed. London: Longmans, Green, Reader, and Dyer, 1874.

—. *On Liberty.* London: J. W. Parker and Son, West Strand, 1859.

—. *Principles of Political Economy with Some of Their Applications to Social Philosophy.* London: J. W. Parker, 1848.

—. *The Subjection of Women.* London: Longmans, Green, Reader, and Dyer, 1869.

—. *A System of Logic, Ratiocinative and Inductive, Being a Connected View of the Principles of Evidence, and the Methods of Scientific Investigation.* London: J. W. Parker, West Strand, 1843.

—. *Utilitarianism.* London: Parker, Son, and Bourn, 1863.

Rinderle, Peter. *John Stuart Mill.* Munich: Beck, 2000.

Schumacher, Ralph. *John Stuart Mill, Reihe Campus. Einführungen.* Frankfurt; New York: Campus, 1994.

Skorupski, John. *John Stuart Mill.* London; New York: Routledge, 1989.

Sowell, Thomas. *On Classical Economics.* New Haven, CT: Yale University Press, 2006.

Spencer, Herbert. *John Stuart Mill, His Life and Works.* New York: Henry Holt and Company, 1875.

Stafford, William. *John Stuart Mill, British History in Perspective.* New York: St. Martin's Press, 1998.

Urbinati, Nadia, and Alex Zakaras. *J. S. Mill's Political Thought: A Bicentennial Reassessment.* Cambridge, New York: Cambridge University Press, 2007.

Marx and ethics

Brenkert, George G. *Marx's Ethics of Freedom.* London: Routledge & Kegan Paul, 1983.

Churchich, Nicholas. *Marxism and Morality: A Critical Examination of Marxist Ethics.* Cambridge: James Clarke, 1994.

Cohen, Marshall, Thomas Nagel, and Thomas Scanlon. *Marx, Justice and History.* Princeton, NJ; Guildford: Princeton University Press, 1980.

Hayes, Calvin. *Popper, Hayek and the Open Society.* London: Routledge, 2009.

Jessop, Bob, and Charlie Malcolm-Brown. *Karl Marx's Social and Political Thought: Critical Assessments.* London: Routledge, 1990.

Jessop, Bob, and Russell Wheatley. *Nature, Culture, Morals, Ethics, Karl Marx's Social and Political Thought; V.8.* London: Routledge, 1999.

Kain, Philip J. *Marx and Ethics.* Oxford: Clarendon, 1988 (1991).

Kamenka, Eugene. *The Ethical Foundations of Marxism.* 2nd ed. London: Routledge and Kegan Paul, 1972.

Lukes, Steven. *Marxism and Morality.* Oxford: Oxford University Press, 1987.

Miller, Richard W. *Analyzing Marx: Morality, Power, and History.* Princeton, NJ: Princeton University Press, 1984.

Peffer, R. G. *Marxism, Morality, and Social Justice.* Princeton, NJ: Princeton University Press, 1990.

Sweet, Robert T. *Marx, Morality and the Virtue of Beneficence.* New York; London: Peter Lang, 1991.

Van der Linden, Harry. *Kantian Ethics and Socialism.* Indianapolis, IN: Hackett Publishing Co., 1988.

West, Cornel. *The Ethical Dimensions of Marxist Thought.* New York: Monthly Review Press, 1991.

Wilde, Lawrence. *Ethical Marxism and Its Radical Critics.* London: Macmillan, 1998.

Leo XIII: Rerum Novarum

Antonazzi, Giovanni, Gabriele De Rosa, Leo, and Catholic Church. Pope (1878–1903: Leo XIII). *L'enciclica Rerum novarum e il suo Tempo.* Roma: Edizioni di Storia e letteratura, 1991.

Bellavite, Enrico, S. Fontana, and Catholic Church. Pontificia Commissio Iustitia et Pax. *La Destinazione Universale Dei Beni: Atti Del Colloquio Internazionale Nel Centenario Della Rerum Novarum, Cittáa Del Vaticano, 14–15 Maggio 1991.* 1st ed. Verona: Edizioni Cercate, 1992.

Blatchford, Robert. *The Pope's Socialism, Pass on Pamphlets; No. 16.* London: The Clarion Press, 1909.

Boutry, Philippe, Ecole francaise de Rome, and Centre national de la recherche scientifique (France). Histoire religieuse moderne et contemporaine. *Rerum Novarum: Ecriture, Contenu Et Réception D'une Encyclique: Actes Du Colloque International, Collection De L'Ecole Française De Rome, 232.* Rome: Ecole française de Rome Palais Farnese, 1997.

Corrin, Jay P. *Catholic Intellectuals and the Challenge of Democracy.* Notre Dame, IN: University of Notre Dame Press, 2002.

De Gasperi, Alcide. *I Tempi E Gli Uomini Che Prepararono La "Rerum Novarum."* 3rd ed., *Dottrina Sociale Cattolica; 4.* Milano: Vita e Pensiero, 1945.

Furlong, Paul, and David Curtis. *The Church Faces the Modern World: Rerum Novarum and Its Impact.* Scunthorpe: Earlsgate Press, 1994.

Gill, Eric, Catholic Church. Pope (1878–1903: Leo XIII). Catholic Church. Pope (1922–39: Pius XI). And Catholic Church. Pope (1922–39: Pius XI). *Social Principles & Directions Extracted from the Three Papal Encyclicals, Rerum Novarum, Quadragesimo Anno, Divini Redemptoris; Arranged According to Subject Matter, Giving All Positive Statements of Doctrine, and Suggestions for a Programme of Social R.* High Wycombe: Hague Gill & Davey, 1940.

Gorce, Matthieu Maxime. *La Politique De L'Eternel: Sociologie, Philosophie, Ecclesiologie, Avec Les Grandes Encycliques De Leon XIII Et De Pie XI, Bibliotheque De Philosophie Contemporaine.* Paris: Presses universitaires de France, 1941.

Knorn, Peter. *Arbeit und Menschenwürde: Kontinuität Und Wandel Im Verständnis der Menschlichen Arbeit in den Kirchlichen Lehrschreiben von Rerum Novarum bis*

Centesimus Annus: eine Sozialwissenschaftliche und Theologische Untersuchung. Leipzig: Benno Verlag, 1996.

Ledure, Yves, and Institut catholique de Paris. *Rerum Novarum En France: Le Père Dehon et l'engagement social de l'eglise*. Paris: Editions universitaires, 1991.

Luciani, Alfredo, and Marvin Herrera Araya. *La "Rerum Novarum" E I Problemi Sociali Oggi*. 1st ed., *Collana Problemi Del Nostro Tempo; N. 76*. Milano: Massimo, 1991.

Manning, Henry Edward. *A Pope on Capital and Labour. The Encyclical "Rerum Novarum."* New ed., *Cath. Truth Soc; S. 104*. London: Catholic Truth Society, 1931.

Reato, Ermenegildo. *Pensiero E Azione Sociale dei Cattolici Vicentini e Veneti Dalla "Rerum Novarum" Al Fascismo (1891–1922)*. Vicenza: Edizioni Nuovo Progetto, 1991.

Ruch. *La Doctrine Sociale De L'eglise d'apres l'encyclique Rerum Novarum et les qutres enseignements des souverains pontifes*. Paris: Maison de la bonne presse, 1931.

Scholl, S. H. *150 Anni Di Movimento Operaio Cattolico Nell'europa Centro-Occidentale (1789–1939)*. 1st ed. Padova: Gregoriana editrice, 1962.

Shuck, Michael J. *That They May Be One: The Social Teaching of the Papal Encyclicals*. Washington, DC: Georgetown University Press, 1991.

Watt, Lewis. *Catholic Social Principles: A Commentary on the Papal Encyclical Rerum Novarum*. London: Burns Oates & Washbourne Ltd., 1929.

Weigel, George, and Robert Royal. *Building the Free Society: Democracy, Capitalism, and Catholic Social Teaching*. Grand Rapids, MI; Washington, DC: Ethics and Public Policy Center, 1993.

Pius XI: Quadragesimo anno

Figl, Thomas. *Die Enzyklika Quadragesimo Anno und Ihr Einfluss auf die Österreichische Verfassung vom 1. Mai 1934, Schriftenreihe des Instituts für Ethik und Sozialwissenschaften*. Wien: Institut für Ethik und Sozialwissenschaften der Kath.-Theol. Fakultät der Universität Wien, 1995.

Himes, Kenneth R., and Lisa Sowle Cahill. *Modern Catholic Social Teaching: Commentaries and Interpretations*. Washington, DC: Georgetown University Press, 2005.

McGowan, Raymond Augustine. *Toward Social Justice; a Discussion and Application of Pius Xi's "Reconstructing the Social Order."* New York: Printed for the Social action department, National Catholic Welfare Conference, 1933.

Müller, Josef Heinz, and Wolfgang Mückl. *Die Enzyklika Quadragesimo Anno und der Wandel der Sozialstaatlichen Ordnung: Beiträge, Rechts- und Staatswissenschaftliche Veröffentlichungen der Görres-Gesellschaft; N.F., Heft 62*. Paderborn: F. Schöningh, 1991.

Nell-Breuning, Oswald von. *Wie Sozial Ist Die Kirche? Leistung und Versagen der Katholischen Soziallehre*. 1st ed., *Schriften der Katholischen Akademie in Bayern*. Düsseldorf: Patmos-Verlag, 1972.

Pieper, Josef. *Thesen zur Sozialen Politik: Die Grundgedanken des Rundschreibens Quadragesimo Anno*. 2. Aufl. ed. Freiburg im Breisgau: Herder, 1946.

Schasching, Johannes. *Zeitgerecht, Zeitbedingt: Nell-Breuning und die Sozialencyklika Quadragesimo Anno nach dem Vatikanischen Geheimarchiv*. 1. Aufl. ed., *Frankfurter*

Arbeitspapiere zur Gesellschaftlichen und Sozialwissenschaftlichen Forschung. Sonderband. Bornheim: Ketteler, 1994.

John XXIII

Bonnot, Bernard R. *Pope John XXIII: An Astute, Pastoral Leader.* New York: Alba House, 1979.

Hebblethwaite, Peter. *Pope John XXIII, Shepherd of the Modern World.* Garden City, NY: Doubleday, 1985.

John and Michael Chinigo. *The Teachings of Pope John XXIII.* London: Harrap, 1967.

Johnson, Paul. *Pope John XXIII. The Library of World Biography.* Boston, MA: Little, 1974.

Pope John XXIII. *Address Delivered by His Holiness Pope John XXIII at the Solemn Opening of the Second Vatican Council October 11, 1962: Address Delivered by His Holiness Pope John XXIII at the Formal Closing of the First Session of the Second Vatican Council December 8, 1962. Vatican Translations.* Washington, DC: National Catholic Welfare Conference, 1963.

Zizola, Giancarlo. *The Utopia of Pope John XXIII.* Maryknoll, NY: Orbis Books, 1978.

Paul VI

Etling, Mark G. *The Relevance of the Property Teaching of Pope Paul VI: An Ancient Teaching in a New Context.* San Francisco, CA: Mellen Research University Press, 1993.

Macchi, Pasquale. *Paolo VI e la Tragedia di Moro: 55 Giorni di Ansie, Tentativi, Speranze e Assurda Crudeltà, Gente Nel Tempo.* Milano: Rusconi, 1998.

Populorum Progressio: Encyclical Letter of His Holiness Pope Paul VI. London: Catholic Truth Society, 1967.

Index

CPSIA information can be obtained at www.ICGtesting.com
260823BV00001B/1/P

9 781441 169914